Life Drive & Death Drive
Libido & Lethe

Life Drive & Death Drive Libido & Lethe

A clear road through Freud's metapsychology leading to helpful findings and new concepts

Cordelia Schmidt-Hellerau

Translated by Philip Slotkin

IPBOOKS.net
International Psychoanalytic Books

International Psychoanalytic Books
New York • http://www.IPBooks.net

© 2024 Cordelia Schmidt-Hellerau

Published by IPBooks Inc
(International Psychoanalytic Books)
Queens, New York
www.IPBooks.net

Originally published in German by Klett-Cotta, © 1995, J.G. Cottasche Buchhandlung Nachfolger GmbH, Stuttgart, as: *Lebenstrieb & Todestrieb, Libido & Lethe. Ein formalisiertes konsistentes Modell der psychoanalytischen Trieb- und Strukturtheorie.*

2003 German edition available from: Psychosozial-Verlag Haland & Wirth, Giessen, Germany.

Previous version of English translation published by Other Press in 2001 as: *Life Drive & Death Drive, Libido & Lethe. A formalized consistent model of psychoanalytic drive and structure theory.*

ISBN: 978-1-956864-78-6

Cover Design by Karola Schmidt-Hellerau and Lawrence L. Schwartz
Layout and typesetting by Noel S. Morado

The theory of the drives is the most important but at the same time the least complete portion of psychoanalytic theory.

Sigmund Freud, 1924

Contents

Preface to the Updated Edition

Well into the 21st century, the importance of Freud's metapsychology has not waned. Worldwide psychoanalysts use its concepts, like the unconscious, the ego and superego, drive and repression - just to name a few. Without them. there would be no psychoanalysis. And yet, a clear grasp of their function and place within the so-called "psychic apparatus" is obscured by the specifics of Freud's theoretical reflections. While searching for answers to clinical questions, he frequently drew on neuroscientific, ontological, mythological and commonsense reflections, creating a maze of arguments one can easily get lost in. His model of the mind is difficult to understand and master.

This is what this book wants to facilitate. In carving out the principles of Freud's metapsychology as it grew from his 1895 *Project of a Scientific Psychology* till his 1938 *Outline of Psycho-Analysis*, I will show that his theory is derived from the general assumption that the mind—like any living system—has a tendency to perpetuate a state of *dynamic stability / homeostasis*, and that the means necessary to achieve this objective can be developed with only two axiomatic notions, *drive and structure*. Holding on to these basic ideas—woven together in Ariadne's thread—allows us to find a clear road through the labyrinth of Freuds theory. The clarification of certain concepts and the resolution of contradictions and inconsistencies made it necessary to introduce a few new notions—as for instance *lethe*, the energy term for the death- and preservative drive—but by and large my main goal has been to work towards a better understanding of Freud's metapsychology.

Nonetheless, reading this book may not be easy. One particular difficulty will likely arise from the fact, that many readers have already made up their minds about the meaning of major concepts, which I will present in a different light. For instance, one of the theorems set up to be "true" is that sexuality and aggression are the basic motivators of the mind. Resistance against rethinking such an assumption can be fierce, almost reflexive; interestingly though, this "conservative" tendency seems to confirm the workings of a preservative drive (a concept, which I hope to resurrect in this book). And in general, theoretical reflections require to refrain from applying experiential knowledge in order to think abstractly about the logic of a system. I would hold though that the rewards of working through this book will reach even beyond an understanding of Freudian psychoanalysis.

In preparing this edition, I shortened the elaboration of some details that could weigh down the reader. However, the cuts never eliminated essential steps in thinking about Freud's theoretical developments. Furthermore, I decided not to include the last chapter of the previous edition, *Prospect: Metapsychology as a bridging conception* (a comparison of A. Luria's model of the brain with Freud's model of the mind), because an extended version of this text is available elsewhere (Schmidt-Hellerau, 2002b, 2018, pp 123-161). Instead, an *Epilogue: Further Developments*, presents a brief summary of some important realizations, which I arrived at only after the first publication of this book in 2001.

I am grateful to the editor of International Psychoanalytic Books, Arnold Richards, who enthusiastically welcomed this new and updated version of my book in his program. I also feel encouraged by my psychoanalytic colleagues, who reassured me that my reflections on metapsychology are useful; their reactions, questions and comments helped me to more clearly articulate my analysis of this theory. Finally, I owe much gratitude to my husband, Fred Busch, whose love and interest in my work over so many years always showed me that I was on a road worth taking.

Brookline, August 2024

Preface

Freud's metapsychology has always fascinated me to a quite exceptional degree. This is because, in his unremitting passion for theoretical reflection on psychic phenomena of the utmost complexity, he succeeded in developing a relatively assimilable model of the mind that remains unparalleled to this day in terms of the differentiated nature of his concepts and their capacity for development. The tremendous freedom and mobility of his thought, the wealth of his ideas, and the playful character of his intellect reach the acme of their power precisely in the metapsychological texts—a power that, notwithstanding all the criticisms leveled against them, has been exerted unfailingly throughout the first century of psychoanalysis and has stimulated many analysts the world over to further thinking. What makes these further elaborations of his basic theoretical concepts both necessary and possible is the openness of the psychoanalytic paradigm—and this openness bears unmistakable witness to its living vibrancy.

The starting point for the review of metapsychology presented here was a contradiction between Freud's conception of a death drive and its association with aggression. I had in fact originally intended only to pursue this contradiction in a short paper on the death drive. However, it soon became clear to me that my critique of the conception of the death drive could not be undertaken in isolation, and I decided to devote a longer essay to drive theory. Having embarked on this project, I realized that a comprehensive discussion of drive theory was not possible unless my treatment also took account of the first topographical theory and the second structure theory. In this way my original modest intention with its relatively circumscribed ambitions grew into the present volume, which is the fruit of seven years of intensive study of Freudian and post-Freudian metapsychology and its critique. The sifting of the logical contradictions and reflection on the lacunae in the conception of the "psychical apparatus" was an exciting and challenging task, which I found incredibly enriching and often also a source of great joy. The road I traveled is documented in this book. It led me to develop a formalized consistent model of psychoanalytic drive and structure theory, in which I present old concepts in a fresh light or a different context, as well as new ones that open up novel perspectives for our thinking on the level of both theory and clinical practice.

The original German edition of this book was published by Verlag Internationale Psychoanalyse, Stuttgart, in 1995. For the French edition, brought out by Delachaux & Niestlé, Lausanne and Paris, in 2000, I had to reduce its length by approximately half because the Collection Champs psychanalytiques does not accept books above 300 pages. In the process of shortening I made sure that all the important steps in my argument remained logically intact, merely cutting some of the details of my work on Freud's texts, and deleting a number of footnotes. Since a slimmer book is more economical and less daunting to the reader, I decided to use the shorter version as the basis for the English edition too, although the text differs in some respects from its French counterpart, and, in particular, many of the notes have been changed.

I am especially gratified by the appearance of my book in English because I moved to Brookline, Massachusetts, in 2000, where I now work in private practice as a Training and Supervising Analyst of the Boston Psychoanalytic Society and Institute and a member of the American Psychoanalytic Association. I should like to express my warm thanks to my colleagues and friends in the New Continent for the sincere and friendly welcome accorded to me here, and for their interest in my work. A particularly enriching experience for me was the close collaboration with my model translator Philip Slotkin—a process that he made both interesting and highly instructive regarding the sorely needed improvement of my knowledge of English. As a number of people have confirmed, his translation has succeeded in conveying the full clarity of my argument—an aspect by which I set much store—as well as my love of language; that is to say, he has transferred my book into the medium of English in the best possible way, and for this I am exceedingly grateful to him. My husband, Fred Busch, spent many hours familiarizing me with the American psychoanalytic landscape and introduced me to my publisher in this country; I wish to express my heartfelt thanks to him for this and, in every respect, for smoothing my path to a new life in the United States. I should like to express my pleasure and gratitude, too, to Michael Moskowitz for championing my book and for including it in his interesting and stimulating list. Finally, my thanks go to Diogenes Verlag, the Zurich publishing house, for its generous contribution to the cost of the translation.

Brookline, December 2000

INTRODUCTION

Metapsychology—Superstructure
or Foundation of Psychoanalysis?

METAPSYCHOLOGY AND
THE METAPSYCHOLOGY DEBATE[1]

It is some years now since a wave of minute and fundamental criticism broke over metapsychology: analysts such as G. S. Klein, Gill, Holt, Schafer, Stolorow, Peterfreund, Rosenblatt, and Thickstun gave vent to the dissatisfaction that had long been smoldering about the state of psychoanalytic theory, thereby unleashing a veritable tempest against the "intellectual tyranny" of a "dogma" that had, in the opinion of these critics, for years blocked the way to any creative progress in the development of psychoanalysis (Mertens 1981, p. 8). A number of suggestions were made with a view to achieving the hoped-for liberation: it was recommended that specific elements of metapsychology, for example the concept of energy, should be thoroughly eradicated (Holt 1976); or the need for a metatheory—that is, a level "above" that of clinical theory—was disputed, thus rendering metapsychology superfluous (Klein 1976); or else metapsychology was to be replaced by a new, contemporary-style model along systems and information theory lines (Peterfreund 1971, Rosenblatt and Thickstun 1977). The storm of the 1960s, 1970s, and early 1980s has now abated, leaving the Witch Metapsychology,[2] somewhat weather-beaten, in its wake. Metapsychology no longer seems to be of interest in

---

1 A shortened version of this introduction was first published in Schmidt-Hellerau 1993; some of the main positions defended in this book are outlined in Schmidt-Hellerau 1997.

2 Cf. Freud's quotation from Goethe's *Faust*: "We can only say: *'So muss denn doch die Hexe dran!'* ('We must call the Witch to our help after all!')—the Witch Metapsychology. Without

the United States today. One would think that argument in this field had been totally exhausted—or even, perhaps, that the struggle to modernize and update psychoanalysis as a science had once and for all eliminated this "serious obstacle to the development of psychoanalysis" (Gill 1988, p. 46), and indeed "effectively destroyed" it (Holt 1985, p. 289). The aggressive character of the attacks on the theoretical foundations of psychoanalysis has not been overlooked. "Who killed metapsychology?" asks M. H. Klein (1989, p. 565), while Holt (1985, p. 307) notes "a kind of moral crisis in psychoanalysis" in the aftermath of the debate. The battle is over, and a heavy, oppressive silence of fundamental perplexity has descended over its theater:

> So here lies the battered and bleeding body of metapsychology at our feet. What are we to do? Is the victim still breathing? Does it have a pulse? What is called for? First aid? Artificial respiration? Cardiopulmonary resuscitation? An ambulance and intensive care? As good physicians, the questions cannot fail to concern us. But as psychoanalysts we are also forced to ask, "Should this battered body be revived at all? Is the effort really worth it?" [Meissner 1981, p. 931]

The intellectual sophistication of the arguments deployed in the meta-psychology debate was evidently paralleled by the accompanying affect, which is manifested not only in the barbaric violence of this image but also in the doubt evinced by the concluding questions. Why has so much aggression been directed against a theory? It is after all a theory that in Europe has survived all the onslaughts on its scientific or clinical utility and continues to stimulate the thinking of analysts on that continent in one way or another. The answer that suggests itself is that this affect-laden attitude of the Americans toward metapsychology is, at least in part, a reaction to the Hartmann school of ego psychology, for the two entities are currently associated, if not indeed equated, in the American mind—for example, Wallerstein (1992) refers not

---

metapsychological speculation and theorizing—I had almost said 'phantasying'—we shall not get another step forward" (1937c, p. 225).

to "metapsychology" but to the "ego psychological metapsychology paradigm." Talking to colleagues from the United States, one clearly senses their relief at having finally overcome this phase, as well as their reluctance to have anything more to do with metapsychology—almost as if the "monolithic hegemony" of the Hartmann era (Wallerstein 1992, p. 13) had traumatized generations of American analysts. We can experience something of this for ourselves by turning to Hartmann's work and finding ourselves at once exposed to his cold breath. Unlike Freud's metapsychological papers, which—at least in the original German— convey a sensuousness that renders the reconstruction of his arguments an exciting and pleasurable intellectual experience, Hartmann's texts are characterized by a total lack of appeal. Laborious, unyielding, and dreary to read, they have been likened by Schafer (1970) to a rocky and impregnable mountain range with distant peaks. Stone's reference in this connection to the "robotlike anonymity of our neoclassical period" (in Smith 1999, p. 470) suggests that the spirit of Hartmann has settled upon the practice of analysis in the United States, where, consequently, "so many analyses are conducted within an atmosphere of hostility" (Busch 1999, p. 48). It is therefore not surprising that many of today's training and supervising analysts, having lain during their own analyses on the hard bed prepared for them at the foot of these great mountains, later came to deplore and combat the coldness and rigidity of their own analytic experience. The palpable relief and enthusiasm with which Kohut's self psychology was espoused in the 1960s and 1970s, involving as it did the recushioning of the analytic couch with abundant empathy and warmth, can perhaps be seen partly as a reaction to the coolness of Hartmannian thought.

What the Americans wanted to get rid of by the combined efforts of metapsychology's critics seems to have been connected with Hartmann's particular kind of ambitious scientific designs, which were manifestly felt to contain something profoundly antipathetic to the nature of the psyche or to analytic thinking. Interestingly, the assault on metapsychology then came from two diametrically opposed directions: whereas the subject appeared for some to be excessively scientific and hence of no use to the practicing analyst, other critics attacked it precisely on the grounds that it was unscientific. Of course, the labels "scientific" and "unscientific" can hide a variety of views and motivations, while positions within science itself are subject to constant change. Leaving aside for the moment the question of the scientific status of metapsychology at the beginning of the twenty-first century, we can at least say that Freudian metapsychology has furnished a comprehensive model of psychic functioning as a whole ("how the mind works") that remains, to this day, unrivaled in terms of the subtlety of its concepts and their amenability to further development. Various aspects of psychic activity have since undergone further elaboration, partly through reciprocal contacts with the findings of neuroscientific research—for example, consciousness (Shevrin et al. 1996, Solms 1997) or affect (Opatow 1999, Panksepp 1999)—and it will be interesting to integrate the individual results of these efforts into an overall model of mental functioning so that they can be understood for the first time in the complexity of their interdependence. However, that stage has not yet been reached. For even today, notwithstanding our liberation from the alleged fetters of an obsolete conception of science in Freud's metapsychological thought, no new, better comprehensive model of the psyche has so far gained acceptance. The best we have remains Freud's old "psychical apparatus."

It is not as self-evident as it might at first seem that the need to invoke a hundred-year-old model today, in the 21st century, wounds our narcissism and feels like an imposition.[3] For if we allow ourselves to be inspired by metapsychology, if we turn the creative potential   of these texts to account, and if, instead of clinging to their letter, we are prepared to play with Freud's

---

3 The recourse to Freud performs an extremely complex function in our trade. Where it is more a matter of duty or embarrassment than of interest—more an adherence to the letter than to the spirit of his works—it sometimes resembles a quasireligious gesture of subordination, which, moreover, is often institutionally encouraged (Kernberg 1996), and has resentment following hard on its heels. This is particularly so because the secret calculation never works out: if the reference to Freud is intended to lay a claim to truth ("Freud already said that..."), this appeal to the founding father of psychoanalysis after all merely earns the reproof that you are operating in a prescientific era—quite apart from the fact that your interlocutor will immediately reach into his pocket for another Freud quotation to refute your argument.

hypotheses and ideas and develop them further, then the acuity of his genius will open up more and more hitherto unforeseen vistas for exploring the complexity of psychic life. It seems to me that the critique of metapsychology from the 1960s to the 1980s was directed mainly toward bringing out the aspects of Freud's model of the psyche that were *wrong*, *untenable*, and *unserviceable*. In contrast to this widespread skepticism about metapsychology, my own approach to Freud's texts has in fact always concentrated on identifying the points that Freud sometimes intuited, sometimes expressed in ways that lend themselves to misunderstanding, but nevertheless got basically right; and from this point of view I have taken an interest in his contradictions and sought to determine the reasons for the logical discontinuities and inconsistencies of his concepts. Freud's metapsychology has thus to this day remained for me a storehouse of ideas and indications, a vastly rich scientific treasure trove the mining of which for the purpose of developing something new (and hence also something of one's own) remains as exciting as it is challenging.

I therefore advocate a creative return to metapsychological thinking. That does not mean that I would like to sweep away the arguments, criticisms, and insights that have accrued from the metapsychology debate. On the contrary, I contend that we should begin with the central objections. It must immediately be conceded that the criticisms are in most cases well founded and to that extent justified; however, the conclusions drawn from them are by no means as compelling as they appear to the critics.

BASIC REQUIREMENTS

The metapsychology developed by Freud over the course of some four decades remained, as he himself knew perfectly well, an incomplete theoretical corpus. His plan in 1915 had been to write a series of metapsychological essays to be assembled in a book entitled *Preliminaries to a Metapsychology*. The intention of these essays was "to clarify and carry deeper the theoretical assumptions on which a psycho-analytic system could be *founded*" (Freud 1916–1917f [1915],

p. 222, note 1, my emphasis). Of the twelve papers written, Freud himself published only five, and his own lifelong critical attitude toward his theoretical efforts is evident, for example, in the much quoted comment that, of the entire body of his metapsychological assumptions and conclusions, "any portion... can be abandoned or changed without loss or regret the moment its inadequacy has been proved" (Freud 1925d [1924], p. 32f.). Hence Freud, whose approach to the building blocks of his theory was always playful, imaginative, and precisely for that reason creative, was very conscious that the pieces of his jigsaw did not fit together without lacunae. Metapsychology does indeed suffer from a lack of systematization, from terminological inconsistency, from the non-operationalization of individual concepts, from logical contradictions, and from a mixing-up of the different levels of abstraction. These are serious shortcomings, particularly as there is no "consistent, coherent and fully integrated theoretical model in psychoanalysis" (Sandler et al. 1973, p. 18). The attempts to tidy up this situation and to fill any missing logical and conceptual gaps date back many years, as I shall now show.

The basic requirements to be satisfied by a psychoanalytic theory were outlined by Rapaport and Gill (1959). In their view, metapsychology ought to consist of a number of propositions, which should contain the necessary and sufficient minimum of independent assumptions, constituting the foundation of psychoanalytic theory. Although Rapaport and Gill did not yet feel able to offer detailed formal definitions of these basic assumptions and terms, they adopted the terms "force," "energy," and "structure," with which it was, in their opinion, possible to work even without recourse to a concrete somatic-physiological substrate: the "forces"—as yet unspecified—were conceived as vectorial, "energies" as addable scalars, and "structures" as hierarchically arranged configurations that generated psychic processes. For Rapaport, whose well-known book on the structure of psychoanalytic theory (1960) represented a more comprehensive "systematizing attempt,"[4] the main tasks to

---

4 According to Rapaport (1960), Freud's theory contains "four distinct models," which "are united in the theory itself, but not in one single model" (p. 20). The four models are: first, the

be performed for the further development of psychoanalysis were clarification of the "dual relationship between the organism and its environment" (p. 62), and a thorough "study of psychological structure formation" (p. 98). He was also convinced that psychoanalysis, like all sciences that seek to define their assertions precisely, urgently needed systematization, and hence also formalization and axiomatization (p. 104).

> Theories can be tested only when they are taken seriously. To test is to mathematize and to mathematize is to discover, in the relations posited by the theory, relationships of a higher order of abstraction. Such abstractions cannot be derived from isolated propositions, but only from the system of relationships which link these to each other. [Rapaport 1960, p. 97]

Rapaport and Gill thus formulated strict criteria for a scientific elaboration of the theoretical foundations of psychoanalysis, thereby marking out the field within which the phalanx of critics of metapsychology subsequently formed up into two opposing camps. The first comprised those who resisted what they saw as the presumptuous application of the criteria of natural-science methodology and theorization to the human science of psychoanalysis, favoring instead a psychoanalytic theory freed from mechanistic thinking, where the methods of the humanities and of hermeneutics would be applied to psychic life (Holt 1965, Klein 1976, Schafer 1976, Stolorow 1978). Ranged against them were those who wanted to see psychoanalytic theory purged at last of all metaphysical, anthropomorphic, and metaphorical elements, so that it could

---

"*reflex-arc (or topographic) model*," which represents the organism's tendency to respond to stimuli by a *directional* reaction; second, the "*entropy (or economic) model*," which, as the basic model of all motivated behavior, postulates a causal relationship between behavior and *tension-reduction processes*; third, the "*Darwinian (or genetic) model*," which includes a systematic presentation of the *regular laws of ontogenesis* (e.g., libido development); and, fourth, the "*Jacksonian (or neural integration hierarchy) model*," which sees the nervous system as a *hierarchy of different levels of integration*, in which the higher levels control or inhibit the lower, and which, by analogy, conceives the systems *Ucs.*, *Pcs.*, and *Cs.*, as well as, later, the structures of the id, superego, and ego, together with their functions, as hierarchically stratified. Rapaport must take the credit for having demonstrated the various model conceptions existing within psychoanalytic theory and having drawn attention to the need for a higher-order, unified model level.

link up with the contemporary findings of biological and neurophysiological research; to this end they advocated a reformulation of clinical concepts in terms of information and systems theory and their transposition into precise cybernetic models (Rubinstein 1965, 1967, Rosenblatt and Thickstun 1970, 1977, Peterfreund 1971, 1975).

However, the fact that two such antithetical objectives for a revised metapsychology could be invoked was due not only to Rapaport's categorical stipulations but also, and principally, to the circumstance that Freud's metapsychology contains and unites both positions. This is evident if only from its language, which comprises a colorful mixture of metaphorical, anthropomorphistic, reifying, physicochemical, biologicalorganismic, and neurophysiological elements. By concentrating on either one or the other aspect of Freud's terms and concepts, both parties were thus equally able to appeal to his writings and to claim that their efforts at revision formed part of his legitimate succession—but this was tantamount to introducing a split into metapsychology. All the same, this process clearly revealed the need for, first, a clarification of terms, and then, as a corollary, a separation of the various descriptive levels of psychoanalysis. All critics were unanimous on this point.

BREAKDOWN OF THEORETICAL LEVELS

As long ago as in 1962, Waelder suggested that the subject matter of psychoanalysis should be divided into six levels:

1. The level of the data of observation in the analytic situation
2. The level of clinical interpretation
3. The level of clinical generalizations
4. The level of clinical theory
5. The level of metapsychology
6. The level of Freud's philosophy

Waelder (1962) characterizes these levels by an increasing degree of abstraction, coupled, in his opinion, with concomitantly decreasing relevance, so that levels 5 and 6 seemed to him "far less necessary" (p. 620). He fails to provide cogent reasons for this appreciation, or any reflections on the consequences of neglecting the position of metapsychology for levels 1 to 4. Aside from this, however, his classification, to which many subsequent authors have referred, constitutes a good foundation for a further reduction to three levels, each subsuming two of Waelder's; this not only affords greater clarity but also compels us to adopt sharper differentiating criteria for such a classification, as we shall see below.

The first level to be identified is surely that of the *analytic situation*, or, more generally, of *psychic phenomenology*; it contains all psychic phenomena (forms of experience, fantasies, etc.) as manifested in, for example, the analytic situation (and elsewhere). The *language* on this level—which is thus also that common to patient and analyst—is *everyday language*. Waelder's separate level of clinical interpretation is also undertaken in the patient's everyday language and operates, as regards terminology, with building blocks from the patient's experiential world—in other words, the *terms* used here are of *high complexity*, pictorial, metaphorical, and multilayered; their *meaning* is in each case *context-related and wholly or partially individually determined* (the kind of "private language" described by Lorenzer 1970), and belongs to a *system* determined by the sociocultural context of understanding afforded by the patient's *individual life history*. The *hypotheses* and *concepts* of this level have the status of *reconstructions* of life history, and the links between them serve as explanations. This first level is already (at least partially) theoretical, in so far as it contains reflections "on" direct experiencing. The *field of reference* is *individual reality*.

The second level comprises *clinical theory*, or, more generally, *psychoanalytic psychology*; subsuming Waelder's levels 3 and 4, it contains the specific concepts—namely, the theory of the neuroses and the theory of technique (e.g., the theory of intervention)—or, in Rubinstein's (1967) classification, the low-level generalizations and correlations[5] on this level, as well as the higher-level hypotheses that seek, by the introduction of new postulates such as the wish-fulfillment tendency or repression, to explain the generalizations and correlations of the low-level hypotheses. The *language* of this level is *specialized*: its terms no longer have direct counterparts in the concrete constituents of the experiential world. Its *terms* are instead names for *constructs*, which relate to perceived processes, structures, and relational configurations of psychic and psychopathological phenomenology; they contain the condensed clinical experience of numerous therapists with a large number of patients and a wide variety of psychic disturbances; and to that extent they are applicable *generally* to a *system* whose reference remains that of the plane of understanding of *clinical experience*. The *hypotheses* and *concepts* of this level have mainly a *pragmatic, generalizing status*. The *field of reference* of this level is *psychopathological and psychological phenomenology*.

The third level is that of *metapsychology*. It includes the usually unspoken presupposition adduced in Waelder's sixth category as Freud's personal philosophy. For our purposes, this will be formulated more generally as one's basic position, in terms of the philosophy of science or epistemology, on the body–mind or, as the case may be, the mind– brain issue, which is the starting point for the formulation of the metapsychological positions. Metapsychology contains all assumptions formulated from this position as to the constituent parts and functioning of the "psychical apparatus." The *language* of this level is one of *pure theory* and to that extent also specialized; it differs from that of the clinical level in that it no longer directly relates to specific (say) clinical and psychological phenomena, but is directed toward the assumed *general principles of organization* whereby both normal and abnormal psychic processes or

---

5 By *empirical generalizations* Rubinstein means statements like: if one person is humiliated by another, the former will tend to have an antipathy toward the latter; the *clinical correlations* comprise statements such as "the behavior of an adult person corresponds to that person's feelings as a child in similar situations," or "exaggerated friendliness corresponds to concealed hostility." In other words, statements on this level are close to everyday psychology, and hence also to psychic phenomenology (in our above classification, however, they would differ from first-level statements because they are general and not individual).

phenomena can be described. The *hypotheses* and *constructs* of metapsychology have an *axiomatic* and primarily *logical status*, and their *system* has the *character of a model*. The *field of reference* of this level covers everything that relates to the *organizational principles of this model*, which forms the ordering framework wherein are specified the precise steps that are logically necessary to refer the hypotheses and postulates of the second level to each other and to link them together (Rubinstein 1967).

A possible objection to such a classification of terms is as follows. Although it seemingly promises greater clarity through the assignment of terms such as "joy" and "impatience" to the level of psychic phenomenology, "depression" and "resistance" to the level of clinical theory, and "drive" and "structure" to that of metapsychology, many terms are in fact used on two or all three levels, so that this breakdown is perhaps after all incapable of overcoming the nuisance of terminological fuzziness and mixing of theoretical levels. This objection could, however, be rebutted on the grounds that, where individual terms are used on two or more levels, the field of reference is the deciding factor. Here are three examples. The psychoanalytic term "to repress" has entered ordinary language and therefore occurs on all three levels: on the first level it denotes the phenomenon of "forgetting" or "not wanting to know"; on the second it stands for a specific defense within a conflictual situation; and on the third, that of metapsychology, it refers to a process assumed to exist for the purpose of maintaining hypostasized equilibrium states within the psychical apparatus. Again, on the first level (the vernacular), the term "narcissism" signifies a particular kind of self-centeredness and vanity; on the clinical level it is used for specific manifestations at a certain stage of development or for a given kind of self and object relationship; while on the level of metapsychology it describes a position and structure defined in libidinal-economic terms within the model conception of the "psychical apparatus." Or take the universally familiar term "Oedipus complex": on the first level it has to do with concrete situations, described as "my father, my mother, and I" or "the janitor, my female neighbor, and I," or which signify love relationships with parent figures; on the clinical level it covers the entire field of aspirations, conflicts, and anxieties belonging to the positive and negative Oedipus complex—that is, the state of being in love, rivalry, castration anxieties, and so forth; and on the metapsychological level it denotes the particular regulative processes necessitated by the concept of triangulation within the "psychical apparatus" construct. The sense in which a term is used is therefore determined by its field of reference—by whether it relates to experienced reality (level 1), clinical phenomenology (level 2), or the assumed organizational principle (level 3). If this is borne clearly in mind, it is then in fact possible to specify precisely one's chosen theoretical level of description in any individual case, and to use, or clearly to define, solely the terms applicable to this level in the sense corresponding to their field of reference.

The following nonpsychoanalytic analogy will help illustrate this idea. Looking at the accompanying fanciful image (Figure 1), we may perhaps see it as an unspecified graphic, but it could also be a microscopic cross-sectional view of a cell, an abstract depiction of an island or coral-reef formation, or a photograph of a cratered landscape on another planet. Alternatively, however, it might conceivably be a drawing illustrating a dream or an experience along the lines of: "I am walking peacefully along the road when a big fat man suddenly comes along and blocks my path."

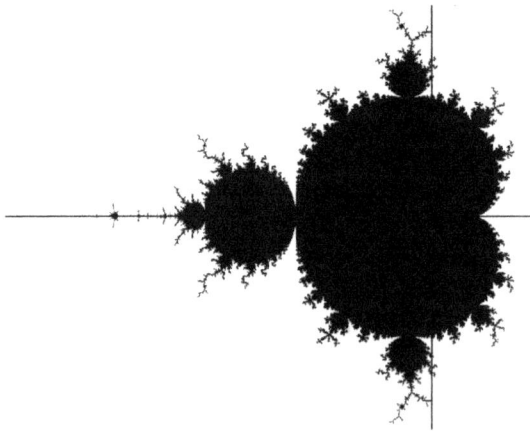

FIGURE 1. Mandelbrot set (Peitgen 1989, p. 140).

If we now take a closer look at Figure 1 (or, if you will, magnify selected areas of the image), then despite the appearance of various irregularities—variants we did not initially perceive—the generality of what we see is always homogeneous and recurring: order exists in this fanciful figure, in that all the selected areas and successive magnifications are *self-similar*. Relating this to our earlier example, we can say that, after a series of such dreams or situations, the analyst observes something constant, recurring, or "self-similar," which reveals to him the structures of this particular personality and its disturbances—for example, a conflict of rivalry within an oedipal pathology.

Figure 2 is a *fractal*. "A fractal object [is a geometrical shape that] looks the same when examined from far away or nearby—it is self-similar" (Mandelbrot 1991, p. 123f.). Hence the higher-order term or name for this and similar figures is "fractal"; this particular fractal is called the *Mandelbrot set*, after its inventor. There are also *Julia sets*, named for the mathematician Gaston Julia; the details are not relevant here. The important point now, however, is that a Mandelbrot set is a computergenerated image derived from a comparatively simple geometrical formula, namely $x \rightarrow x^2 + c$ (in which x is any complex variable and c is a constant). This little formula can now be used to produce an infinite number of forms astonishingly similar to those occurring in nature, thus enabling us to grasp something of the order that exists in the chaos of dynamical systems, as the following quotation indicates.

> The theory of nonlinear dynamical systems affords us an insight into growth and other processes in both animate and inanimate nature. It takes us a step nearer to the secret of nature—how a small number of natural laws could give rise to the multiplicity of different phenomena and forms we see when we look out of the window, into a telescope, or through a microscope. If this world were merely chaotic, it would be hopeless. Precisely the harmonious *mixture* of *order* and *disorder*, of unity and diversity, in the forms of trees, clouds, snow crystals, or coastlines, all of which are the result of nonlinear dynamical processes, gives us the impression of *naturalness* and *beauty*. Biological evolution needs the genetic variability resulting from the structured

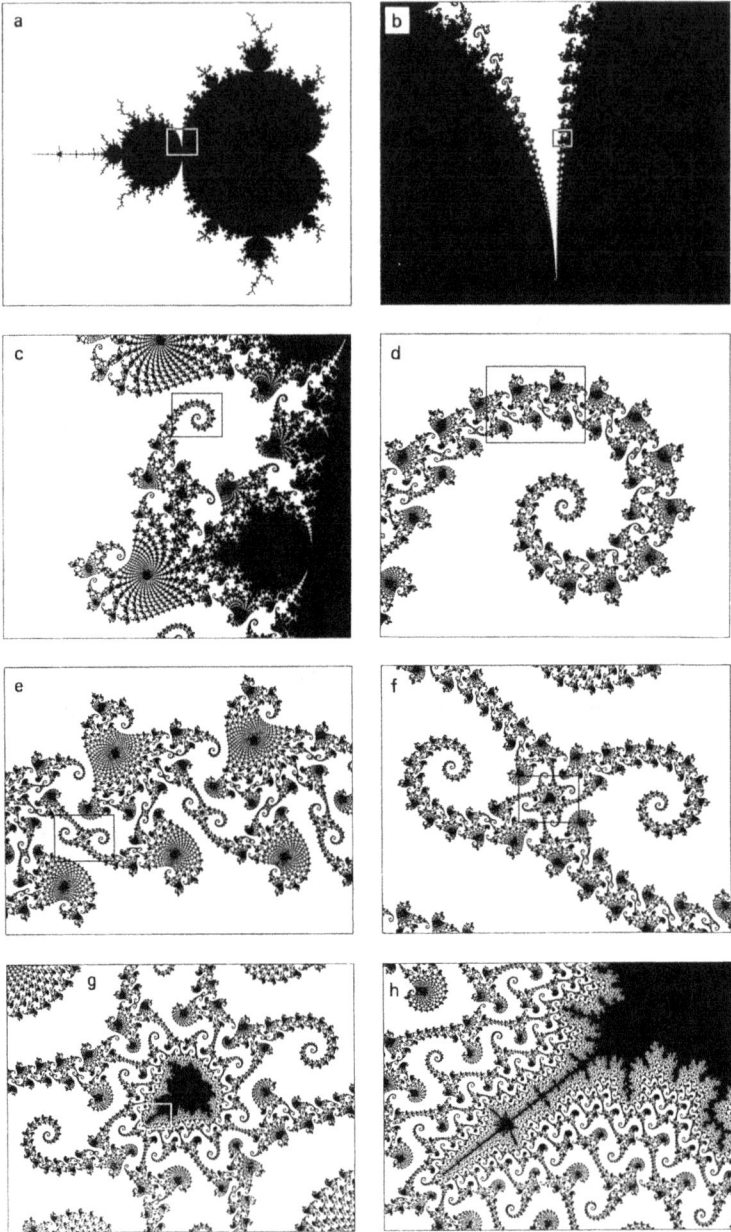

FIGURE 2. Series of successive magnifications alongside the Mandelbrot set (Peitgen 1989, p. 141).

control and amplification of small fluctuations just as the human intellect does for the purpose of bringing forth and formulating new ideas. In this way, the law supplies us with the unity and order of nature, and chance with its diversity and wealth. What imparts particular fascination to our looking into the world is the *interplay of law and chance*. [Martienssen 1989, p. 98f., my emphasis (translated for this edition)]

Another interesting aspect of this example for our purposes is that, whereas fractal geometry can be used to generate forms and figures deceptively similar to those occurring in nature, such as a snowflake, a fern leaf, or the crown of a tree (Peitgen 1989), it is not yet clear "how conclusions may be drawn from the fractals found [in nature] as to the nonlinear laws that generate them" (Grossmann 1989, p. 109 [translated for this edition])—that is, how it might be possible to derive any underlying (mathematical) laws from the heterogeneous multiplicity of psychic phenomena and disturbances. To discover this is regarded as one of the major scientific challenges of our time, particularly as it is now generally accepted "that the geometry of the nonlinear, structured world is fractal" (ibid. [translated for this edition]).

Our mini-discussion of fractal geometry included a computer graphic, the application of the term fractal or Mandelbrot set to it, and, finally, the mathematical expression $x \rightarrow x^2 + c$. Three clearly distinguishable *languages* are in evidence here, which are respectively *graphic, verbal*, and *mathematical. Although they cannot be meaningfully mixed, they nevertheless all relate to the same object.* Transposing this to our breakdown of levels in psychoanalysis, we readily admit that the comparison is not absolutely perfect, but it does serve the purpose of once again clarifying certain situations. For example, the diversity of psychic phenomena and forms of expression (the phenomenological level) corresponds very well to the multifarious forms of the fractal figures (the graphic level); moreover, it can be shown that both the term "fractal" (the verbal level) and the associated specific formula (the mathematical level) are *inherent* in the computer graphic (because these figures have precisely this name and were derived from these formulae) *although they do not occur concretely in it*. In exactly the same way, we can say that both the clinical and the metapsychological concepts are *inherent* in psychic phenomenology *although they do not occur concretely within it*. In other words, a formalized conception of metapsychology in the restrictive sense proposed here has the consequence that its terms and concepts are used in distinct ways. It thus becomes evident that entities like the drive or the id are inherent as organizers or laws in the outward manifestations of the psychic; however, they do not occur *as such*, but are merely concepts in a model suitable (just as the simple formula $x \rightarrow x^2 + c$ is conceived as an infinite store of images) for describing the organizational principles capable of generating the infinite diversity of the psychic. Hence the point of this comparison is to draw attention as clearly as possible to the *differences in the terminological languages of the three postulated levels*, all of which nevertheless relate to the same natural phenomenon of the psychic. For we *all* repeatedly fall victim to a kind of mental short-circuit whereby we see the constructions of metapsychology reflected in the concrete phenomena—or not, as the case may be. This is no doubt because the former are *inherent* in the latter, but we are not absolved on that account from the mental effort, in the development of our argument, of distinguishing again and again between the theoretical levels and the different denotations and connotations of their terms.

SCIENTIFIC REDUCTIONISM AND ANTHROPOMORPHISM

This bold excursion into the alien world of fractal geometry will now help us to assess the objections to metapsychology and the resulting attempts to revise it, the most important of which we shall now briefly review one by one in detail. Obviously, for example, no one would seriously accuse a mathematician experimenting with the formula $x \rightarrow x^2 + c$ of adopting a reductionistic, mechanistic, and denatured approach to nature. This at once brings us to a first group of objections, according to which metapsychology gives rise to a depersonalized, dehumanized—that is, precisely, a scientific—

view of the human individual (Schafer 1976, Gill 1977), based on a causal and reductionist epistemological approach, seeking causes instead of intentions and meanings. According to this view, this results in the disappearance of the "individual's self-comprehension as an active agent who defines and creates situations... behind depersonalized terms of seemingly greater scientific dignity" (Saperstein and Gaines, in Mertens 1981, p. 42 [translated for this edition]) that take no account of "the responsibility of individuals and the fact that meaningful interactions have been actively brought about" (Schafer, in ibid., p. 14 [translated for this edition]). All we can say here is that this not only is the case but also is intended to be so. Human beings, as individuals molded by their life history, do not appear on the plane of metapsychology; nor, however, does this individuality disappear from it, because it is not at issue there in the first place. The beauty of fractal figures does not become visible or unfold in the mathematical formula. Precisely the comparison with fractal geometry makes it clear that the considerations, assumptions, and hypotheses of metapsychology have nothing to do with reductionism of content, but concern the general organizational principles whereby individuality becomes possible at all.

Schafer subjected both metapsychology and clinical theory to a radical linguistic analysis and showed how what were originally metaphorical constructions become concretized, reified, and anthropomorphized in them: [6]processes and actions are nominalized and thereby transformed into entities, out of which the metapsychological constructions are ultimately composed. That is true. Reification and the provisional assumption of the existence of certain entities for the purposes of exact definition are admittedly part and parcel of the normal process of theorization, but everyone is also familiar with formulations, positively characteristic of Freud's style, such as "that the ego

---

6 Freud himself anticipated this objection in his lectures: "I am now prepared to hear you ask me scornfully whether our ego-psychology comes down to nothing more than taking commonly used abstractions literally and in a crude sense, and transforming them from concepts into things—by which not much would be gained" (Freud 1933a, p. 60). On this point, see also Hartmann et al. (1946) and Beres (1965).

gives itself up because it feels itself hated and persecuted by the super-ego, instead of loved," the super-ego "here again [appearing] as the representative of the id" (Freud 1923b, p. 58). Such passages really do sound as if Freud were dealing, in his theoretical considerations, with affairs of the heart and of state—but that is also one reason why his works are so exciting and entertaining to read. Schafer adduces such examples and others to demonstrate the unscientific nature of psychoanalytic theoretical language, and it must be admitted that he is right: such formulations really belong in the field of psychic phenomenology—that is, on the first level; that is the stage on which love and hate are played out, and where we observe all the variegated manifestations of psychic life, whereas only their organizational principles ought to find expression on the metapsychological level. Even if such formulations are merely a stylistic device (of a kind, as it happens, common in other academic disciplines too), theoretical psychoanalysis does admittedly make excessive use of such idiom, in the process often succumbing to the seductions of its own chosen images. The problem essentially concerns the manner of conducting the theoretical argument, which, given the complexity of terms in the phenomenological field, will be based now on one connotation or level of meaning and now on another, with the consequence of concealed discontinuities in the logical chain that can be subsequently brought to light only with difficulty.

Now Schafer concludes from this that a new language for psychoanalysis is needed, and indeed he immediately offers as an alternative the "action language" of his own devising, which accepts no more than the four basic terms of "meaning," "action," "reason," and "situation." However, these terms place Schafer wholly on the first theoretical level, for meaning, action, reason, and situation, in the senses in which he uses them, belong to the field of psychic phenomenology: his theoretical language is that of a practitioner speaking in precisely this way to his patient: "That was a *situation* in which you *did* this or that for this or that *reason*, and it *means* this or that for you." Nor does Schafer (1978) intend anything different, because he takes the restrictive view that psychoanalysts "should develop no more theory than they need for their method" (p. 176). But have the requirements of—or the theoretical background assumptions needed by—a clinician for his practice in fact already been established? At any rate, from the point of view chosen here, Schafer is wrong in his belief that the "metapsychology that is to be replaced presents the person as a mental apparatus" within which forces and structures are at work (p. 187). Metapsychology presents not "the person as an apparatus," but merely the so-called psychical apparatus itself, which is nothing other than a model construction in which hypotheses about the function of structures and processes within a system are accommodated. Schafer's substitution of his own theory of action language for psychoanalytic theory logically corresponds to an abolition of metapsychology. For this reason, Schönle (1981) rightly censures him for failing to provide an overall systemic conception of his new metapsychology, or indeed any theoretical level on which the simple specification of action, event, and person is elaborated; while Rawn (1979) concludes that without reifications and permanent structures there would also be no regularities, no laws, no science, and ultimately no psychoanalysis.

Hence Schafer's attempts at revision, too, come to grief because he fails to distinguish clearly enough between the various theoretical and conceptual levels of psychoanalysis. For this reason, one can only agree unreservedly with the insistence of G. S. Klein (1973, 1976) and Gill (1976) on a strict separation of clinical theory and metapsychology. As Klein (1976) demonstrates, Freud always nurtured the hope that it would one day be possible to develop a neurophysiological model of the psyche. The scientific concepts—such as structure, force, and energy—that have been incorporated into metapsychology and constitute its focal points can, however, in his view *not* be *derived* from the psychoanalytic method, so that metapsychological assumptions are *not abstractions* of clinical propositions. As the example of fractal geometry clearly shows, all this can be accepted without reservation. (The mathematical formula [level 3] cannot, or at least cannot yet, be derived from the formed natural configuration [on level 1], or, of course, from the terms chosen for it, even that of self-similarity [on level 2]; nor does it constitute an abstraction of these.) But Klein (1976) now concludes that metapsychology is merely an expression of Freud's philosophy of science; it is in his view neither essential to nor expressive of the psychoanalytic enterprise, but merely irrelevant to it, because it throws overboard the fundamental intent of psychoanalysis, which is to unlock meaning and make it accessible to the conscious mind. From theabove point of view, one can only repeat that such a meaning cannot arise in the first place without a mathematical formula—that is, without the regular laws that metapsychology seeks to formulate; although psychoanalysis as practiced is concerned to unlock meanings, metapsychology is not. Klein has here failed to abide by his own stipulation of a strict separation of theoretical levels.

Gill (1976) likewise points out that metapsychology differs from clinical theory not in a higher degree of abstraction, but in the fact that it uses a different scientific frame of reference, and he therefore suggests "that the term metapsychology should be restricted to propositions about the material substrate, both neurological and biological, of psychic functioning" (p. 71). This can be accepted in an inclusive (but not an exclusive) sense. Although Gill agrees with Rubinstein that, for example, "there is a material substrate for an unconscious wish—or for a conscious wish, for that matter" (p. 95), and does not deny the need for interdisciplinary work, he nevertheless considers it sufficient to accommodate the wish as such within an autonomous "pure" psychological theory. He concludes, first, that "Metapsychology is not psychology" (p. 71, title), and, second, that one theory—the clinical theory—is enough (Gill 1977, p. 582). In view of the foregoing considerations, we cannot agree with this second conclusion, although we can perhaps accept the first— but the following question then arises: If metapsychology is not a psychology, what is it? Is it then not precisely a theory for what Gill (1976) assigns to it— that is to say, for "neuropsychological and biopsychological propositions" (p. 71, note)? Let us accept this result, for the time being. Even if Gill considers that research data from the neurosciences and biosciences are not "relevant to psychoanalysis" (p. 92), he is cautious enough to recommend a wait-and-see attitude open to the findings of future research, while holding that, in the present state of psychoanalytic theory, "it makes no sense to say globally that one accepts or rejects metapsychology" (p. 104).

MONISM OR DUALISM

This brings us to a fundamental question, which many critiques of metapsychology fail to answer explicitly even though the choice of reply determines the direction of the argument. It is therefore important to be perfectly clear on this point. At issue is the age-old body– mind question, or, in more modern terminology, the mind–brain debate. An almost infinite range of positions have been adopted by philosophers of science, epistemologists, neuropsychologists, and others, and I do not propose to enter the lists myself here. However, no one who engages in the critique of metapsychology can avoid making the fundamental choice between monism and dualism. After all, whatever individual standpoints are distinguished within these two camps— whether the endpoint of one's work is the theory of identity, functionalism, epiphenomenalism, or a neuroepistemological or interactionist view—the basis of all these considerations, once fully differentiated, is the decision as to whether the psychic and the somatic are to be regarded as two distinct spheres, perhaps somehow synchronized or interacting but in principle separate (the dualistic position), or in the last analysis are to be traced back to something common, whatever it may be (the monistic position). In conceiving his psychoanalytic theory—that is, metapsychology—a dualist can initially disregard any findings of neurobiological or physiological research; but strictly speaking he must then, as it were after the event, explain whether this abstracted field of the psychic bears any relation to the somatic, and if so how it is related to or connected with it, for instance in somatization processes of all kinds. The monist, on the other hand, is faced from the beginning with the problem that the dualist tackles only at the end of his theorization, if at all: since he cannot conceive of any psychic process occurring totally independently of somatic-physiological processes (and possibly also vice versa), he must take account, in his theorization and outlining of a metapsychology, of all, or part, of the existing body of physiological knowledge. In other words, the monist's theorization must satisfy the minimum requirement that, for him, a theory of the organizational principles of psychic functioning shall *at least not conflict* with a theory of the organizational principles of physiological functioning. Since no definitive answer can at present be given to the question "Monism or dualism?," and since there are good arguments on both sides, neither position deserves to be discredited. Objectively, after all, the choice of one or other of these positions is merely an *initial hypothesis*, concerning which the question necessarily arises: What *consequences* will ensue if I take this hypothesis as my starting point? And later: Is the theory constructed on the basis of this initial hypothesis capable of accurately describing the relevant phenomena and if possible of accounting for them?

In his paper "Psychoanalytic Theory and the Mind–Body Problem," Rubinstein (1965) presents a comprehensive discussion of the "monism or dualism" question, and adopts a position that I can substantially accept: like Hebb (1955), he holds that there is no such thing as a mind without a body, and that therefore no psychological theory can be conceived completely independently of physiology—in particular, of neurophysiology. Phenomenal events, such as the experiences of wishing, thinking, perceiving, or dreaming, are always accompanied by bodily sensations that can be perceived with greater or lesser clarity, as well as by measurable physiological changes. Every phenomenal event may therefore be said to have a (neuro)physiological correlate; that is the hypothesis of an empirical parallelism.

> We must remember that, although mind and brain can be conceptually separated, they cannot be thought of as factually separable unless we adopt the dualistic view. It follows that, however indirectly and merely implicitly, a statement about the mind is also a statement about the brain. Accordingly, a theoretical psychological model, even if quite abstractly formulated, cannot be completely devoid of existential, i.e., neurophysiological, meaning. [Rubinstein, in Peterfreund 1971, p. 3]

Rubinstein now goes a step further, saying that statements about correlated events are also correlated but not mutually translatable without a change of referential field—that is, without a *translation* from one *language* into the other, because phenomenal and neurophysiological (or protoneurophysiological) statements belong to different languages. If two statements are correlated, this means that, if one of them is true, so too is the other; correlated statements are logically, but not empirically, equivalent. It thus turns out that the different solutions to the body–mind problem concern the contradiction between *logical equivalence* and *empirical difference*. See Figure 3.

Dualism postulates two different spheres of existence, the psychic and the somatic. The events of each are completely independent of one another but perfectly synchronized (metaphysical parallelism), or are deemed to be causally linked in the body-to-mind direction (epiphenomenalism) or in both directions (interactionism). At any rate, these theories interpret empirical difference as transempirical—that is, metaphysical—difference. Monism, by contrast, interprets empirical difference as transempirical identity. From this point of view, two correlated events are fundamentally one,[7] but appear in different forms, as psychological and (neuro)physiological events, so that they belong in the world of what can be subjectively experienced and in that of the objectively observable. Putting this once again in different language, namely the terminology of Feigl (1958, quoted in Rubinstein 1965, p. 39), we may say that correlated phenomenal and neurophysiological terms have the same denotation but different connotations. Of the theories mentioned here, epiphenomenalism and identity theory are stated to be the most accepted and discussed, interactionism as a rule being rejected because it implies a discontinuity in the causality of the physical world.

---

7 As formulated by von Weizsäcker (1971), the identity hypothesis is as follows: "Consciousness and matter are different aspects of the same reality" (p. 315 [translated for this edition]).

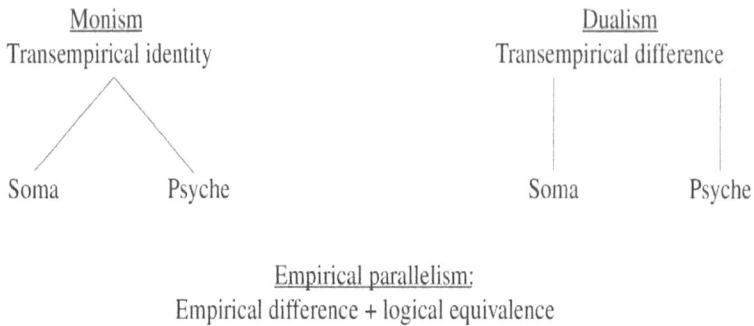

| Monism | Dualism |
| Transempirical identity | Transempirical difference |

Soma   Psyche   Soma   Psyche

Empirical parallelism:
Empirical difference + logical equivalence

FIGURE 3.

As Rubinstein shows, in the position of empirical parallelism it must be clearly realized that phenomenal and (proto)neurophysiological statements are correlated but not directly mutually translatable; they are *empirically always different* even when transempirically identical. This, in his view, is the only strictly empirical general formulation of the body–mind problem (Rubinstein 1965, p. 40). Phenomenal terms, such as those inherent in the statement "P desires O," are thus not directly translatable into neurophysiological terms. This is, however, not the case for theoretical statements, such as postulates, assumptions, and hypotheses: if our premise were that theoretical assertions are not translatable into neurophysiological statements, we should have opted for a dualistic interpretation, because a statement cannot be translated into another if the two statements have different references. If we presume, on the other hand, that the theoretical statements of psychoanalysis are translatable into neurophysiological statements (that is, that the referents of metapsychological statements are also neurophysiological events), this would mean that at least *some* neurophysiological statements can be referred to psychological statements, as both epiphenomenalism and identity theory assume. Rubinstein concludes from this that we can keep open the choice between epiphenomenalism and identity theory only by adopting a monistic position in the interpretation of psychoanalytic theory (metapsychology) (p. 41).

Hence our choice of initial hypothesis already determines our conception of a psychoanalytic theory—that is, of metapsychology and its terms. Rubinstein

(1965) discusses three different possibilities. First is a *psychological interpretation of psychoanalytic theory*; this means that the high-level terms of the theory have as referents purely psychological entities only, and are therefore not translatable into neurophysiological terms. Such a conception of metapsychology would mean that we have opted for a dualistic theory. Second, we may decide on a *metaphorical interpretation of psychoanalytic theory* by starting from the assumption that the terms have only metaphorical significance. This is the position of an "as-if dualism" or "pseudo-dualism" (p. 46): if the terms have only metaphorical significance and we at the same time hold that there is a correlation between psychic and physiological processes, we are admitting that the terms do not have real referents. This interpretation, according to Rubinstein, avoids the body–mind problem at the cost of degrading the theory to low-level status. The third and last possibility is a *neurophysiological interpretation of psychoanalytic theory*. This assumes that the high-level terms of metapsychology refer to neurophysiological events or entities—that is, that these theoretical terms of psychoanalysis are wholly translatable into neurophysiological terms; as Rubinstein notes, this is a possibility that Freud alludes to on several occasions, and which he may be said to have worked toward (Freud 1914c, p. 78f.). Rubinstein manifestly opts for this third interpretation, because at the same time it offers an elegant solution:

> On this combined view the high-level theoretical terms would be definable *both* neurophysiologically *and* in terms of psychological relationships. Statements including these terms would thus be verifiable in two directions: physiologically and psychologically. [p. 47]

According to this conclusion, then, metapsychological statements would be of such a nature as to be verifiable (and falsifiable?) in *both* directions—of physiological and of psychological events. Metapsychology, understood in this way as a high-level theory, would thus form a bridge between psychology and physiology; it would, as it were, lie midway between them, and would be precisely what Freud postulates for the metapsychological term *drive*, namely *a supraordinate boundary theory, formulated in terms straddling the boundary between the psychic and the somatic.*[8]

However, Rubinstein (1965) retreats from this position—and here I can no longer follow him—when he continues: "Thus interpreted, psychoanalytic theory would be *in part* a metaphorical expression of neurophysiological theory, or, as I would prefer to say, it would be a *protoneurophysiological model*" (p. 47). But in his view this interpretation of metapsychology is not possible, because its high-level terms are at present precisely *not* translatable into neurophysiological terms. For instance, structure is stated to be an anatomical concept, although there are so far no indications that it might one day be possible to define something like the id, ego, or superego in strictly neuroanatomical terms. Moreover, energy, Rubinstein goes on, is a vitalistic concept and is precisely for that reason not usable in neurophysiological sense; the physicochemical term *energy* is a nondirectional magnitude, that is, a scalar, which is defined solely by its magnitude; the notion of psychic energy, on the other hand, as used, for instance, in the context of "libidinal cathexis," is a goal-directed quantity and hence vectorial (p. 44). However, this interpretation of psychic energy does not distinguish between the terms "drive" and "drive force" on the one hand and "psychic energy" and "drive energy" on the other: while the term "drive" or "drive force" is used to describe a vectorial quantity characterized by both its *direction* and its *magnitude*, "psychic energy" can, conversely, perfectly well be employed in a scalar sense as, precisely, the *magnitude* activated or made available by the drive (the magnitude of the vector is a scalar quantity). Formulations such as "libidinal cathexis" may from this point of view be regarded as elliptical or *pars pro toto* stylistic devices: the drive is responsible for direction, whereas its magnitude, or what is being directed, is psychic energy. Concerning the objection to the term "structure," we need only adduce Freud's repeated rejection of any direct equation of his psychic topography with

---

8 As long ago as in 1948, Wiener expressed "the conviction that the most fruitful areas for the growth of the sciences were those which had been neglected as a no-man's land between the various established fields" (Wiener 1948, p. 8).

specific neuronal structures in the brain (e.g., 1900a, p. 536; 1915e, p. 174); his topographical theory and later structural theory define positions within his *theoretical* model and not anatomical concepts. In any case, there is no reason to rule out the possibility that a precise formulation of the relations between these metapsychologically postulated structures and the cortical functions of the human central nervous system might after all one day be feasible.

However, one issue is even more important than the definition of metapsychological terms. Rubinstein first suggests that the required high-level terms should be such that they refer *at one and the same time* to neurophysiological and psychological relationships, and goes on to postulate that psychoanalytic theory, at least in part, ought to be a metaphorical expression of a *neurophysiological* theory or, as he would like to call it, a *protoneurophysiological* model. If this "proto" is to be understood in the sense of a "prototype," or—perhaps better—of a "proto-science,"[9] this would imply that metapsychology does not yet exist in a mature—as it were, formalized (mathematized)—form. At the same time, however, the requirement of proto-*neurophysiological* terms, or a proto-*neurophysiological* model, draws attention to a distortion of perspective in the originally intended mediating or bridge function of metapsychology. Just as in this case, from the point of view of psychoanalysis or of psychology in general, the metatheoretical terms ought to be proto*neurophysiological*, so, from the standpoint of physiology, the metatheoretical terms should be proto*psychological* ones; in other words, the terms of the metatheory should actually be proto-psychoneurophysiological. Rubinstein (1967) ought then to be reminded of his original aspiration: "Protoneurophysiological terms are not neurophysiological terms. They merely in a general way *point* to neurophysiological events; and for the most part these are yet to be discovered" (p. 75). This after all means that metatheoretical terms with proto-psycho-neurophysiological scope, as last mentioned, would merely *refer* to both psychological and physiological processes, but not

---

9 The term *proto-science* was used by Andrew Lang in his view of myths as a kind of primitive, first, or primal form of science (Kirk 1974, p. 53f.).

that the metatheoretical terms "energy" and "structure" correspond *directly* to a physicochemical term "energy" and an anatomical term "structure." Understood in this way, a metatheory (in the sense of a meta-psychophysiology) would be characterized by a specific departure from both the former and the latter conception of the relevant terms. The psychoanalysts' charge that metapsychology does not fit in with clinical and psychic phenomenology (the patient's manner of experiencing) finds its counterpart in the critique voiced by Rubinstein and others that metapsychological terms are inconsistent with biophysics and neurophysiology.[10] See Figure 4.

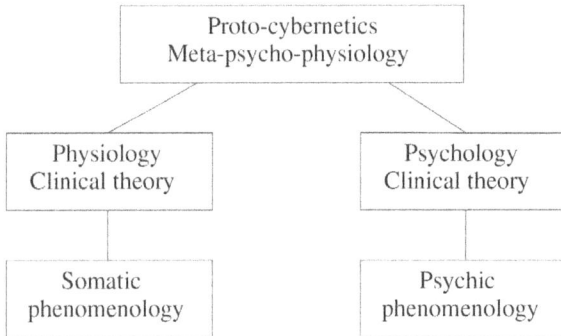

```
                  ┌─────────────────────────┐
                  │    Proto-cybernetics    │
                  │  Meta-psycho-physiology │
                  └─────────────────────────┘
                   /                       \
    ┌────────────────────┐        ┌────────────────────┐
    │     Physiology     │        │     Psychology     │
    │   Clinical theory  │        │   Clinical theory  │
    └────────────────────┘        └────────────────────┘
              │                              │
    ┌────────────────────┐        ┌────────────────────┐
    │      Somatic       │        │       Psychic      │
    │   phenomenology    │        │   phenomenology    │
    └────────────────────┘        └────────────────────┘
```

FIGURE 4

10 A number of objections have been raised to the idea that it might be possible to formulate a higher-order theory valid *simultaneously* for the somatic and the psychic. One of the soundest is the *complementarity thesis*. This notion, due to Niels Bohr (which has recently been invalidated in the field of the nanosciences), concerns the fundamental limitation of science—for example, that an electron can, by virtue of the instruments used for observation, be detected and described only as *either* a particle *or* a wave. In this sense, Edelheit (1976) argues that neurophysiological and psychological concepts are always complementary; neither are reducible to or subsumable into the others, and they therefore should be kept isolated from each other. Noy (1977) for the same reasons recommends that metapsychology should be seen as a "multimodel system," based on different models rather than a single one.

INFORMATION AND SYSTEMS THEORY

From this Rubinstein (1965) concludes that psychoanalytic theory should rid itself of its obsolete postulates and introduce new theoretical terms compatible with contemporary neurophysiological concepts; and he gives *information* as an example of such a concept. This proposal is perfectly consistent; after all, a combination of information and systems theory would satisfy many of the requirements applicable to a modernized theory of psychoanalysis: information theory is a mathematical theory concerned with both the quantitative *and* the structural exploration of information, so that it conforms to the mathematizing tendency of the sciences as already described by Rapaport; and systems theory, as a *supraordinate exact and empirical universal science* that concerns itself, independently of specific contents (qualities), solely with the structures (interrelationships and interactions) of a system could assume the meta-position or trans-position demanded by Rubinstein and by Holt (1965)—that is, a mediating or boundary position between psychology and physiology. All this argues in favor of the idea that information and systems theory (or, taken together, cybernetics) constitutes the appropriate framework for a higher-order metatheory in the boundary area between psychic and somatic processes. That, indeed, is the position of Holt (1965), Peterfreund (1971), and Rosenblatt and Thickstun (1977), who, like Rubinstein, dispute the sense of an interpretation of metapsychology as a purely psychological theory entirely cut off from the world of the natural sciences, and who therefore advocate the addition to clinical theory of a new metatheory, for which information and systems theory would constitute the appropriate reference framework.

Peterfreund (1971) examines the problem of how scientifically reliable data can be derived at all from a psychoanalytic process, given that, in this process, the analyst and the analysand are two highly complex, multilayered systems that constantly alter and mutually influence each other in still unknown ways. This, however, he argues, is a general biological problem: all living systems are complex multilayered systems, which change and are changed, and are nevertheless regulated homeostatically. Psychoanalysis, in his view, deals only with a selected portion of a natural phenomenon of this kind, just as physicists and biologists do, and it would therefore be unusual if the *basic logical structure* of an appropriate psychoanalytic theory were completely different from that of the theories of other disciplines concerned with natural biological phenomena. After all, it is repeatedly objected, the natural sciences have long completed the shift, described by Norbert Wiener in 1948, from the "power engineering" paradigm of the nineteenth century (operating with systems in which masses or their energy equivalents are moved by forces) to the twentieth-century "information engineering" paradigm (concerned with signal transmission processes), whereas psychoanalytic theory, with its drive-energy model, remains bogged down in the obsolete "power engineering" paradigm (Rosenblatt and Thickstun 1977, p. 542).

In his comprehensive discussion of the basic terms of systems theory, Peterfreund (1971) therefore defines information, structure, and process. From a biological point of view, the term "information" always refers to a pattern of physical events or to the relationship between such patterns; a pattern arises out of a series of causally interconnected signals responsible for the encoding and decoding of information. The signals and patterns may vary or be changed from one form to another; however, what remains the same in each case is the information conveyed. Hence the information does not exist independently of matter and energy, but it is not the same as energy: its essential aspect is the pattern. For Peterfreund, who always uses the term "information" in this strictly physical, nonpsychological sense, psychic experience corresponds to the route whereby information is communicated, or transmitted, within the CNS. "Structure" and "process" in this sense are also conceived as basic biological concepts: according to J. G. Miller (1965), the term "structure" tends to be used rather in a static sense to describe a particular configuration of matter, energy, and information within a system at a given point in time (transverse section)—a kind of "frozen action"—whereas "process" concerns dynamic changes in matter, energy, and information over a given period of time (longitudinal section). The organism's various information-processing control systems are, like the associated structures and processes, organized hierarchically (Peterfreund 1971).

Peterfreund (1971) formulates his psychoanalytic informationsystems theory as follows on the basis of these fundamental positions:

1. The CNS is an information-processing system of high capacity and complexity.
2. The organism is endowed with a large number of hierarchically organized, feedback-regulated information-processing programs and with open program and memory capacities, which are in part subject to maturation.
3. Existing programs are adapted and reprogrammed (learning) by the arrival of new information.
4. Psychic experiences during waking and sleep (thoughts, fantasies, affects, dreams, etc.) are conceptualized as phenomena that correspond to or parallel the activity of specific complex hierarchically arranged programs.
5   Pathological experience could then result from defective or inappropriate programming, and conflicts from a form of programming logically incompatible with the aimed-for objective.
6. Control, adaptation, organization, and integration (the ego functions) are the properties of an optimized information-processing system.
7. The psychoanalytic process is a learning process with the properties of a complex feedback-regulated system between the analyst and the analysand. [p. 147ff.]

No objections can be raised to these fundamental theses. However, their application implies something like the following. Walking is the result of the activity of an information-processing program responsible for walking, and defective walking is due to an error in or crash of this program. The same applies to other examples. For instance, derealization and depersonalization are stated to be dramatic clinical examples of far-reaching programming deficiencies. Repression is described as the exclusion of information or programs from processes associated with consciousness. Or, more fully: during sleep we operate on a generally lower level of organization and activity, and have less sensory input, and so forth, hence the idiosyncrasies of dreams; in other words, there is no need for the mechanisms of the dream work and censorship described by Freud, for the assumption of wish fulfillment, for the idea that dreams are the guardian of sleep, or for the theory of the primary and secondary processes; these are all limited and inappropriate if the particularities of dreams are understood as the consequence of a failure of the information-processing systems active in waking life. Differences between sleeping and waking are therefore "explained" as differences in information processing—in simple language, then, waking results from the activity of "waking" programs, while nonwaking and the particular features associated with it are consequent on the nonactivity of these "waking" programs (Peterfreund 1971).

In this way, Rosenblatt and Thickstun (1977a), too, are ensnared by their own model construction. In their view, the key to a workable concept of motivation lies in the addition of what they call "appraisal processes," such as feelings or affects. Motivational systems (e.g., a "need system" or "defense system") are complex hierarchically organized behavioral systems containing appraisal loops (p. 295). Here are some examples. A central drive state is the integration of all currently activated motivational systems. Attention and repression are seen as regulated by all simultaneously activated motivational systems and their appraisal processes. Perception consists in a passage through a number of appraisal processes of simultaneously activated motivational systems. The storage of memories is strongly influenced by the motivational systems activated at the time of their inscription, and memory retrieval is likewise controlled via an integration of the activated motivational systems. Learning, which depends on the processes of perception and remembering, is influenced by the appraisal processes of the activated motivational systems. In this connection:

We would define motivation as *the integrate or composite of the appraisal processes of all currently activated motivational systems*. Motivation thus involves selection (including assignment of priority), direction, organization, and invigoration of action—but no hypothetical force or energy, although the felt aspects of the appraisal processes may have an experiential quality of urgency or drivenness. [Ibid.,   p. 301]

Briefly, then, motivation is the activity of all activated motivational systems, and everything is ultimately attributable to "the integrate or composite of the appraisal processes of all currently activated motivational systems," thus disposing of the obsolete terms "drive" and "energy"—although the term "motivation" (or "motivational system") is in fact just as much a construct as "drive." My account of the intentions and endeavors of Peterfreund and of Rosenblatt and Thickstun may perhaps seem a somewhat one-sided oversimplification. However, in bringing out the ultimately *tautological* structure of this argument, I am concerned to show that the substitution of (at the time) modern cybernetics for old-fashioned metapsychology has hitherto merely diluted the explanatory potential of psychoanalytic theory: the dynamics of psychic functioning have, as it were, been processed out of existence by systems theory (Friedman 1972[11]). Damson (1974) has rightly drawn attention to the fallacy in Peterfreund's argument whereby he seeks "to achieve two completely different objectives with a *single* instrument (cybernetics), namely a formal-theoretical objective and at the same time a reorientation in content of the corpus of psychoanalytic thought" (p. 272

---

11 Friedman (1972) here identifies a conceptual deficiency in Peterfreund's theory: whereas it is stated to be an attempt to eliminate *intentionality*, its author is, in Friedman's view, unable to show within the theory itself how the motives and programs that control behavior are developed, learned, modified, and switched on and off; nor, he objects, would programs seek, for example, to fulfill themselves (a notion revealing a latent anthropomorphism in Peterfreund too): "None of this means that an information-systems theory of the mind is untenable. Indeed, it must be granted that a theory of the mind is a theory of the brain, and if nerve impulses can be discussed in terms of information systems, so in principle can mental functioning. But Peterfreund's theory does not reinterpret the core models of psychoanalysis. Peterfreund has only shown that one can easily talk about the mind in computer terms, and thus in terms of other sciences" (Friedman 1972, p. 553).

[translated for this edition]). However, as this author says, owing to its high degree of abstraction cybernetics could be applied to any number of sciences—precisely because it is not concerned with the content of a theory but seeks only to bring out its organizing and structural aspects. On the level of content, therefore, a reorientation cannot be expected from the application of cybernetics.

BOTTOM-UP AND TOP-DOWN RESEARCH STRATEGIES

The work of Peterfreund (1971) highlights yet another problem in the critique of metapsychology. He admittedly recognizes that theories generally tend toward ever greater universality and abstraction, and that the different hierarchically organized levels of scientific explanation have different referential systems and languages, so that rules of correspondence must be established in order to link theoretical laws to observable facts; yet he nevertheless attempts direct testing of his high-level theory on examples from practice or psychic phenomenology, such as, for example, the depersonalization phenomena mentioned earlier or a simple walk in the street. He thereby leaves out an important step in translation, namely the clinical stage; as Rapaport (1960) had already noted, it "is doubtful that the long hierarchic chain of intermediary concepts interposed between the major explanatory constructs and the observables can be bypassed, and that direct relations can be found between them" (p. 36). Why, then, does Peterfreund proceed in this way? Why does he not remain on the "high level" of theory, considering that he is, after all, seeking to investigate the *logical structures* of psychoanalytic *theory*? He answers the question himself, maintaining that there is a broad consensus that "modern science begins with observation" (Peterfreund 1971, p. 24). That is also the point made by all the critics who pillory metapsychology for its remoteness from practice; these authors are typified by Langs, who makes the following demand in his contribution to a journal issue devoted to the methodology of psychoanalytic research:

Models, like hypotheses, should be generated by clinical observation and evolve into fundamental theories of human functioning only as they are borne out by evidence. One cannot formulate theories in the absence of data and then search for data to support the resulting concepts. Such concepts are inevitably cultural prescriptions disguised as metapsychology. [Langs 1989, p. 308]

The demand that empirical research should take priority is, however, based on an illusion about the potential of both our thinking and our perception. This has three elements: first, the assumption that we are capable of thinking up theories in complete independence of our experience or perception (pure "creatures of the intellect"); second, the notion that pure prior observation can lead us more objectively to the connections inherent in phenomena; and, third, the idea that we can experiment without presuppositions. In fact, all perception starts with presuppositions, which lie not in the object but in the subject of the research; and the same presuppositions that structure and limit our perceptions also structure our thinking. This epistemological problem, which has exercised minds at least since Kant and has long been an issue in the natural sciences too, acknowledges the fact that our cognitive capacity necessarily depends on biological structure (as can easily be overlooked in view of the highly complex organization of the central nervous system and the diversity and richness of human intellectual and mental activities); in line with a monistic position on the mind– brain issue, it indicates that our empirical researches and the "bottom-up" theories derived from them possess the same structure, dignity, or deficiencies as our theory-based research endeavors, the "top-down" strategies. The fact that the two approaches complement each other and form a circular model—with simultaneous uninterrupted mutual influencing of models and data (Moser 1989, p. 166)—points to the existence of both internal *processes of adaptation* and a fundamental, biologically or structurally determined endosystemic *situation of "fitting-together"* (Hartmann 1939, p. 38ff.); neither approach ought therefore to be dismissed. On this assumption, therefore, a revision of metapsychology without any reference to the aspects of psychoanalysis concerned with clinical phenomenology no longer constitutes a problem. On the contrary, "theory is the product of theory-making" (Rapaport 1960, p. 36). Again, if it is admitted that the weakness of metapsychology lies mainly (or partially) in its logical contradictions, lack of terminological consistency, and absence of systematization, then our first task should be to apply logic to the detection and elimination of these discontinuities in the logical chain, to arrive at solid and consistent definitions of terms, and thereby to contribute to a systematization of metapsychology.

However, is this feasible? Peterfreund, for whom metapsychology was "completely unacceptable" from the outset, takes the view that metapsychology with its fundamental assumptions should be abandoned in favor of a new paradigm, and that any attempt to revise it would be doomed in advance to failure (Peterfreund 1975, p. 536). Conversely, Holt (1965), like Amacher (1965), demonstrated not the discontinuity but the continuity of Freud's thought—even concerning his attachment to the Helmholtz-Brücke school—pointing out that Freud's model is endowed with at least five feedback loops and is thus no less self-regulating than a cybernetic model. Notwithstanding serious objections to individual elements of metapsychology (e.g., the reflex arc model, the notion of energy, and the principle of constancy), this author considers that psychoanalysis can, with relatively few modifications, emerge from its encapsulation and get back into the mainstream of scientific advance—but only by consistent pursuit of Freud's aspiration to forge a link between biology and psychoanalysis (Holt 1965). In the view of G. S. Klein (1996), the foundations of psychoanalytic theory could be laid in two possible ways. The first would be an attempt to systematize Freudian metapsychology by winnowing, reinterpreting, and reconciling (clarifying) the inconsistencies in his thinking over time, while at the same time highlighting the existing consistencies; the chief test of the success of such an enterprise would be the parsimony of integration and its logical cohesion. Second, specific important root assumptions could be selected and used as points of departure for an independent formulation of basic psychoanalytic principles. Klein opts for the latter alternative: for him the apparent advantage of this selective approach is that it allows him simply to pass over problematic concepts of metapsychology.

However, first Hartmann (1939) and later Rapaport (1960) pointed out that revisers who confine themselves to rejecting or replacing individual concepts without at the same time explaining how their revisions affect the theory as a whole obscure the existing structural unity of metapsychology:

> The theory of psychoanalysis grew by successive spurts in the fifty years of Freud's work. Additions and revisions make it appear more like a patchwork than an architectonic design, since their consequences for the structure of the system have often remained a matter of a passing comment by Freud or isolated papers by other psychoanalysts. This in itself bespeaks a looseness of the theory and the lack of an explicit canon according to which revisions and additions are   to be fitted into its system. *Yet psychoanalytical theory does have an impressive structured unity; though it is hidden under the layers of progressive additions and modifications, and has not been disentangled and independently stated.* [Rapaport 1960, p. 101, my emphasis]

It is a stony path indeed that Rapaport is suggesting here! It involves nothing less than an *archaeology of the argument structure* underlying the metapsychological papers. But, once again, is this feasible? How is it to be done? And why ought it to be feasible? Let us start with the last question: it is feasible because the "patchwork"—"mosaic" might be a better word—of psychoanalytic theory *in Freud's thought* has a unity and *virtual consistency* of its own. My thesis is as follows. Given normal mental health, we are *in principle* unable to think wrongly, because the correct specifically human process of thinking is *structurally* embodied in the design of our cognitive organ; our thinking can, of course, mislead us into all kinds of erroneous conclusions and logical fallacies, which then, along the lines of the secondary elaboration of our dreams, mask the sources of our (logical) errors, as well as the underlying *correctness, accuracy,* or *appropriateness* of our insights, with a confusing fabric of justifications. Freud reflected on this situation as follows:

> [I]n what do the *logical faults* consist? Stated briefly, in the nonobservance of the *biological rules* for the passage of thought. These rules lay down where

it is that the cathexis of attention is to be directed each time and when the thought-process is to come to a stop. They are protected by threats of unpleasure, they are derived from experience, and they can be transposed directly into the rules of logic— which will have to be proved in detail. Thus the intellectual unpleasure of contradiction, at which the passage of testing thought comes to a stop, is nothing other than the [unpleasure] accumulated for the protection of the biological rules, which is stirred up by an incorrect thought-process. *The existence of biological rules of this kind can in fact be proved from the feeling of unpleasure at logical faults.* [Freud 1950c/1950a (1895),[12] p. 386]

In reading Freud's metapsychological writings, we can therefore turn precisely this "feeling of unpleasure at logical faults" to account as a *signal* and, in each of the relevant passages, work to uncover the *correct* pathways of his thought that lie concealed beneath a colorful plethora of seemingly plausible arguments. Precisely in this sense, I have steadfastly adhered to the principle that it is possible to read Freud's metapsychological texts (like any other utterance, such as a dream or a story), and, by distinguishing between their superficial and deep structure, to bring out the *conceptual unity* and *logical consistency* of this theory. This unity and consistency should therefore be the focus of our endeavors in the following, notwithstanding all the manifest logical discontinuities of metapsychology and the manifest vagueness of many of its terms; for these shortcomings (aside from the insidious snares of a complex phenomenology-based terminology) ultimately prove again and again to be partly attributable to the simple fact that Freud *did not* distinguish between the different levels of theoretical statements, so that the pieces of the overall corpus of metapsychology in our possession have come to be situated on completely different levels of abstraction, each having so to speak been refined to different

---

12 [Translator's note: Strictly speaking, "1950c" stands for the complete German edition of the 'Project' presented in the supplementary volume (*Nachtragsband*) to the *Gesammelte Werke*; there is no English translation. However, "1950a" by itself is used for *The Origins of Psycho-Analysis*, so that, throughout this book, "1950c/1950a" should be understood as the version of the 'Project' featuring in Volume 1 of the *Standard Edition*.]

degrees. In other words, there are differences in the degree of formalization, not only within the various works published during a creative career spanning more than forty years but also within each individual work (for instance, theoretical considerations alongside clinical vignettes), as well as within concepts developed over the course of a number of works or even in some cases of his entire oeuvre (e.g., libido). However, in referring to psychoanalytic theory, we do, after all, have in mind the fiction of a unified level of abstraction or formalization. Distortions were therefore bound to arise in the conduct of the relevant arguments and in our conception of the terms concerned— and we realize at the same time that metapsychology, accommodated as it now is on these different levels, does, when referred to these levels, have a certain "correctness." So if matters sometimes appear askew, this is partly because of our expectation of a unified level of abstraction. This is a justified demand, so that our task must now be to achieve the necessary unification in the level of formalization of metapsychological concepts. That will indeed entail a laborious process of excavation and development.

But how is this to be done? If we hold fast, in the teeth of all objections, including those of content, to our aspiration, based on some form of monistic answer to the mind–brain question, to place metapsychology once and for all in the boundary zone between the mental and the somatic, then not only would "drive" be a "boundary term," precisely in Freud's sense, but metapsychology, too, would become a "boundary science" between psychology and physiology: it would become a *meta-psycho-physiology*, whose "proto"-terms would *refer* to both the psychic and the physiological. Again, if we remain faithful to the notion that the basic ideas of information and systems theory—or their combination, cybernetics—constitute the most suitable *formal* frame of reference for a higher-order theory of this kind, even if the first attempts did not succeed, we could then assert that Freud's essays, which were intended as *preliminaries* to a metapsychology, can be read anew in the sense of a *proto-cybernetics of psycho-physiology*. In choosing the term "*meta*psychology," Freud could be said, subject to the possibilities of his time, to have indicated the path along which his theory would be able to proceed.

So is metapsychology a superstructure or the foundation of psychoanalysis? That was the question posed at the beginning of this introduction. Both designations may be found in Freud: the intention of his metapsychological writings is "to clarify and carry deeper the theoretical assumptions on which a psycho-analytic system could be *founded*" (Freud 1916–1917f [1915], p. 222, note 1, my emphasis), while he at the same time regarded these as a "*speculative superstructure* of psychoanalysis, any portion of which can be abandoned or changed without loss or regret the moment its inadequacy has been proved" (Freud 1925d [1924], p. 32f., my emphasis). Let us consider first the "speculative superstructure." Consistent with this phrase is the idea of a metatheory, understood as a third level "above" the levels of clinical theory (in psychology and physiology) and the phenomenology that can be experienced both in everyday life and in (psychic and somatic) therapeutic practice; as an image, this conforms to the requirement that metapsychology should be a high-level theory and, so to speak, a theory on the highest level of abstraction, and that metapsychological theorization should correspond to a top-down strategy. However, such images must be handled with care, because they contain sympathetically resonating associations that may color our attitudes. For instance, the idea of "above" and "below," "high" and "low,"— that is, a "higher" degree of abstraction, or a "high-level" as opposed to a "low-level" theory—may be misunderstood as implying higher or lower *quality*, rather than being seen as a purely quantitative distinction denoting "more" or "less" generalization, abstraction, or concreteness. Furthermore, the idea of a "superstructure," together with Freud's invitation, quoted above, to replace individual parts of the theory should they prove inadequate, might tempt us to assume that the theory of psychoanalysis could be changed like a hat according to the fashion of the day—that we could try on this one or that, first the power engineering model, then cybernetics, and today chaos theory, depending on the requirements of the moment—without any significant repercussions for psychoanalysis. All the critics who wish to abolish large swathes of metapsychology or to replace it completely by something else appear to take this view, or at least a similar one.

The situation is, however, different if metapsychology is seen as a basis or foundation; it then immediately becomes clear that individual components cannot be ripped out without rocking or seriously jeopardizing the entire structure. This theory can then on no account be declared superfluous or simply abolished without in effect causing the entire edifice to collapse. Some may think this entirely reasonable or necessary. However, the idea of metapsychology as the basis and foundation of psychoanalysis clearly proves to be more than just an image if it is recognized as an attempt to conceptualize the unity of psyche and soma. If this unity is present (as the monistic position assumes), then it is the foundation of the psychic; then it determines the laws of psychology and physiology; and then there can be no question of aspiring to abolish a theory that seeks to conceptualize something of this unity.[13] To that extent, metapsychology, as I understand it, is certainly the foundation of psychoanalysis, even if it can at the same time, in other respects, also be seen as a kind of superstructure.

A NOTE ON THE STRUCTURE OF THIS BOOK

The formalized model of psychoanalytic theory put forward here will be developed by means of a chronological reading, detailed examination, and elaboration of Freud's metapsychological writings. His clinical contributions, theory of the neuroses, case histories, papers on technique, and essays on applied psychoanalysis will be either disregarded or considered only to the extent that they contain passages on metapsychological issues. In our attempt to follow every step of theway traveled by Freud in the construction of his

---

13 See also Grubrich-Simitis (1988, p. 29): "It is conceivable that the contribution to a possible solution of the body–mind problem might one day be counted among the undying Freudian achievements—along with the discovery of the unconscious and of infantile sexuality and the invention of the psychoanalytic method—and that in this 'in-between area' the modernity and viability of Freud's thinking would again be borne out. At the frontiers of our knowledge we should, with a gay naturalness, dare to indulge in creative fantasy, which also means, we should have the courage and the capacity to play."

theory, we shall encounter contradictions, logical discontinuities, lacunae, or gaps in his presentation that will induce us to reflect, leading us now to a deeper understanding of his intentions and now to alternative answers to outstanding questions. The proposed solutions yielded by this approach will each be noted and carried forward to the next stage of theoretical conceptualization. Our chronological reading will therefore be paralleled by the genesis of a model of psychoanalytic theory that is novel in so far as it did not previously exist in such explicit form, as well as by virtue of the new ideas and insights it contains, which could not have accrued without this review. However, in so far as this analysis allows the fundamental structures of Freud's model of the psyche, as already outlined in rudimentary form in his metapsychology, to achieve their fullest expression, it can also perfectly well be seen as conservative in the best sense of the word.

Metapsychology is here treated in accordance with the restrictive conception I have expounded in this introduction: all metapsychological terms and concepts are used as constructs, and when they are combined to form propositions, hypotheses, and postulates, the combination is subject solely to the laws of logic. It must therefore always be borne in mind that, in referring here to, for example, a drive, the ego, or the oedipal phase, we mean not the concrete phenomena encountered in our practice but only conceptualizations of processes and structures, to which hypothetically determined laws and functions are assigned. Let me emphatically stress this point again before proceeding to the main part of this book. We more or less take it for granted that an entity such as "the id" has only a theoretical, and not a concrete or real, existence; but even such a basic term as "the unconscious" can be defined in different ways (it was, of course, to preclude such variations that Freud substituted the term *id* for the *Ucs.*). Every analysand and every practicing analyst has, after all, experienced the existence of the unconscious through its effects, so that we shall constantly have to remind ourselves that the unconscious (as a phenomenon) can be experienced, but not *the system Ucs.*, which is a component of our metapsychological constructions. Within this restrictive conception of metapsychology, a question such as "Is there such a thing as a death drive?" is therefore a concretistic misunderstanding—or else it must be reformulated as "Is it practical, or necessary, or heuristically appropriate, or logically correct, or compatible with our other assumptions, to introduce the *theoretical construct* of the 'death drive' into our model of the psyche?"[14] Hence the level of metapsychology will be reserved here solely for the assumed organizational principles whose existence we postulate when we hold that certain regularities are exhibited in psychic processes. On the other hand, it is in practice virtually impossible to confine our examination wholly to formal aspects and to disregard content completely; a text composed in this way would be quite indigestible and either almost unreadable or readable only with difficulty. For this reason, the phenomena will repeatedly be given a voice; this is indeed an automatic result of work on Freud's texts. In dealing with, for example, the Oedipus complex, we shall refer to the child, the mother and father, and castration anxieties, but always with the object of bringing out and presenting in theoretical terms the organizational principles within the "psychical apparatus" that underlie these relationships. Since this feat of discrimination, which must constantly be accomplished anew, is one of the most difficult mental hurdles to be overcome in this conception of metapsychology, I shall remind the reader of it from time to time, especially at points where the distinction is critical.

On the assumption that the theoretical common ground of all psychoanalysts is embodied in Freud's metapsychological works, I have decided to engage myself and the reader in a discussion with Freud alone; he is after all an extremely potent interlocutor, who still merits our entire attention and concentration. On the other hand, the psychoanalytic thinking of every one of us has been partly molded by the scientific contributions, proposed theoretical solutions, and further developments of psychoanalysts from the post-Freudian period to the present day; their work has changed our vision,

---

14 As long ago as in 1935, Bernfeld pointed out that Freud had repeatedly stressed that the drive "is a scientific term very remote from observable circumstances, and that it is therefore not a matter of distinguishing whether a particular drive 'exists,' but of whether it is desired to 'assume' its existence" (Bernfeld 1935, p. 125 [translated for this edition]).

decisively deepening and in some cases also modifying our understanding of certain concepts. Whether or not we realize it in each individual case, anyone who sets out today to read and understand Freud (or to do so anew) stands on their shoulders. The corpus of literature on metapsychology alone is vast: critical, constructive, and illuminating contributions exist on every issue and concept. Over the years I have read a great deal on the theoretical foundations of psychoanalysis, but certainly by no means everything. To contain the volume of this book within acceptable limits, I have had to confine the references in my footnotes to a small number of authors. Given the abundance of interesting publications on metapsychology, it is surely inevitable that others before me will have had the same or similar ideas, and come to the same or similar conclusions, on various matters. This would merely argue in favor of these views. (Many contributions on clinical theory, too, include longer or shorter passages on metapsychological issues.) In consequence, I may perfectly well have occasionally taken up an idea originated by another author, used perhaps in a different context. While I am therefore not concerned to claim priority for the individual reflections put forward in this study, I do assert sole authorship of *the version presented here of the formalized model of Freudian metapsychology as a whole*, including the introduction of the term *lethe* in connection with Freud's conception of the death drive. It would have been interesting to end by comparing this model with other metapsychological or psychoanalytic models (considered in each case as a whole), but this idea too had to be dropped on grounds of space. In such an enterprise, in fact, a choice has to be made as to whether to go for depth or for breadth. What I have attempted is a deep-going examination of the entire breadth of Freud's metapsychology; and I commend the resulting model to the psychoanalytic community for further in-depth discussion across the breadth of the contemporary literature on the theory of our discipline.

I

FOUNDATIONS OF THE MODEL

(analysis of Freud's writings
from 1895 to 1905)

GENERAL FUNCTIONAL PRINCIPLE
AND QUANTITATIVE ASPECT

"A project for a Scientific Psychology," which dates from 1895, is Freud's first metapsychological work and stands at the beginning of the development of psychoanalysis. In this early theoretical contribution, Freud was attempting to draft a "Psychology for Neurologists" (Freud 1985c [1887–1904], p. 127); more accurately, his aim was twofold: "to examine what shape the *theory of mental functioning takes* if one introduces quantitative considerations, a sort of *economics of nerve forces*; and, second, ... [to furnish] *clear assumptions about normal mental processes*," as a background against which to arrive for the first time at "a satisfactory *general conception* of neuropsychotic disturbances" (p.129, my emphasis). He first used the term *metapsychology* in a letter to Fliess dated February 13, 1896: "I am continually occupied with psychology— really *meta*psychology" (p. 172). Then, two years later, when he was no longer working on the "Project," he again spelled out what the word meant for him: "It seems to me," he wrote to Fliess in connection with his work on *The Interpretation of Dreams*, "that the theory of wish-fulfillment has brought only the psychological solution and not the biological—or, rather, metaphysical— one. (I am going to ask you seriously, by the way, whether I may use the name metapsychology for my psychology that leads behind consciousness.)" (p. 301f.). This shows that the term "metapsychology," which the "Project" ushers in, was intended from the beginning to designate the theoretical place where psychology and biology meet *conceptually*—that is, on a theoretical, abstract level.

It is astonishing to see how many of the central notions of psychoanalysis are introduced in this early *sketch*: the *principle of inertia*; the *principle of constancy*; the *pleasure/unpleasure principle*; the *primary* process and the *secondary* process; the distinguishing of *unconscious, preconscious,* and *conscious*; the *ego* as a separate agency; *cathexis, discharge, inhibition, defense,* and *repression*; *hallucination* and *reality testing*; the *wish-fulfilling tendency of dreams* and the resemblance of dreams to neurotic symptoms; the importance of speech; and the rudiments of a theory of cognition. It will be shown here that, in addition, the basic elements of psychoanalytic *drive and structure theory* are already clearly outlined in the "Project." This work thus contains the theoretical foundations of psychoanalysis; it is really a project for a metapsychology. For this reason, Strachey, who from the beginning recognized the richness of this essay, published for the first time in 1950, considers it "no exaggeration to say that much of the seventh chapter of *The Interpretation of Dreams*, and, indeed, of Freud's later 'metapsychological' studies, has only become fully intelligible since the publication of the 'Project'" (Freud 1900a, p. xv).

This early work of theory, which did not appear complete [in German] until 1987, is not easily accessible even after a number of readings, and the "Project" is consequently one of Freud's least read texts.[1] The difficulty is that, while following the detailed (and often involved) description of the assumed "neuronal" pathways, one has to keep in mind, as it were at a higher level, the fundamental guiding ideas that governed the construction of Freud's model. However, if one manages to avoid total absorption by the concrete *content* of the individual statements and instead to concentrate more on the *structure of the argument*, then, on a more abstract level, one begins to discern the contours of a *model of the organizational principles of psyche and soma*—a model that remained fundamental to Freud's entire metapsychology. For this reason, our approach here takes the form of an attempt to follow the progression of Freud's

---

1 Fuller introductions to and discussions of the "Project" may be found in, for example, Pribram (1962, 1965), Wollheim (1971), Pribram and Gill (1976), Drews and Brecht (1982), Sulloway (1979), and Jones (1953–1957); on the singular importance of the "Project" for the foundations of psychoanalytic theory, see Peters (1960), Pribram (1969), and Basch (1975).

thinking—the *logical structure of the model he built*—and in so doing, it is perfectly acceptable to begin by imagining a neurone[2] as a concrete neurone, provided that we bear in mind that the neurone, or, as the case may be, the nervous system, is portrayed as a *functional unit,* and that, from the point of view of metapsychology, we are concerned solely with the *organization* of such a functional unit (or a different one). In other words, what matters for our purposes is not whether the state of neuroscientific knowledge to which Freud refers has now been superseded,[3] but *how* Freud reflected on what he held to be the case in order to construct a theoretical model of mental functioning.

From this vantage point, we can now consider the individual hypotheses underlying the general functional principle and the quantitative aspect of Freud's model of the mind.

(a) *Initial Position*

Freud opens the "Project" by declaring his "intention . . . to furnish a psychology that shall be a natural science: that is, to represent psychical processes as quantitatively determinate states of specifiable material particles, thus making those processes perspicuous and free from contradiction" (1950c/1950a [1895], p. 295). He thereby shows that he is concerned in this work not with the *experiential dimension* of the psychic—its contents, the "what" of psychic life; not, that is, with a *theory directed toward understanding*— but with the "quantification" of psychic processes at least to the extent that they can be assigned a *plus* or *minus* sign, or, as the case may be, a *zero* symbol, and arranged within a model in quantitative terms (i.e., as *more* or *less*); and the constituents of this model are Freud's quasi-"material particles." The initial hypothesis underlying his "general scheme" (ibid.) is thus that psychic processes

---

2 [Translator's note: The older spelling "neurone" is used here throughout in preference to the more modern "neuron" for the sake of consistency with the *Standard Edition.*]

3 Pribram and Gill (1976, pp. 34, 61) demonstrate by a number of examples that Freud's "Project" anticipates many of the findings of later neurophysiological research, and that his *conception* of the neurone and outline of neuronal *functions* are substantially correct and have not been superseded to this day.

conform to specific (logical and mathematical) laws and that they can be represented on a formalized level within a model (the psychical apparatus).

(b) First Principal Theorem: The "Principle of Inertia"

Freud immediately states that the system to be constructed (the psychical apparatus) is to have the tendency to remain in a permanent (stable) state; if it is driven out of this state by the action of forces of some kind, every form of activity is to have the aim of returning it to the original state. In other words, if the psychical apparatus, starting from its initial position, is exposed to the "supply" of a certain quantity of excitation, it will immediately attempt to get rid of it by "discharge": the supply of excitation (plus) and its discharge (minus) together satisfy what we may call the zero principle: $(+e) + (-e) = 0$. Since zero (i.e., any value arbitrarily taken as zero) is to be the *stable* initial position of the system, the *zero principle* (Freud's *principle of inertia*) is, in purely formal terms, simply a principle of regulation in the service of *homeostasis* (or, if you will, of the system's *dynamic stability*). This is the proposition of the first principal theorem and the fundamental principle of the model: *any departure (in this case, a supply of incoming excitation) from the reference value (in this case, zero) leads to measures on the part of the system (in this case, discharge) that restore the system's state to its reference value—that is, equilibrium—through homeostatic regulation (in this case, the principle of inertia).* The simplest way of representing this is as follows:

input variable $(+e)$ → law: zero principle → output variable $(-e)$

(c) The φ System

The activator of the psychical apparatus is in each case a quantitative stimulus. Freud distinguishes between exogenous and endogenous stimuli. The quantities of the *exogenous* or *environmental stimuli* (e.g., a ray of light falling on the eye, or a blow on the hand) are broken down by the "nerve-ending apparatuses" of the sense organs into quotients of their physical magnitude, and then pass via afferent pathways to a group of neurones, which Freud calls

φ (i.e., peripheral) neurones, that together form the φ *system* (p. 302), whence they are "discharged" again via the motor neurones of the efferent pathways. The principle of inertia is thus satisfied in the φ system by way of a *reflex movement*, in which the discharge ("flight from the stimulus") is proportional to the supply (magnitude of the stimulus)—thus restoring the initial position of the system (homeostasis):

exogenous (sensory) $\rightarrow$ φ system $\rightarrow$ motor discharge supply of stimulus

(d) The ψ System

The situation is more complicated in the case of the *endogenous* stimuli, such as "the major needs: hunger, respiration, sexuality" (p. 297); here, simple motor discharge would not eliminate the cause of the stimulus, because new quantities of excitation are constantly being produced inside the organism. These arise continuously, but it is only periodically, by "summation," that they attain a given minimum necessary stimulatory value, which then passes directly to the nucleus of the "ψ group of neurones" (ψ meaning psychic), the ψ *system*. The ψ system is "exposed" to this quantity of "Qs... without protection and in this fact lies the *mainspring* of the psychical mechanism" (p. 315f.): the result is an urgency for discharge of the stimulus, which in this case means an urgency for satisfaction of the need; this, however, is possible only "subject to particular conditions, which must be realized in the external world" (p. 297), so that what Freud calls a "specific action" is now necessary. The paradigm of such a process is the following series: hunger—screaming/search behavior—appearance of the nourishing object/nourishment—supply of nourishment—termination of the hunger stimulus. The sequence is now:

endogenous $\rightarrow$ ψ system $\rightarrow$ specific $\rightarrow$ termination
stimulus   action   of stimulus

(e) *Principle of Constancy*

As Freud acknowledges, this sequence extends beyond the model of a simple reflex movement: the specific action constitutes a much more complex process than simple discharge; it is an accomplishment that consumes more energy than is supplied by the cause of the stimulus alone.

> In consequence, the nervous system is obliged to abandon its original trend to inertia (that is, to bringing the level [of $Q\acute{\eta}$] to zero). It must put up with [maintaining] a store of $Q\acute{\eta}$ sufficient to meet the demand for a specific action. Nevertheless, the manner in which it does this shows that the same trend persists, modified into an endeavour at least to keep the $Q\acute{\eta}$ as low as possible and to guard against any increase of it—that is, to keep it constant. All the functions of the nervous system can be comprised either under the aspect of the primary function or of the secondary one imposed by the exigencies of life. [p. 297][4]

Hence "the exigencies of life" develop the *principle of constancy* out of the "trend to inertia": the ψ group of neurones must equip itself with (i.e., must store) a minimum of quantities of excitation in order to be capable at all times of effectively countering an increase in quantities of endogenous excitation within the organism by the performance of the specific action. However, even if the system deviates from its "zero level," the new term *principle of constancy* already indicates the persistence of the "principle of inertia": a new homeostatic ("zero") value is established, which must now be kept constant and restored whenever it is departed from.

(f) *Second Principal Theorem: The "Neurone Theory"*

To facilitate understanding of this process of storage—of both the quantity of excitation and the specificity of the action—Freud formulates what he calls his *neurone theory*, which is interesting in that it already contains essential

---

4 Freud distinguishes between Q (quantity in general, of the order of magnitude in the external world) and $Q\acute{\eta}$ (quantity of the intercellular order of magnitude).

propositions of his subsequent structure theory and theory of structural development. He writes:

> The main substance of these new discoveries is that the nervous system consists of distinct and similarly constructed neurones, which have contact with one another through the medium of a foreign substance, which terminate upon one another as they do upon portions of foreign tissue, [and] in which certain lines[5] of conduction are laid down in so far as they [the neurones] receive [excitations] through cell-processes [dendrites] and [give them off] through an axis-cylinder [axon]. They have in addition numerous ramifications of varying calibre.
>
> If we combine this account of the neurones with the conception of the $Q\acute{\eta}$ theory, we arrive at the idea of a *cathected* neurone filled with a certain $Q\acute{\eta}$ while at other times it may be empty. The principle of inertia finds its expression in the hypothesis of a *current* passing from the cell's paths of conduction[6] or processes [dendrites] to the axis-cylinder. A single neurone is thus a model of the whole nervous system with its dichotomy of structure, the axis-cylinder being the organ of discharge. The secondary function [of the nervous system], however, which calls for the accumulation of $Q\acute{\eta}$, is made possible by the assumption of resistances which oppose discharge; and the structure of neurones makes it probable that the resistances are all to be located in the contacts [between one neurone and another], which in this way assume the value of *barriers*. [p. 297f.]

Freud is here focusing on the nerve cell as a "model of the whole nervous system"—in other words, he is concerned not so much with the process within a concrete nerve cell as with a principle possessing general validity within the system as a whole. The most important point here is that there

---

5 [Translator's note: Freud's word *Richtungen* should actually be translated as "directions."]

6 [Translator's note: This is a translation of the German word *Zelleitungen*. The complete German edition (1950c [1895]), however, has *Zelleib*, which means "cell's body."]

is a "certain *Richtung* [direction] of conduction," in which the "current" flows; moreover, it flows from the "cell-processes" (dendrites) in the afferent direction via the "*Zelleib*" ["cell body"] (nerve cell) to the "axis-cylinder" (axon) in the efferent direction. In the language of the model, this may be expressed as follows. The process is *directional*: the input variable (supply of a quantity of excitation [plus]) and the output variable (discharge of a quantity of excitation [minus]) are vectorial magnitudes (that is, they are determined by value and direction). The principle of inertia is the homeostatic regulation that proceeds from the nerve cell in the direction of the axon; hence the nerve cell operates as a switch, as a control center, or, if you will, as a controller that contains the homeostatic law. This is illustrated by Figure I–1.

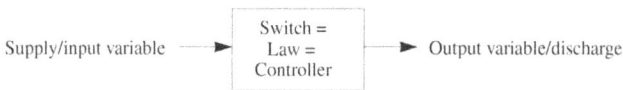

Figure I–I

This basic principle also applies within the afferent and efferent pathways: in order to reach a "central" switch or controller, the stimulus must cross a number of thresholds in the contact barriers; its discharge is likewise controlled by such thresholds. The above configuration can therefore be subdivided again—in principle, any number of times—the contact barriers also being assigned the function of switches, or, so to speak, of subcontrollers or microcontrollers (subordinate levels) in relation to a central main controller or macrocontroller (supraordinate level), as shown in Figure I–2.

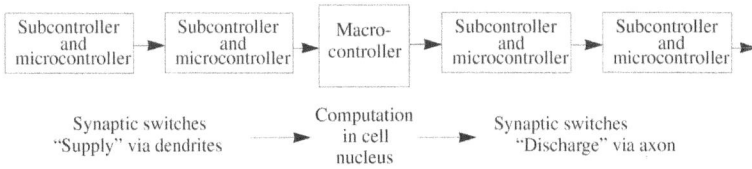

Figure 1–2

(g) Facilitation

Since the paths of conduction (of the nervous system) have multiple segments, the endogenous stimuli must overcome various resistances or thresholds before they reach the neurones of the ψ system. At each barrier in the path of conduction, therefore, a summation of the quantities of excitation is initially necessary; the barriers controlling conduction to the ψ system become permeable only when a given quantity is reached. At this point a *facilitation* arises and *partially persists* after the passage of the excitation—and, moreover, "the facilitation which remains after the passage of Q consists, not in the lifting of every single resistance but in its reduction to a necessary remaining minimum" (p. 317). This is now significant for the direction of future passages, as the next passage of endogenous excitation preferentially involves pathways (neurones) whose contact resistances already have a lower threshold value—that is, pathways that are *facilitated* and thus allow faster discharge. Freud thus assumes that "the process of conduction itself will create a differentiation in the protoplasm and consequently an improved conductive capacity for subsequent conduction" (p. 298f.). This interesting point in his theory must not be underestimated, because it states that the (repeated) passage of certain quantities of excitation through the "neuronal" pathways influences the controller value or switching principle (the synapse): in other words, the *process of conduction itself is structure-forming: the energetic activity of the system leads to the formation of structure!*[7]

---

7 Already in 1960, Rapaport had declared structure formation to be one of the central issues of psychoanalytic theory. Applegarth (1971), who also believes that the central question

(h) *"Information Processing" by the System ("Complication")*

With the introduction of facilitation through the partial lowering of resistances, Freud finds an initial answer to the question of how the system he has constructed can *learn*. However, a second question then immediately arises: Does a quantitatively greater stimulus in this case always produce a stronger psychic effect in ψ? Freud makes a distinction:

> Here a special contrivance seems to be present, which once again keeps off Q from ψ. For the sensory path of conduction in ψ[8] is constructed in a peculiar fashion. It ramifies continually and exhibits thicker and thinner paths, which end in numerous terminal points—probably with the following significance: a stronger stimulus follows different pathways from a weaker one. For instance, [1] $Q\acute{\eta}$ will pass only along pathway I and will transfer a quotient to ψ at terminal a. [2] ($Q\acute{\eta}$) will not transfer a double quotient at a, but will be able to pass also along pathway II, which is narrower, and to open up another terminal point to ψ (at β). [3] ($Q\acute{\eta}$) will open up the narrowest path [III] and will transfer through γ as well. This is how the single φ path is relieved of its burden; the larger quantity in φ will be expressed by the fact that it cathects several neurones in ψ instead of a single one. The different cathexes of the ψ neurones may in this case be approximately equal. If $Q\acute{\eta}$ in φ gives rise to a cathexis in ψ, then [3] ($Q\acute{\eta}$) is expressed by a cathexis in ψ1 + ψ2 + ψ3. Thus quantity in φ is expressed by *complication* in ψ. By this means the Q is held back from ψ, within certain limits at least. [p. 314f.]

---

of psychoanalysis, as a general psychology, has to do with the nature of psychic structure and the mechanisms of structure formation sees the "Project" as an ambitious attempt by Freud to develop a structural theory of this kind (ibid., p. 397) and, moreover, as an attempt to do so in such a way that *a connection between psychology and neurophysiology becomes unavoidable* (ibid., p. 386).

8 [Translator's note: The *Standard Edition* here has the Greek letter misprinted as φ.]

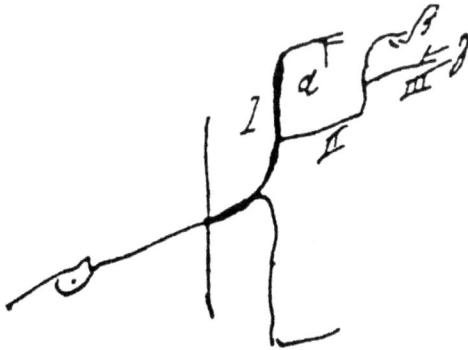

Figure 1–3. Ibid.

This can be imagined in simplified form as follows: a quantum of excitation exceeds the threshold of pathway I; pathway I passes only a certain quantity; there remains a residual quantity that is sufficient to pass through the "thinner" pathway II; and so on. Hence a larger quantum will give rise not to a greater threshold reduction in pathway I, and a consequent stronger stimulus in ψ, but to the distribution of the excitation over a number of pathways, and will thereby—and this is the crucial point in Freud's assumption of "complication" (divergence)—*generate a specific pattern of excitation*, which will be different in each case. In other words, the *information* corresponding to a given quantum of excitation is in effect converted, transformed, or "reformatted," so that information is preserved while the transfer of excitation, or consumption of energy, decreases.[9] In this way the "Project" not only reflects the hierarchical "construction of the

---

9 Pribram and Gill (1976) emphasize the importance of the distinction between energy and information, which originates in thermodynamics, whose first law concerns the *conservation* of energy and whose second law relates to its *organization*. The first states that an interaction between systems is limited by the fact that each action gives rise to an equal and opposite reaction. The principle of inertia enunciated in the "Project" corresponds to this. The second law deals with the quantitative change in the organization of energy systems involved in these interactions (conversion of energy). A similar distinction proved relevant in communications engineering: the quantity of energy required to maintain a system (radio, for example) does not bear any direct relation to the information processing carried out (e.g., a news bulletin, a symphony, a sports commentary, or merely the station's call sign). The amount of *organization*

nervous system out of several systems" (p. 306), but is, from its very design, already a surprisingly modern information processing model.

(i) The System's Memory

Freud's purpose in introducing the concept of contact barriers is wholly concrete. It is clear to him that a "psychological theory deserving any consideration must furnish an explanation of 'memory'" (p. 299). The problem of such an explanation lies in the fact that "it must assume on the one hand that neurones are permanently different after an excitation from what they were before, while nevertheless it cannot be disputed that, in general, fresh excitations meet with the same conditions of reception as did the earlier ones" (ibid.). The problem is solved by his assumption that the thresholds of the contact barriers in the neuronal pathways are permanently changed, whereas the (input) receptors of the neurones remain unaltered. The learning process of the ψ *neurones* (i.e., the memory of the ψ system) then consists firstly in the reduction of the resistance of the contact barriers, a reduction that differs in each case by virtue of the magnitude (quantity) and frequency (also a quantity) of a stimulus—that is, in the *facilitation* of the pathways—and secondly in the *distribution* ("complication") of the passages of excitation, that is, the different paths—associations (patterns)—that are thereby established. Now associations consist of nothing other than connections, or switches, that link different "neurones" together. Freud thus comes to the following general conclusion: "*Memory is represented by the facilitations existing between the ψ neurones*" (p. 300). Again, since memory after all has to do with the *particular* "preferred pathways" taken by the passage of an excitation, Freud immediately adds that "*memory is represented by the differences in the facilitations between the ψ neurones*" (ibid.).

---

that characterizes a communication was given the name *information* by Claude Shannon and Warren Weaver in 1949, a good half-century after Freud's "Project."

(j) *Building Blocks of a Hierarchical Organization*

It is impossible to overlook the paramount importance of the contact-barrier theory of the "Project" for metapsychology's subsequent theory of structural development. However, we shall now specifically show once again that it also demonstrates the great parsimony of the basic theoretical assumptions and the *stringency* of the entire model design. As we have seen, the principle of inertia set forth in the first principal theorem can be reduced to the formula in Figure I–4.

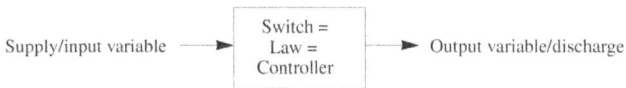

Supply/input variable ⟶ | Switch =
Law =
Controller | ⟶ Output variable/discharge

Figure I–4

We have recognized that the working of the contact barriers in Freud's "neurone theory" is based on the application of this principle of inertia: the contact barriers in the pathways also function as controllers of this kind, classifiable according to their position as microcontrollers, subcontrollers, or macrocontrollers. The various controllers (barriers in the pathways) incorporate modifiable laws (threshold values), differing according to the degree of their facilitation and their position, which they apply in order to restore the initial state of *homeostasis*. Any measure (switching operation) that brings the system, at whatever stage of its organization, into a *dynamically stable equilibrium* (the principle of inertia or of constancy) can be understood as a form of homeostatic control. These few assumptions already contain the foundations of the "psychical apparatus" model, as described not only in the "Project" but also in the later versions of Freud's metapsychology: *the entire system is hierarchically structured, regulated specifically according to hierarchical level, and made up simply of (input and output) variables (the subsequent drives) and controllers or switches (the subsequent structures).*

(k) *Cathexis*

Freud's reflections on the contact-barrier theory had started from the assumption that the psychical apparatus (and, within it, the ψ system in particular) had to lay up a certain store of quantity in order to perform the specific action. This process of "storing" quantities of excitation can now be imagined roughly as follows: if the passage of an excitation proceeds from its source via the φ and/or ψ neurones to some kind of "discharge," climbing through the various interposed contact barriers as if up a staircase—that is, if the thresholds become "higher" (the pathways "narrower") step by step (relative to the magnitudes transported)—then a certain store of quantities of excitation can as it were "get stuck" on each step; this will be precisely the store of excitation that is no longer strong enough to cross the next threshold in the sequence. Freud calls this storage of quantities of excitation at each level of the hierarchy a "cathexis." *The facilitation of the contact barriers and the cathexis of the ψ nuclear neurones*[10] *are therefore the result of one and the same quantitative passage.*

(l) *Inhibition*

On the basis of this assumption of a cathexis of the ψ group of neurones, Freud now develops a "third powerful factor," *inhibition*. He writes:

> If an adjoining neurone is simultaneously cathected, this acts like a temporary facilitation of the contact-barrier lying between the two, and modifies the course [of the current], which would otherwise have been directed towards the one facilitated contact-barrier. A *sidecathexis* thus acts as *an inhibition of the course of Qή* … If we suppose that a *Qή* enters a neurone *a* from outside (φ),

---

10 Within the ψ system, Freud distinguishes between the ψ *nuclear neurones* and the ψ *neurones of the pallium*: since the excitation of the φ system (which receives the exogenous stimuli) itself gives rise to an endogenous stimulus within the psychical apparatus, and the latter after all is supposed to be capable of distinguishing precisely between exogenous and endogenous stimuli—i.e., between *outside* and *inside*— he introduces a *topography of representation* by suggesting that "the ψ neurones should be divided into two groups: the neurones of the *pallium* which are cathected from φ and the *nuclear* neurones which are cathected from the endogenous paths of conduction" (p. 315).

then, if it were uninfluenced, it would pass to neurone *b*; but it is so much influenced by the side-cathexis *a*—a that it gives off only a quotient to *b* and may even perhaps not reach *b* at all. [p. 323f.]

This completes the development of the deciding factors that both control and (quantitatively) modify the passage of excitations within the psychical apparatus. To recapitulate, the passage of excitation leads to *facilitation* of the contact barriers—to a change in the controllers' resistance (that is, in their switching laws)—so that the excitation is routed in specific divergent directions (those of least resistance); the neurones' *divergence* and *cathexis* reduce (modify) the quantities of excitation and contribute to a further control of their passage, because each cathexis, in the form of a *"side-cathexis,"* can effect a further facilitation; this kind of control constitutes an additional *inhibition* for the course of the excitation. Here, then, Freud is already introducing his theory of the *primary* and *secondary processes* (for the secondary process is substantially characterized by the inhibition of discharge). All these considerations show him at work on a theory of the *control of passages of excitation within his model*; in other words, he is attempting to establish on a general level why a given stimulus follows an absolutely specific path, and which path it follows.

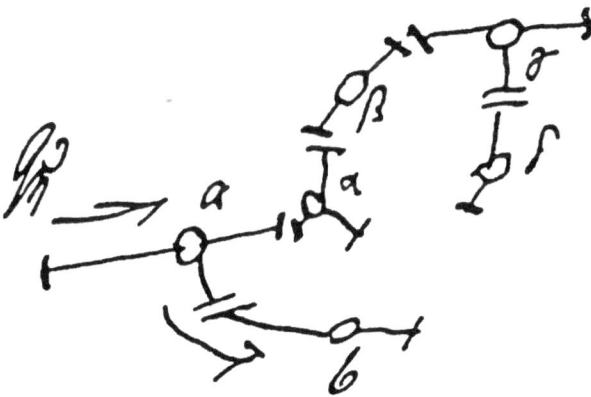

Figure 1–5. Ibid., p. 324.

(m) Introduction of the "Ego"

These theses now prove important for the introduction of the ego. The ego is conceived as a *hierarchically supraordinate (macro)structure*—namely, as an *organization* in ψ that influences the passages of excitation in a particular way. Freud imagines its genesis as follows:

> [T]he regularly repeated reception of endogenous *Qή* in certain neurones (of the nucleus) and the facilitating effect proceeding thence will produce a group of neurones which is constantly cathected and thus corresponds to the *vehicle of the store* required by the secondary function. Thus the ego is to be defined as the totality of the ψ cathexes, at the given time, in which a permanent component is distinguished from a changing one. [p. 323]

This is a *formal* definition of the ego. It states that the ego is composed, or consists, of a group, or network, of cathected neurones; in other words, it is the totality of "a complex of neurones which hold fast to their cathexis, a complex, therefore, which is for short periods at a constant level" (p. 369)—that is, a series of controllers whose operation is integrated (i.e., associated controllers), which, at least "for short periods," operate together by switching principles on approximately the same level—and in the process it so happens that "a permanent component is distinguished from a changing one." This means that the ego has at its disposal, firstly, a *permanent* part made up of cathected ψ neurones with a relatively higher level of organization—corresponding to constant homeostatic regulation at ego or secondary-process level—and, secondly, an additional *changing* part consisting of neurones that are manifestly only temporarily cathected (to a higher degree) and therefore do not belong to the ego's primary stock of neurones. This *interaction* of the ego's permanent nuclear stock, which is no doubt greater, with the fluctuating proportions of elements (neurones) that operate only temporarily at ego level, already constitutes the rudiments of the *dynamic organization of the ego*.

(n) Satisfaction of Needs: Origins of an Object-Relations Theory

Having sketched out this formal ("neurophysiological") model of the ego, Freud develops its *psychological* counterpart, by demonstrating the consequences of *interaction with an object* for the formation of the ego's structure: if, for example, "hunger"—that is, the endogenous stimuli corresponding to hunger—has overcome the various contact barriers and reached the ψ nuclear neurones, then, according to Freud, ψ "is at the mercy of [the quantity] Q, and it is thus that in the interior of the system there arises the impulsion which sustains all psychical activity. We know this power as the *will*—the derivative of the *drives*" (p. 317).[11] What now occurs is as follows.

> The filling of the nuclear neurones in ψ will have as its result an effort to discharge, an *urgency* which is released along the motor pathway. Experience shows that here the first path to be taken is that leading to *internal change* (expression of the emotions, screaming, vascular innervation). But... no such discharge can produce an unburdening result, since the endogenous stimulus continues to be received and the ψ tension is restored.[12] The removal of the stimulus is only made possible here by an intervention which for

---

11 Here as nearly everywhere else in the *Standard Edition*, Strachey translates Freud's term *Trieb* as *instinct*; sometimes, however, it is rendered as "motive" (e.g., *Triebkraft* as *motive force*). Freud in fact distinguished very precisely between *Trieb* and *Instinkt* (see footnote 1, p. 213, this volume). Now *Trieb* is understood in this book in a very specific formalized sense (to denote a vector, or unidirectional force), which differs fundamentally not only from the ethological notion of instinct (as a complex structured action or fixed pattern of action) but also from the more complex psychological concept of "motive." For this reason *instinct* and *instinctual* have here been tacitly replaced by *drive* in all quotations from the *Standard Edition*. This has occa sionally necessitated minor stylistic amendments. *Instinct* is retained only where Freud himself uses the word *Instinkt*. Holt, who advocates the abolition of the concept of *Trieb* and its replacement by "wish," points out "that Freud worked productively for his first 15 years as a psychoanalyst without the concept of *Trieb*, relying primarily on wish as his motivational term" (Holt 1976, quoted in Pribram and Gill 1976, p. 57). The passage quoted above, however, proves that Freud worked from the beginning with the idea of the drive, even if it only appears explicitly for the first time in his published oeuvre in an insertion, dating from 1915, in the *Three Essays on the Theory of Sexuality*, in a form analogous in every respect to his 1895 conception: "The source of a drive is a process of excitation occurring in an organ and the immediate aim of the drive lies in the removal of this organic stimulus" (Freud 1905d, p. 168).

12 [Translator's note: "and restores the *y* tension" would be a more accurate translation.]

the time being gets rid of the release of *Qή* in the interior of the body; and this intervention calls for an alteration in the external world (supply of nourishment, proximity of the sexual object) which, as a *specific action*, can only be brought about in definite ways. At first, the human organism is incapable of bringing about the specific action. It takes place by *extraneous help*, when the attention of an experienced person is drawn to the child's state by discharge along the path of internal change. In this way this path of discharge acquires a secondary function of the highest importance, that of *communication*, and the initial helplessness of human beings is the *primal source* of all *moral motives*. [p. 317f.]

It is thus clear that Freud incorporates the "external object" into his theory of the psychical apparatus from the beginning. The description of the first decisive interactions between mother and child thus contains the *basic schema* of every relationship between *inside and outside*—and hence the origin and nucleus of a *psychoanalytic theory of object relations*—while at the same time furnishing a pattern for the structuring processes, or processes of adaptation and learning, within the psychical apparatus: a "helpful object" for the first time makes possible the "specific action" that eliminates the urgency and, at the same time, the cause of the endogenous excitation, namely hunger. The result is an experience of satisfaction "which has the most radical results on the development of the individual's functions" (p. 318). What happens is that links are forged between (1) the specific neurones of the ψ nucleus that are affected by this urgency, (2) a cathexis of specific neurones of the ψ pallium that are excited by the (visual, olfactory, gustatory, tactile, auditory, etc.) perception of the helpful object, and (3) the "information of the reflex discharge" (which also takes the form of sensory excitations) that leads to a cathexis elsewhere in the ψ pallium, where it so to speak produces a "motor image" of the specific action. "A facilitation is then formed between these cathexes and the nuclear neurones" (ibid.). By virtue of this facilitation, every new endogenous excitation of the same kind—that is, every urgency generated by a *need stimulus* from the same source—will lead, in accordance with the "basic law of *association by simultaneity*," to a series of sensory excitations (equivalent to an *"object image"*) and "sensory excitations (from the skin and muscles)" (ibid.)—that is to say, a *"motor image."* Hence an *endo-senso-motor association* between *need, object, and action* is facilitated—and this association forms the basis of *hallucination.*

(o) The ψ System

A fresh difficulty now arises. If the object images and motor images once associated are recathected—that is, "remembered" (hallucinated)—upon each

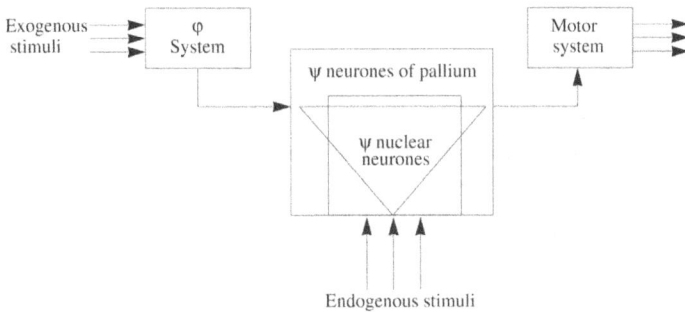

Figure I–6. Diagrammatic representation of the φ-ψ system. The three vertices of the triangle stand for the need (*drive stimulus*) (bottom), the *object image* (left), and the *motor image* (right), which are all excited together in hallucination, combined into a pattern of association (that is, a wish).

drive stimulus from the same source, how is the psychical apparatus then to tell whether the image of the object summoned up by an endogenous stimulus is a hallucination (reproduction) or a perception of reality (reception), and, consequently, to decide when it is appropriate to perform a motor action? Freud links the answer to this question, at least in part, to the conception of *consciousness*—and the phenomenon of consciousness, which every psychology both finds interesting and needs to explain, has, after all, not yet been elucidated within his model. He reflects as follows.

During perception the φ and the ψ systems are in operation together; but there is one psychical process which is no doubt performed exclusively in ω—reproducing or remembering—and this, speaking generally, is *without quality*. Remembering brings about *de norma* [normally] nothing that has the peculiar character of perceptual quality. Thus we summon up courage to assume that there is a third system of neurones—ω perhaps [we might call it]—which is excited along with perception, but not along with reproduction, and whose states of excitation give rise to the various qualities—are, that is to say, *conscious sensations*. [p. 308f.]

Here consciousness is the subjective side of one part of the physical processes in the nervous system, namely of the ω processes; and the omission of consciousness does not leave psychical events unaltered but involves the omission of the contribution from ω. [p. 311]

At first sight, Freud seems to be trying to resolve the issue of perception and consciousness tautologically by the introduction of neurones of perception or consciousness (ω for its resemblance to the "W" of *Wahrnehmung*, the German word for perception)—that is, with the aid of an *ω system*: consciousness is equated with the activity of neurones of consciousness, and omission of consciousness with the inactivity of these neurones. However, with the complex of the ω neurones, Freud is introducing a *third* system; this fact alone should preserve us from the temptation to dismiss the ω neurones overhastily as a tautological pseudo-explanation for consciousness. For all the variant forms of Freud's models are characterized by a *duality of variables* and a *triad of controllers*—for example, the systems φ, ψ, and ω; the *Ucs.*, *Pcs.*, and *Cs.*; or the structures id, superego, and ego. Does this *ω* system, then, have some special aspect that could not be conceptualized by the two systems introduced previously?

Let us now follow Freud as he sets about incorporating the *ω* neurones into his system. The idea is that the *ω* system is excited *upon every external perception* from φ via ψ, or direct from φ; the ψ excitation will then result in an ω discharge, information of which will in turn pass to ψ—because ψ registers all *changes* (whether increases or decreases) in endogenous excitations, and hence also those in φ and ω. "*The information of the discharge from ω is thus the indication of quality or of reality for* ψ" (p. 325). This applies in the first place to all simple perceptual processes.

However, an intense endogenous excitation in ψ alone—that is, if "the wished-for object is abundantly cathected" (ibid.) or sought—could give rise to an indication of quality of this kind in ω. The initial question as to the distinction between a mnemic image (hallucination or wish) and a perception of reality, which is so important for the organism's selfpreservation, can therefore be answered *quantitatively* only by saying that the processes in ψ must be subject to a (quantitative) inhibition in order for them not to trigger an indication of *reality* in ω. This inhibition is now made possible by the ego, that "network of cathected neurones well facilitated in relation to one another" (p. 323), which, precisely, distributes a part of the quantities of excitation in the direction of the facilitated contact barriers among the cathected neurones (including "side-cathexes"), binding the quantity of excitation present and thus reducing the level of excitation. By the "hypothesis of what is, as it were, a *bound state*" in the neurones, Freud reconciles two opposing requirements, "strong cathexis and weak displacement" of quantities; and this is the very state that makes the process of thought, or intense attention, possible (p. 368f.)—characterizing the *secondary process* as opposed to the *primary process*. The residual "unbound" ("freely mobile") quantities in ψ then no longer suffice to produce in ω the indication of quality for the perception of reality. This allows Freud to add the following explanation: "It is accordingly *inhibition by the ego which makes possible a criterion for distinguishing between perception and memory*" (p. 326).

(p) *The Function of Speech*

However, the process of remembering is also able, and intended, to reach consciousness, and what is conscious is, after all, supposed to be connected with discharge, however minimal, in ω. The problem is as follows:

> Indications of quality come about normally only from perceptions; it is thus a question of obtaining a perception from the passage of Qή. If a discharge

were linked to the passage of $Q\acute{\eta}$ (in addition to the [mere] circulation), then, like every movement, it [the discharge] would furnish information of the movement. After all, indications of quality themselves are only information of discharge.... It is a question, however, of receiving discharges of this kind from all cathexes. They are not all motor, and for this purpose, therefore, they must be brought into a secure facilitation with motor neurones.

This purpose is fulfilled by *speech association*. This consists in the linking of ψ neurones with neurones which serve sound-presentations and themselves have the closest association with motor speech-images. In any case, from the sound-image the excitation reaches the word-image and from it reaches discharge. Thus, if the mnemic images are of such a kind that a part-current can go from them to the sound-images and motor word-images, then the cathexis of the mnemic images is accompanied by information of discharge, which is an indication of quality and also accordingly an indication of the consciousness of the memory. [p. 364f.]

Remembering or thinking can thus become conscious only subject to the use of "motor word-images," or "*indications of speech-discharge*": "they put thought-processes on a level with perceptual processes, lend them reality and *make memory of them possible*" (p. 366). The slight innervation of the motor apparatus of speech, triggered by an activated associative network, produces the indications of discharge (i.e., the quantitative amount) necessary for satisfying the criteria of consciousness within the model. That is to say, *conscious thinking is always coded in the form of speech*. We now have a firm criterion for a quantitative distinction between perception and ideation (conscious or unconscious reproductive thinking, or memory), and all that remains to be shown is how the two can be made to coincide, for example for the purpose of need satisfaction.

(q) The "Reality Principle"

If it is borne in mind "that perceptual cathexes are never cathexes of single neurones but always of complexes" of neurones (p. 327), and, in addition, that the need likewise excites an entire associative chain of neurones belonging to the ψ nucleus and the ψ pallium—that is, also a *specific complex of neurones*—it will readily be conceived that "[b]iological experience" (the requirement of the principle of constancy—in this case, the persistence of states of disequilibrium) will teach "that it is unsafe to initiate discharge if the indications of reality do not confirm the whole complex but only a part of it" (p. 328). This is an interesting point, because we are now dealing with the excitation of *two neuronal complexes connected in parallel*, one of which (the perceptual complex) is required to *confirm* the other (the need complex, or wish). The "activation of the wish" will therefore trigger, or "cathect," a specific *pattern*, a specific associative series, in ψ, and lay it down as a reference for the overall perception in the searching movement (selective perception); it is only upon the appearance of a perception in the outside world, which activates a corresponding *matching pattern* in ω via the φ and ψ neurones of the pallium, that the specific quantitative amplification (a kind of "doubling") that initiates final "discharge" will occur via the feedback to ψ. This could also be put as follows. The associative pattern of the memory trace in ψ contains the neuronal excitations of the need stimulus, the satisfying object, and the satisfying action; the associative pattern of the (external) perception in ω contains (in favorable cases) only the excitation values of the (matching) satisfying object; hence the performance of the satisfying action *completes* the pattern in combination with the need stimulus and thereby makes it a better match overall. From this point of view, matching, too, would in formal terms be simply a kind of "equilibrium state" of two patterns of excitation (on a higher hierarchical level).

The postulate of the ω system thus introduces a *reference value* that manifestly performs the function of an *integration* or, if you will, *comparison of pattern formations of neuronal (or psychic) excitation complexes*. This can be pictured as follows. In the simple process of "disinterested contentment"— that is, what might be described as a need-free perception (as, for example, in the situation of "evenly suspended attention")—the ψ neurones of the pallium and the ω neurones are excited from φ, and their discharge, as an indication of quality or reality, gives rise to the amplification of excitation in the ψ neurones of the pallium that results in the phenomenon of conscious perception. Conversely, in a state of need-induced tension, a *specific* pattern of associated neurones is excited in the y nucleus and the ψ pallium; the pattern of excitation of any merely random perception will *not match* this pattern (it will seem "insignificant"), and will therefore remain quantitatively subliminal

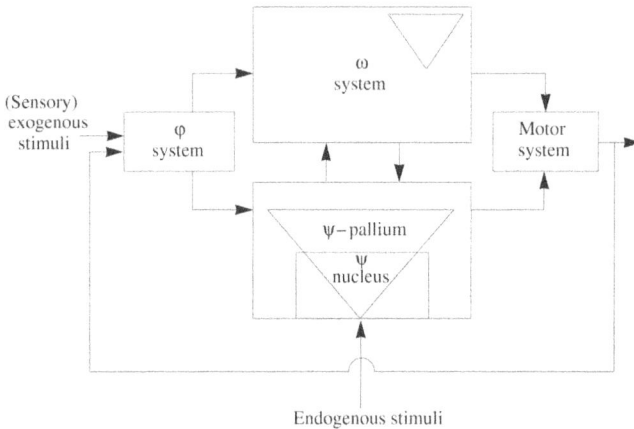

Figure 1–7. This diagram is merely a simplified representation of the systems constructed by Freud in the "Project" and the referencing processes that take place within them. In the process of need satisfaction in reality, the smaller triangle in the ω system (the perceptual pattern) is required to be brought into coincidence with the larger triangle in the ψ system (the need pattern—i.e., the wish); the *need pattern* is the *reference* for *orientation* and *coordination with the perceptual pattern*: the latter makes the organism better able, on each succeeding occasion, deliberately to bring about an experience of satisfaction, and/or to perform a "specific action."

overall, because a comparison of patterns between the excitation complexes in ψ and ω, which are superimposed like two filters, now occurs—and it is only in the event of an *optimum match between the patterns* that the necessary quantitative amplification takes place for triggering in ω the indication of reality for conscious perception of the object "that promises satisfaction." In other words, then, ω is the system crucial both to consciousness and to distinguishing between internal and external perceptions—mainly by comparing and, where appropriate, integrating and processing the patterns of different excitation complexes on two levels; the ω system thus operates on a more complex level than the ψ system, so that it belongs on a higher hierarchical plane. Moreover, since Freud links consciousness to ω, the ω system by definition corresponds to the later *system Cs.*, while the ψ processes of the 1895 ego may be said to correspond to the system *Pcs.*; similarly, in the eventual structure theory of 1923, the ego would have its roots in ψ and include ω.

CONSTRUCTION OF THE PSYCHICAL APPARATUS

The beginnings and foundations of psychoanalytic theory (metapsychology), and hence also the model of the "mental apparatus," were for a long time—and indeed mostly still are—placed in Chapter 7 of *The Interpretation of Dreams* (1900a). This is mainly because the entire generation of the "founding fathers" of psychoanalysis knew nothing of the existence of the "Project"; hence their starting point was—besides the theoretical parts of his studies on hysteria, published before 1900—Freud's dream book, and the literature they bequeathed to us has passed on this position to our own times. Yet we have known since 1950 that, in Chapter 7 of *The Interpretation of Dreams*, Freud merely takes up again the central themes of his "Project for a Scientific Psychology." Rather than dwell on a rereading of the basic hypotheses of the "Project," with which we are already familiar, we shall therefore concentrate on the following two questions. First, what does the *psychical apparatus* here introduced by Freud look like, and how does it work? Second, how does Freud understand the interplay of forces between wish and defense—that is, what *drive* concept is contained implicitly or explicitly in this chapter; how does he tackle the problem of *repression*, hitherto unsolved on the theoretical level; and how are both presented as constituent parts of the conception of the psychical apparatus?[13]

The *D-P-M* System

The fundamental hypothesis underlying Freud's (1900a) development of a "mental apparatus" is that "psychical events are determined" absolutely (p. 514): in the psychic sphere nothing is unregulated or arbitrary, and there are no "trains of thought without purposive ideas" (p. 529). This determinism is connected with the assumption of a *chronological and spatial orientation* of psychic events. Freud proposes that the "mental apparatus" should be imagined as consisting of several "agencies" or "systems"—he refers to them for "the sake of brevity... as 'ψ-systems'" (p. 537)—which have a specific structure and through which psychic processes proceed in *succession*. Psychic events thus take place in a particular *direction*:

> Accordingly, we will picture the mental apparatus as a compound instrument, to the components of which we will give the name of 'agencies,' or (for the sake of greater clarity) 'systems.'... The first thing that strikes us is that this apparatus, compounded of ψ-systems, has a sense or direction. All our psychical activity starts from stimuli (whether internal or external) and ends in innervations. Accordingly, we shall ascribe a sensory and a motor end to the apparatus. At the sensory end there lies a system which receives perceptions; at the motor end there lies another, which opens the gateway to motor activity. Psychical processes advance in general from the perceptual end to the motor end. Thus the most general schematic picture of the psychical apparatus may be represented thus [see Figure 1–8]. [p. 536f.]

---

13 The genesis and interpretation of dreams will not, however, be discussed here; on this subject, see Schmidt-Hellerau (1991).

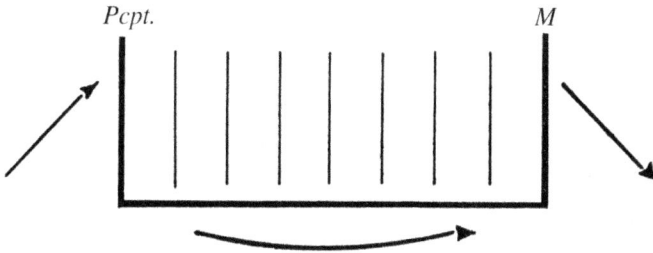

Figure I-8. Ibid., p. 537.

Freud is thereby postulating exactly the same as in the "Project"—that is, an apparatus within which processes take place *in a particular direction*, namely from the perceptual (*Pcpt.*) to the motor (*M*) end. Since the function to be performed by this reflex apparatus is "to avoid an accumulation of excitation and to maintain itself so far as possible without excitation" (p. 598)—because "the accumulation of excitation ... is felt as unpleasure and ... it sets the apparatus in action with a view to repeating the experience of satisfaction, which involved a diminution of excitation and was felt as pleasure" (ibid.)—we again have before us the familiar simple schema:

(*Pcpt.*-)input → law: → (*M*-)output
variable (+ E)   zero principle   variable (– E)

As in the "Project," Freud now goes on to consider how permanent memories can arise out of perceptual stimuli: "We shall suppose that a system in the very front of the apparatus receives the perceptual stimuli but retains no trace of them and thus has no memory, while behind it there lies a second system which transforms the momentary excitations of the first system into permanent traces" (p. 538). It is only at this point that Freud refers for the first time to the "[e]vidence afforded by dreams" in relation to another "portion of the apparatus," the critical agency, which he places at the motor end. He calls it the *preconscious*, or *system Pcs.*, and describes the system behind it as the *unconscious*, or *system Ucs.*, "because it has no access to consciousness *except via the preconscious*, in passing through which its excitatory process is obliged to submit to modifications" (p. 541). A footnote from 1919 adds the following: "If we attempted to proceed further with this schematic picture, in which the systems are set out in linear succession, we should have to reckon with the fact that the system beyond the Pcs. is the one to which consciousness must be ascribed—in other words, that *Pcpt.* = *Cs.*" (note 1). Freud's schematic picture of the psychical apparatus now appears as in Figure 1–9.

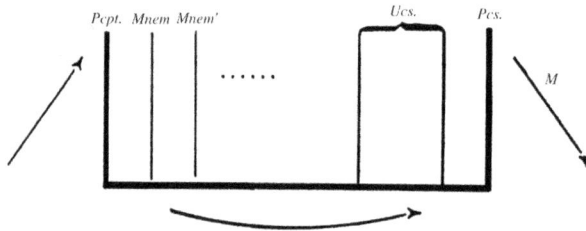

Figure 1–9. Ibid.

The basic schema is again of a supply of excitation proceeding via *Pcpt.* through the mnemic systems, the *Ucs.*, and the *Pcs.* to motor discharge. It is clear from the diagram that the mnemic systems—and the *Ucs.* is manifestly also a particular complex of such mnemic systems— have the function of switches or controllers responsible for (or at least involved in) the restoration of homeostasis. After all, as we know from the "Project," the immediate discharge of a stimulus cannot by itself restore the equilibrium state of the system as a whole: the endogenous needs of the organism call for a "specific action," which constitutes a more complicated sequence of regulative measures. Having reached this point in the construction of his model, Freud turns again to the paradigm of the "experience of satisfaction" to provide a plausible account of the formation and differentiation of the psychical apparatus on the levels of both phylogenesis and ontogenesis (p. 565f.). As in the "Project," he first posits an endogenous stimulus, namely the internal "excitation" resulting from "somatic needs," which corresponds "not. . . to a force producing a *momentary* impact but to one which is in continuous operation"; second, "outside help," the "perception" of the satisfying object; and, third and last, the "experience of satisfaction," which, as the end result of a motor action that must be coordinated between subject and object, "puts an end to the internal stimulus." What is important in this process is the "link that has been established" (an initial structure) between these three elements of the experience of satisfaction, which produces a "mnemic image" that can thereafter be summoned up as a *hallucination* upon every recurrence of internal excitation. This first activity of the psychical apparatus, namely cathexis (activation) of the memory trace of an experience of satisfaction in the state of need, leading to hallucination, is described by Freud as the "primary process" (p. 601). The primary process is thus not confined to the discharge of excitation in the form of a reflex, but already includes structured processes such as the cathexis (activation) of associative complexes; in other words, the system *Ucs.* is structured (on a primary basis), and the primary process taking place within it is a firstorder psychic process.

The "experiences in the mnemic systems" are the associations that have arisen in the experience of satisfaction between specific (endogenous or exogenous) stimuli, object images, and motor images. The "accumulation" or "summation" of such "experiences," which corresponds to the continuous formation of structure, a differentiation of the associative network, leads to the genesis of a second system, whose activity "diverted the excitation arising [directly] from the need along a roundabout path which ultimately, by means of voluntary movement, altered the external world in such a way that it became possible to arrive at a real perception of the object of satisfaction" (p. 599). Freud calls the activity of this second system the "secondary process" (p. 601). The secondary process arises in consequence of higher complexity of structure or associative network formation in the mnemic systems; it is a second-order psychic process, and thus differs from the primary process not fundamentally but in degree. In relative terms, "the activity of the *first* ψ-system is directed towards securing the *free discharge* of the quantities of excitation, while the *second* system, by means of the cathexes emanating from it, succeeds in *inhibiting* this discharge and in transforming the cathexis into a quiescent one, no doubt with a simultaneous raising of its level" (p. 599). The secondary process inhibits the hallucination—or, if you will, limits it (quantitatively) to a mnemic image that can now act as a signpost, in the form of "exploratory thought-activity" (p. 600), toward achievement of the situation of satisfaction.

Freud assembles the psychical apparatus from a number of different systems, and, following his account of the *Ucs.* and the *Pcs.*, must of course now also elucidate the system *Cs.* and the relationship between consciousness and hallucination, memory, perception, and thought. As in his reflections on the ω system in the "Project," he explains here (p. 574) that, although the organ of consciousness has two "sensory surfaces," it can receive excitations from three sources: first, stimuli from the "periphery of the whole apparatus, the perceptual system"; second, "excitations of pleasure and unpleasure... attaching to transpositions of energy in the inside of the apparatus"; and, third, the "mnemic system of indications of speech," which comes into being only in the course of development. In this way the linear pattern outlined by Freud (Figure 1–9) reveals a circular process that admits simple perceptions to consciousness only by way of the *Ucs.* via (a minimal) *M* discharge; and here—that is, continuing in the direction of the arrow starting from motor activity and in effect impinging again on the system *Pcpt.* from below—we see the duplication or referencing, as established in the "Project," of two different "perceptual filters," which produces the amplification necessary for consciousness only when the "external" and "internal" patterns of excitation match—that is, when both "sensory surfaces" have been excited homologously. In principle, nothing new is added to this by the "mnemic system of indications of speech," because the latter, as a subsequent acquisition, as it were sits atop the motor system and merely furnishes the indications of discharge necessary within this conception, which are then registered in *Pcpt.* In Freud's view of the psychical apparatus, thought is bound up with the use of indications of speech, and consciousness with the coinciding of associative patterns of the perceptual system (whether endogenous or activated exogenously) with corresponding patterns from the "*overlying* sense-organ of the *Cs.* system" (p. 616, my emphasis). Here again, we see that the system *Cs.*, which is excited according to the degree of integrability (matching) of patterns of two systems, operates on a higher level of organization (secondary process) than the primary process, which has a comparatively "simpler" structure.

Before proceeding further, let us briefly recapitulate. In the "Project," the development of the structures that form the psychical apparatus is portrayed as a process commencing with the linking (association) of an endogenous stimulus (drive) in the ψ nucleus with a complex perceptual stimulus (object image) and a motor discharge (motor image) in the ψ pallium. Whenever a psychic process takes place, either existing associations between these three pillars of drive activity are energized, or else new ones are facilitated. The associative network of the mnemic systems is thus extended and becomes fully differentiated during the course of development. In this process these three cornerstones of drive activity might well influence each other, in which case the drive stimulus would likewise energize the memory trace of the satisfying object and of the associated satisfying action, just as, conversely, a given pattern of action would summon up a drive-satisfying object image, or the perception of an object could stimulate a drive-related action. All these cases would involve the *completion* of learned patterns of excitation—which is connected, in formal terms, with the idea that this completion corresponds to a homeostatic regulation.

In contrast to this three-dimensional model from the "Project," Freud had, in *The Interpretation of Dreams*, outlined what was at first only a two-dimensional (linear) model, in which the drive as the initiator of every psychic event was contained only implicitly (in the form, firstly, of quantitatively determined releases of pleasure and unpleasure, and, secondly, of wishes, which alone can set the psychical apparatus in motion). Conversely, Freud explicitly places the perceptual stimuli on one side and motor activity (to which he also assigns the system of indications of speech) on the other; and between them he puts the mnemic systems, which allow differentiated (inhibited) exchanges between the two sides.

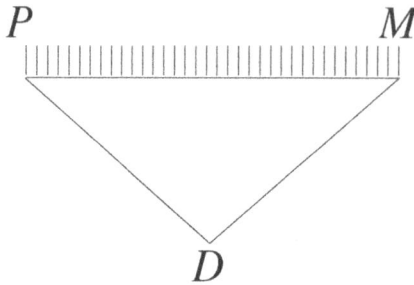

Figure I–10.

If we now combine the configurations from the two works—adding the position of the endogenous stimuli from the "Project" (Figure 1–6) to the linear schema of *The Interpretation of Dreams* (Figure 1–8)—we obtain a model that is again made up of the familiar three pillars (Figure 1–10). It includes a "drive system" (D) that supplies endogenous stimuli; a "perceptual system" (P^{14}) that receives sensory (exogenous) stimuli, which are then stored as object images in the memory traces; and a "motor system" (M) that is responsible for discharge, and whose "motor images" (in particular, of the specific action) are also recorded in the form of memory traces (the barred line). Freud sees the "motor system" primarily as an executive organ close to consciousness— partly because of the "indications of speech discharge," which are in his view subliminal motor innervations ("motor word images"), and which he therefore also places at the right-hand end of the diagram.

This is the basic model of all passages of psychic excitation, valid from the "Project'" on. As will be shown in the next section, it is the *simple schema of the wish*, for every wish can be seen as a memory trace associating a drive impulse

---

14 From now on I shall use the single letter *P* rather than Strachey's abbreviation *Pcpt.*, which is too cumbersome for repeated use, especially in my concept of the *D-P-M* system.

with an object image and a motor image, and (as will become increasingly clear below) it holds for all psychic processes, from those of the microlevel—because it represents the *elementary unit of the memory trace*—right up to those of the macrolevels with their complex structures and organization.

Extroversion and Introversion of Psychic Processes

Let us now attempt to conceptualize *wish* and *defense*, by classifying the "interplay of forces" of *drive* and *repression* in two categories: the *absolute directionality of all psychic processes* on the one hand, and the *distinction between primary and secondary process* on the other.

Let us begin with the relationship between drive and wish. By the beginning of Chapter VII of *The Interpretation of Dreams*, the reader already knows very well that dreams are wish fulfillments, and that what is being fulfilled is a repressed infantile sexual wish operating from the unconscious. Freud resolutely repeats this important result of his many dream analyses several times in his final chapter: "Dreams are psychic acts of as much significance as any others; their drive force is in every instance a wish seeking fulfillment" (p. 533). The wish expressed by a dream has its *"drive roots"* (p. 524, my emphasis) in the unconscious, and "owing to this latter factor we shall take the unconscious system as the starting-point of dream-formation. *Like all other thought-structures, this dream-instigator will make an effort to advance into the* Pcs. *and from there to obtain access to consciousness"* (p. 542, my emphasis). The "drive force" of dreams thus operates in a particular direction, namely, from the *Ucs.* to the *Pcs.*, and thence to the *Cs.*, or—to use a spatial metaphor—*from inside to outside*. Why should this be, and what is the detailed mechanism?

Freud tells us that the "drive forces [are] of organic origin" (p. 603). The paradigms are hunger and sexuality. These forces originate from an endogenous stimulus, a somatic excitation, and induce the apparatus to undertake measures appropriate for discharging the excitation direct or for reducing it by means of a specific action. In other words, a need/desire whose persistence gives rise to tension/unpleasure develops an urgency/craving for satisfaction/fulfillment, which is experienced as pleasure. The (successful) completion of this process leaves behind a memory trace that furnishes the basic pattern in accordance with which all subsequent drive processes of the same kind will tend to proceed. As soon as a certain level of excitation has accumulated, it urgently seeks discharge, precisely because:

> the *accumulation of excitation*... is felt as unpleasure and... it *sets the apparatus in action* with a view to repeating the experience of satisfaction, which involved a diminution of excitation and was felt as pleasure. A *current of this kind* in the apparatus, *starting from unpleasure and aiming at pleasure*, we have termed a "wish"; and we have asserted that *only a wish is able to set the apparatus in motion* and that the *course of the excitation in it is automatically regulated by feelings of pleasure and unpleasure*. The first wishing seems to have been a hallucinatory cathecting of the memory of satisfaction. [p. 598, my emphasis]

This important passage clearly demonstrates the distinction between a drive and a wish: a "current... in the apparatus, starting from unpleasure and aiming at pleasure," is what Freud terms a wish, and he adds that "only a wish is able to set the apparatus in motion." Unpleasure is, however, the phenomenal equivalent of an "accumulation of excitation," and pleasure that of its "diminution." A drive   is a process of excitation in the organism, or, in formal terms, an input variable that initiates (in the switch) homeostatic measures of regulation, namely the "current... starting from unpleasure and aiming at pleasure." This current has a starting point, the excitation of the need (the endogenous stimulus); it proceeds in a specific direction, toward the satisfying object; and it comes to an end, with the successful completion of the satisfying action. When these three fixed points in the drive process come together (each already representing a complex association of excitations—for example, the image of the object is made up of visual, auditory, olfactory, tactile, kinesthetic, and other elements), the *combination* is a wish. *A wish is therefore identical, not with the drive, but with the association, activated by the drive excitation, between drive, object image, and motor image. In other words, a wish embraces the entire memory trace and not just the drive*: "The first wishing seems to have been a hallucinatory cathecting of the memory of satisfaction." "Wish" is therefore a *more complex concept* than "drive," so that it perhaps belongs rather on the level of clinical theory; however, if the term "wish" is to be used in metapsychology, it must be understood in the sense that the memory trace activated by a drive excitation produces a *pattern of excitation* that can operate again as a unity (the quantity of excitation resulting from this passage) on the next higher level (e.g., the system $Cs./\omega$).

Turning now to the terms *resistance* and *censorship*, let us begin by assuming that the wish activated by a drive is directed *from inside to outside*. Freud (1900a) had observed in his analyses of dreams that "this path leading through the preconscious to consciousness is barred... during the daytime by the censorship imposed by resistance" (p. 542). This censorship resulting from resistance is the second component of the "interplay of forces": it *opposes* the drive-induced wish. If the wish stemming from the drive is directed from inside to outside, then the censorship resulting from resistance must, so to speak, be exercised from outside to inside, so that these spatial metaphors could, in formal terms, stand for a plus sign and a minus sign respectively. This "endopsychic censorship," which is fully effective in waking life, is held by Freud to be appreciably reduced, if not abolished, in sleep, and it is only this reduction in the functional level of censorship that in his view allows the drive-induced wish to be expressed to some extent and hence permits dream formation (p. 526). On the phenomenological level, the censorship is manifested by "[d]oubt whether a dream or certain of its details have been correctly reported" (p. 515f.), and by "modifications to which dreams are submitted under the editorship of waking life" (p. 515), which may extend even to partial or complete "forgetting" of the dream (p. 517); it finds expression on the level of content by "withdrawal of psychical value" (p. 516) from the principal elements of the dream, in which the central drive-related wish is contained, or by their "displacement" on to something insignificant (p. 531). These characteristic processes of the censorship—doubt, forgetting, withdrawal of psychic value, and so forth—correspond formally to a *subtraction*, a *minus* sign. As Freud now explains, all these features of dreams and of their reporting, the fact of their "not being recognizable as wishes and their many peculiarities and absurdities are due to the influence of the psychical *censorship* to which they have been subjected *during the process of their formation*" (p. 533, my emphasis). In other words, a dream's complex structure is always the result of an interplay of wishes and censorship:

$$\text{Dream} = \text{wish } (+) + \text{censorship } (-)$$

Let us take a closer look. The censorship imposed by resistance is directed in the opposite direction to the drive-induced wish, which seeks to pass from the *Ucs.* toward the *Cs.*, the result being a dynamic—an "interplay of forces"— whose outcome can only be a *compromise*, and all these "peculiarities," in whose guise the wish ultimately reaches consciousness in the form of a dream, are already manifestations of a compromise outcome of this kind. If we call one of these forces or variables the "drive," then we ought really to regard the other force or variable, which operates in the opposite direction, as *repression*, for drive and repression are antagonists *par excellence*. The process of repression thus corresponds exactly to what is deemed to apply to the drive: repression is a *directional* process, which has a point of departure (in this case the *Cs.*) and a point of destination (in this case the *Ucs.*). Hence the drive is directed from the *Ucs.* to the *Cs.*, whereas the direction of repression (in this case, Freud's censorship imposed by resistance) is from the *Cs.* to the *Ucs.* From the purely formal point of view, we can assign a plus sign to the drive and a minus sign to repression, which is directed in the opposite sense; repression would then have to be "subtracted" from the tendency of the drive, thus reducing the residual quantities of drive excitation to a factor potentially below the threshold of consciousness. The drive and repression, as directional values or forces, can accordingly be seen as two variables whose combination in a controller permits the maintenance of homeostasis. Again, just as a wish is a more complex structure than a drive with a resultant effect tending in the same direction as the drive, so the censorship is a process with a more complex structure than, but whose resultant effect operates in the same direction as, repression. After all, the censorship excises individual parts or sections out of the overall pattern of the memory trace (e.g., the image of the object), replaces them (or parts of them, such as the nose or hairstyle) by others, displaces them, withdraws value from them, and so forth. Indeed, sometimes *the censorship too appears to proceed by way of specific associative patterns*, which might contain an object image and a motor image,[15] so that the censorship is in a way a negative association.[16] This means, as a first approximation, that the wish and the censorship, in formal terms, constitute two quite different patterns of opposite sign, which are as it were compared with and referenced to each other to yield the observed compromise formations. The censorship (like the wish) is thus in fact already a clinical concept, which, when used for metapsychological purposes, ought again to be seen as an *aggregate* unity or *pattern of excitation*, whose resultant is a *directed* force. Considered in this way, the terms "wish" and "censorship" as used by Freud stand in the same antagonistic relationship to each other as drive and repression. However, drive and repression will continue to be regarded here as simple basic variables.

Yet Freud not only assigns the censorship the function of "exclusion from consciousness," but also takes another step: "Further, we found reasons for identifying the critical agency with the agency which directs our waking life and determines our voluntary, conscious actions" (p. 540); and finally:

---

15 "Unconscious intrapsychic conflicts are never simple conflicts between impulse and defense; rather, the drive derivative finds expression through a certain primitive object relation (a certain unit of self and object representation); and *the defense, too, is reflected by a certain internalized object relation*" (Kernberg 1980, p. 155, my emphasis).

16 Freud (1916–1917f [1915]) made a highly interesting comment along these lines in a footnote to "A Metapsychological Supplement to the Theory of Dreams": "I may add by way of supplement that any attempt to explain hallucination would have to start out from *negative* rather than positive hallucination" (p. 232, note 1). Green (1980) has undertaken a thorough study of "negative hallucination," which he sees as the result of one of the "components of primary repression: massive decathexis, both radical and temporary, which leaves traces in the unconscious in the form of "psychical holes." These will be filled in by recathexes, which are the expression of destructiveness which has thus been freed by the weakening of libidinal erotic cathexis" (p. 146).

"Thus the censorship between the *Ucs.* and the *Pcs.*, the assumption of whose existence is positively forced upon us by dreams, deserves to be recognized and respected as the watchman of our mental health" (p. 567). Functions of control and volition are thus also ascribed to the censorship, whose existence as the guarantor of "our mental health" is recognized. This means that *the interplay of forces between wish and censorship is the normal state of affairs in all psychic life, because the homeostasis of the system can be maintained in no other way than by the interaction of drive and repression*—and "mental health" is the expression of a dynamic and stable equilibrium of this kind within the psychical apparatus.

Freud's "interplay of forces" thus describes a normal condition that applies to both sleep and the waking state. However, in waking life the conspicuously odd compromise formations of dreams are less obvious and more refined (they possess the attributes of the secondary process); here they emerge most clearly in neurotic symptoms. These, too, are to be understood as the compromise outcome of a conflict between drive and repression: "Or more correctly, one portion of the symptom corresponds to the unconscious wish-fulfillment and another portion to the mental structure reacting against the wish" (p. 569, note 1). In other words, action and re-action (or reaction formation) in this situation oppose and manifestly hold the balance between each other—for the function of such symptoms is as follows: "On the one hand, they allow the *Ucs.* an outlet for the discharge of its excitation, and provide it with a kind of sally-port, while, on the other hand, they make it possible for the *Pcs.* to control the *Ucs.* to some extent" (p. 581). The equation in this case is:

symptom = (*Ucs.*) wish   + (*Pcs.*) reaction formation/
          fulfillment (+)   censorship (−)

Formulated in this way, the "interplay of forces" between drive and repression, wish and censorship, now becomes for Freud an "interplay of excitations between the preconscious and the unconscious" (p. 564). What does this mean? On one level, Freud presents the situation as if drives were being assigned to the unconscious, repression on the other hand being the province of the preconscious. This is not new, and also corresponds to the 1923 classification, in which the ego is characterized as the repressing agency. However, his starting point had been two opposing "forces," drive and repression, but now he is invoking two "psychical agencies, one of which submitted the activity of the other to a criticism" (p. 540)—an "interplay of excitations between the preconscious and the unconscious"—so that he is asserting that both *systems* are "capable of being excited." This need not confuse us, because this is another antagonism that fits Freud's model. We should realize, though, that this antagonism is now being postulated between *systems*, so that different degrees of complexity will be involved in each of the antagonistic tendencies postulated here. In this configuration, *drive* and *repression* are situated on the simplest level; *wish* and *defense*—or the censorship—will already constitute a more complex, more comprehensive, or more structured level; and the antagonism between the (macro)structures of the systems *Ucs.* and *Pcs.* is even more complex. This means that structures, too, irrespective of their level of complexity, can be conceived as unities, whose *activation* within the psychical apparatus exerts antagonistic effects in the form of the directional forces of drive and repression. This point gives rise again and again to theoretical confusion, and is therefore extremely important: *the activation (output) of the systems (Ucs., Pcs., and Cs.) leads to effects that can be treated as, but are not identical with, drive and repression. Within a cybernetic model of the psychical apparatus, the systems (or structures) are assigned, rather, the function of controllers or switches, whereas drive and repression constitute the variables controlled by these controllers.*

It is appropriate to turn now to the relationship between drive and repression on the one hand and inhibition on the other, and between both of these entities and the primary and secondary processes. In his schematic portrayal of the psychical apparatus, Freud had described "as 'progressive' the direction taken by psychical processes arising from the unconscious during waking life" (we ourselves used the metaphor "from inside to outside"), whereas, for him, dreams had "a 'regressive' character" (p. 542). He had described the progressive direction of psychic processes as advancing from an endogenous stimulus (drive) to a perception (of an object), culminating in a motor action (discharge). The memory traces of such *passages* (the associated excitation complexes) are stored in the various mnemic systems "interposed" between drive excitation and discharge, and it is this associative network of "experiences in the mnemic systems," which increases in density during the course of development, that, according to Freud, divert "the excitation arising from the need along a roundabout path" (p. 599). This "roundabout path" between excitation of the drive and its discharge signifies an "inhibition," a retardation of the passage of the drive *in the progressive direction*. The following initial statement can therefore be made about the passage of a drive excitation. At the lowest level, where the excitation is triggered, the tendency is for immediate discharge (this is a central characteristic of the primary process); but the trend toward discharge is retarded, or *inhibited*, by the roundabout paths (structures) established in the mnemic systems—and this inhibition characterizes the secondary process.

Now Freud had described voluntary action, which, being preconscious or conscious, ought surely to be ascribed to the secondary process, as a consequence of the operation or involvement of the censorship. In contrast to the *progressive* direction of the drive discharge inhibited in the secondary process, however, we had assigned the censorship, and the repression operative within it, a direction opposed to that of the drive—that is, in effect, a *regressive* direction (or, more accurately, one proceeding from outside to inside). *In the preconscious secondary process, therefore, an inhibited progressive drive tendency operates together with a likewise inhibited regressive tendency toward repression, the inhibition in both cases being due to the mnemic systems.* This would mean that the term "inhibition" applies, in the case of both the drive and repression, to the relationship between the passages of excitation and the "roundabout paths" of the associated mnemic systems—the basic rule here being that, the more ramified the associative network, the more differentiated the homeostatic regulation will be.

However, if the term *inhibition* relates exclusively to the roundabout paths, to the distribution of the passages of excitation over the associative network of mnemic traces, we must postulate not only an inhibited interaction of drive and repression of this kind in the secondary process, but also an interaction of drive and repression (the same type of "interplay of forces") for the primary process in the unconscious, the interaction in this case being only *relatively* "more uninhibited." The notion that primary processes are "uninhibited," or, as Freud puts it, "unbound," would then be true only *relative* to the secondary processes; in other words, the primary processes too should not be imagined as wholly "uninhibited" (unstructured). A point usually overlooked is that, according to Freud, the *Ucs.*, at the beginning of the development of the psychical apparatus, also undergoes structuring, albeit more primitive, by the mnemic systems; this primitive structuring consists in the "unconscious wishful impulses,"—a "wide sphere of mnemic material"—constituting the "core of our being" (p. 603f.); and we have, after all, deemed such wishful impulses and mnemic material to be an association of drive excitation, an object image, and a motor image. From this point of view, the unconscious wishes contain from the beginning the structures of the basic subjectobject relations that are recorded in the memory traces of the first situations of satisfaction—relations within which the *"releases of pleasure and unpleasure automatically regulate the course of cathectic processes"* (p. 574). Primitive regulative measures of this kind, or at least their rudiments, also of course constitute the hallucinations ascribed to the primary process, which then help to permit for the first time a modicum of drive deferment. Hence the working of the system *Ucs.* and its primary process can be imagined in no other way than as structured, albeit loosely, and to that extent subject to *primary inhibition* by precisely the associative pathways already laid down in the first memory traces of the *Ucs.* In other words, the degree of inhibition is predetermined by the density of the associative network of the mnemic systems; and this, although insignificant in the primary process of the unconscious, is a very important factor in the secondary process of the *Pcs.* and *Cs.*

THE ANTAGONISM OF DRIVE AND REPRESSION

Having elaborated the fundamental structures and functions of the psychical apparatus in the "Project" and in Chapter 7 of *The Interpretation of Dreams*, Freud turns, in his next major theoretical work, the *Three Essays on the Theory of Sexuality* of 1905, to the conceptualization of the drive. In the two contributions discussed so far, the process of excitation and satisfaction of the drive was described in each case with reference to the example of hunger and the ingestion of nourishment. Freud (1905d) commences his reflections on sexuality by taking up this idea again: "The fact of the existence of sexual needs in human beings and animals is expressed in biology by the assumption of a 'sexual drive,' on the analogy of the drive of nutrition, that is of hunger. Everyday language possesses no counterpart to the word 'hunger,' but science makes use of the word 'libido' for that purpose" (p. 135).

Freud has thus already introduced the *two basic drives*: the "drive of nutrition," which is manifested in hunger, and the "sexual drive," to whose manifestations he applies Moll's term "libido"; and we also receive an immediate indication that Freud sees the sexual drive as "[analogous to] the drive of nutrition."

The sexual *object* and *aim* are distinguished from the sexual *drive* (p. 135f.). Using examples from sexual pathology (homophilia, pedophilia, and zoophilia), Freud demonstrates the need "to loosen the bond that exists in our thoughts between drive and object. It seems probable that the sexual drive is in the first instance independent of its object; nor is its origin likely to be due to its object's attractions" (p. 148). In other words, the sexual *drive* is understood, in genetic terms (as in biology) as an endogenous, somatic process: the specific *object* comes to be associated with it only through experience. Although the *aim* of the sexual drive is ultimately elimination of the drive stimulus through satisfaction, Freud defines it in terms of action: "The normal sexual *aim* is regarded as being the *union* of the genitals in the *act* known as copulation, which leads to a release of the sexual tension and a temporary extinction of the sexual drive—a satisfaction analogous to the sating of hunger" (p. 149, my emphasis).

By this differentiation within his concept of the drive, Freud has retained the basic components of the model described in the previous section: the sexual drive can consequently be assigned to the D system, the sexual object to the P system, and the sexual aim to the M system. It is important to note that he here defines the drive as independent of its object or aim in any particular instance. This means that object and action, although no doubt genetically preformed, are variable to a certain extent in individual developmental history, whereas drives and their development are constants. This now calls for detailed examination. Freud introduces quite a number of new terms in these *Three Essays*—for example, the "origins" and "roots" of the drive, "erotogenic zones" or "sources" of excitation, "component drives," "drive components," and various "classes of drives." It will surely be helpful to reflect on the places to be assigned to each of these notions within his model.

Let us begin with the D system. Freud's starting point is that "something innate in *everyone*" *underlies* every form of sexual activity. "What is in question are the innate constitutional roots of the sexual drive" (p. 171). What is innate is not only the presence of a sexual drive but also the sequence of steps in its maturation, from the oral phase, via the anal and phallic phases, to adult genitality. Although appropriate environmental influences do of course promote the development of infantile sexuality, it is obvious, as Freud points out, that "seduction is not required in order to arouse a child's sexual life; that can also come about spontaneously from internal causes" (p. 190f.). Freud is here in effect indirectly invoking a higher-order mechanism or switch (say, in the central nervous system), which, within the D system in his schema, performs control functions for the steps in the maturation of the sexual drive.

Pursuing the line of development of the sexual drive, we immediately come upon the "erotogenic zones," which constitute an important "source" of sexual excitation, and the "component drives" assigned to them (p. 168). Freud mentions a number of different erotogenic zones. The most prominent, in order of activation, are the mouth, anus, and genitals, followed by the skin (in particular, the mucous membranes), in regard to sensations of touch, temperature, and pain. In addition, however, there is the eye, for the "scopophilic drive," while, on an even more general level, excitation may result from any "rhythmic mechanical agitation of the body. Stimuli of this kind operate in three different ways: on the sensory apparatus of the vestibular nerves, on the skin, and on the deeper parts (e.g., the muscles and articular structures)" (p. 201). Freud has manifestly conceived the "erotogenic zones" as corresponding to the various sense organs: he mentions the erotogenic zones of the proprioceptors, exteroceptors, thermoreceptors, nociceptors, telereceptors, and vestibular receptors, all of which, as *sense organs*, are assignable to the *P* system within the model. In the 1905 edition, he even refers explicitly to "an organ capable of receiving stimuli (e.g., the skin, the mucous membrane, or a *sense organ*). *An organ of this kind* will be described in this connection as an *erotogenic zone*—as being the organ whose excitation lends the drive a *sexual character*" (p. 168, note 1, my emphasis). Briefly, then, an *erotogenic zone* is initially no more than a *sense organ*, which conveys sensory stimuli from the *P* system. The erotogenic effect, however, is also subject to certain conditions— for example, "that the accumulation of the sexual substances creates and maintains sexual tension; the pressure of these products upon the walls of the vesicles containing them might be supposed *to act as a stimulus upon a spinal centre, the condition of which would be perceived by higher centres* and would then give rise in consciousness to the familiar sensation of tension" (p. 213, my emphasis). Such passages demonstrate Freud's manifest preference for an *organizational principle*—namely, for the interaction of certain portions of the "central apparatus" (p. 215) with the peripheral erotogenic zones; in the model, this means the interaction between a drive excitation of central origin (*D*) and an erotogenic zone excited peripherally (*P* system), both of which contribute to the excitation of the relevant component drive. Freud thus conceives the sexual drive as a control mechanism of the central nervous system, to be assigned only as such to the *D* system. The erotogenic zones, whose excitations lend "the drive a sexual character," on the other hand, belong to the *P* system. In concrete terms, the erotogenic zones react both to stimuli projected by the CNS and to those generated peripherally (e.g., by manipulation). The excitation of a component drive triggers a manipulation (an action, which is equivalent to a drive aim), for which the other drive, that of nutrition, provides the model for the specific action—the motor image (*M*)—and a manipulation "analogous to... sucking" will now constitute the satisfying action that eliminates the internal sensation of stimulation. Freud also considers that a component drive bound up with an individual erotogenic zone is at first satisfied *autoerotically*, because it *as yet lacks an object* (*or object image*), and he is thus able to specify the "three essential characteristics of an infantile sexual manifestation: at its origin it attaches itself to one of the vital somatic functions; it has as yet no sexual object, and is thus auto-erotic; and its sexual aim is dominated by an erotogenic zone" (p. 182f.).

These hypotheses can be incorporated in our model of the psychical apparatus as follows. There must first be a series of sensory impressions from the *P* system, which—by "attachment" to feeding and care interactions with the object—are stored in the mnemic systems, before an "object image," a psychic representative of the (part) object that satisfies the need, is *constellated*, becomes *differentiated* from the erotogenic zone (or, as we might perhaps say, *rises above the erotogenic zone*), and *establishes* itself on the *P*-system side of our diagram; this representation, or "object image" (object representation), will henceforth be permanently associated with this (component) drive.

Considering that Freud calls sexuality "the most unruly of all the drives" (p. 161), he has surprisingly little to say about repression in the *Three Essays*. We must therefore examine whether repression is not dealt with here in some other way, for example on the level of phenomenology. It turns out that the discussion of the perversions and neuroses affords repeated opportunities for tackling the issue of repression in connection with symptoms. We read, for instance, that the hysterical character "shows a degree of sexual repression... , an intensification of resistance against the sexual drive," from which Freud concludes that it is possible to "clear up the enigmatic contradiction which hysteria presents, by revealing the *pair of opposites by which it is characterized— exaggerated sexual craving and excessive aversion to sexuality*" (p. 165, my emphasis). Neurosis therefore comes about when the component drives "innate in *everyone*" remain unintegrated and also unsatisfied, being instead repressed, whereas "in the most favourable cases, which lie between these two extremes"— that is, between "hypertrophy" (an *excess*) of the individual component drive in perversion and its "excessive" (and hence unsuccessful) repression (a *deficiency*) in the symptomatic neuroses—"bring about what is known as normal sexual life" (p. 172). In sum, normal sexual life results from a normal "conflict" of opposites between drive and repression, so that, formally, drive and repression may continue to be seen as two variables of opposite sign.

Aside from the reference to repression in connection with hysterical symptoms, further terms associated with defense are encountered in Freud's treatment of the latency period. He mentions "barriers against sexuality" (p. 232), and "mental dams" used "to suppress effectively" the impulses of the component drive ("disgust, feelings of shame and the claims of aesthetic and moral ideals" [p. 177]). "One gets an impression from civilized children that the construction of these dams is a product of education, and no doubt education has much to do with it. But in reality *this development is organically determined and fixed by heredity*, and it can occasionally occur without any help at all from education" (p. 177f., my emphasis).

Just as the sexual drive was conceived in terms of its biological genetic origins, so Freud describes repression—or rather the entities in the *Three Essays* that we have deemed to be its phenomenal equivalents, namely the "barriers against sexuality" and the "construction of these dams"—as a development "*organically determined and fixed by heredity*" (my emphasis). In other words, not only the phases of maturation of the component sexual drives but also those of the associated measures of repression are *genetically determined*; the task of education here is merely that of "following the lines which have *already been laid down organically* and... impressing them somewhat more clearly and deeply" (p. 178, my emphasis). If, then, the D system in the model is supposed to correspond to the CNS control mechanisms of the (component) drives, which are fixed by heredity, the D system would also be responsible for the concomitant control of repression, whereas the specific manifestations of repression (disgust, shame, and morality) would be accounted for by the interaction of the D system with the activation of the various erotogenic zones of the P system and the object images established above them, as well as the specific defensive actions of the M system.

As we have seen, the *Three Essays* contain repeated references to oppositions of various kinds—between perversion and neurosis, drive and repression, psyche and soma, and progression and regression. Further detailed consideration of the fundamental organization of psychic processes, which all prove to be "directional," reveals yet another directional opposition, which is that of the *objects* of the drive, and hence of the *direction* of the drive within the subject–object dimension: *inward* (subject) and *outward* (object). It can then be shown on the *phenomenal* level that oral incorporation (greed) and anal retention (avarice), understood as sexual component-drive impulses, are *inwardly* directed psychic processes; both are opposed in direction by the "repressing measure" of disgust, which is expressed in a desire to "spit out" and "repel"—that is, in an *outwardly* directed psychic movement. Conversely, the component-drive impulses of anal and phallic exhibition then seek *outward* discharge, and the defense mechanism appropriate to them consequently takes the form of an *inwardly* directed tendency, shame, which endeavors to take back, or reconceal, the visible to some extent.

Within the model of the psychic apparatus as conceived by Freud in *The Interpretation of Dreams*, we provisionally assigned a progressive direction to the drive (or the wish resulting from it)—that is, advancing from the *Ucs.* to the *Cs.*—and an (in effect) regressive direction to the opposing repression. A qualification is now in order, as both the drive and repression display progressive and regressive tendencies. However, if the activation of both the component drives and the corresponding repression follows a genetically determined plan of maturation, so that both are intrinsically progressive steps in development, then the terms "progression" and "regression" ought to be, as they normally are, reserved for the genetic (and topographical and structural) aspect, whereas the notions of *introversion* and *extroversion* should be applied to that of *directionality* (of the drive) *within the subject–object dimension*. We do indeed find again and again that Freud himself thought, and developed his ideas of the psychical apparatus, in such dimensions, albeit without making this explicit every time. Hence the *introduction of the terms introversion and extroversion in relation to psychic processes directed toward subject and object respectively, in the context of the directionality of drive and repression processes*, while in principle not new, is nevertheless important for the further differentiation and integration of the various concepts within a formalized consistent model of psychoanalytic drive and structure theory. The following initial schematic generalization could then be proposed: an introversive, subject-directed drive impulse is always matched by an extroversive repression, while an extroversive, object-directed drive tendency is balanced by an introversive repression.

II

ELABORATION OF THE MODEL

(analysis of Freud's writings
from 1910 to 1915)

THE PRINCIPLE OF STRUCTURAL DEVELOPMENT

Repression as a Drive

The next step taken by Freud in the development of his theory, although seemingly no more than incidental, is here deemed a *fundamental*—and not merely provisional or temporary—position in his drive-repression theory; it is of *central importance* to the construction of the model and to all the considerations that follow in this book, as we shall now see.

In a short paper, "The Psycho-Analytic View of Psychogenic Disturbance of Vision" (1910i), Freud declares on the basis of his reflections so far that the drive system is dualistic. He distinguishes the sexual drives from the self-preservative or ego drives, determines the relationship between drive and idea, and finally defines *repression as a drive—specifically, as the drive opposed to the relevant other drive*. The following passage illustrates the development of these notions:

> Our attention has been drawn to the importance of the drives in ideational life. We have discovered that *every drive tries to make itself effective by activating ideas that are in keeping with its aims*. These drives are not always compatible with one another; their interests often come into conflict. *Opposition between ideas is only an expression of struggles between the various drives*. From the point of view of our attempted explanation, a quite specially important part is played by the undeniable *opposition between the drives which subserve sexuality*, the attainment of sexual pleasure, *and those other drives, which have*

as their aim the self-preservation of the individual—the ego-drives. As the poet has said, all the organic drives that operate in our mind may be classified as "*hunger*" or "*love*." [p. 213f., my emphasis]

In both the "Project" and *The Interpretation of Dreams*, Freud had used "hunger" as a paradigm of the drive, and described for it the fundamental pattern "endogenous stimulus—external object—specific action" that unites the *D*, *P*, and *M* systems in the model in an association of simultaneity (of excitation).[1] Hunger, or, if you will, the self-preservative or ego drive, was thus the first drive to be described by Freud, and came to be the foundation of his understanding of the drives; and he had assumed that the process in the case of the sexual drive was the same as that with the ego drive. He had also explained that, at the beginning of development, the component drives of sexuality— that is, the sexual drive—were "attached" to this self-preservative ego drive, because the "sexual and ego-drives alike have in general the same organs and systems of organs at their disposal" (p. 215f.); for this reason Freud also postulates that the excitation and satisfaction of the ego drive stimulates (co-excites) the sexual drive until the two drives become "detached" from, and enter into a conflict (of interest) with, each other. That, in a nutshell, is Freud's first drive theory, which reduces "all the organic drives that operate in our mind" to these two fundamental drives, the ego drive and the sexual drive.

The second thesis advanced by Freud here is that "every drive tries to make itself effective by activating ideas that are in keeping with its aims"—that is to say, the various groups of ideas allow deductions as to the drives that underlie them. This is in itself nothing new: Freud had already shown in the "Project" and in *The Interpretation of Dreams* how, after a series of identical experiences,

---

1 Brierley (1944) was the first to point out that the hypothetical *unity of experience*, which corresponds to a hypothetical *process unity*, is not an atomic impulse, affect, or representation, but should be seen as a *relationship of impulse* (*D*), *affect* (*M*), *and presentation* (*P*). "Hypothetical units are convenient figments to illustrate the parallelism between subjective reaction and objective wave of activity but, in fact, the simplest conscious experience is probably the equivalent of a whole series of processes. The point it is sought to emphasize is that, whether viewed subjectively as experience, or objectively as process-activation, mental life is a sequence of adaptive responses" (p. 100).

an endogenous stimulus (in the ψ nucleus/in the D system) summons up a particular object image (in the ψ pallium/in the P system) (a hallucination or idea). This theorem is thus inherent in Freud's theory from the outset and is an important point in his metapsychology: *ideas are controlled by the drives and express drive impulses*; however, they are not identical to the drives, so that the term "drive" *cannot* be replaced in psychoanalytic theory by "idea" or "representation."

On the basis of these assumptions—drive dualism and the relationship between drive and idea as described—conflict is now defined as the incompatibility of different (simultaneously activated) ideas, while "[o]pposition between ideas is only an expression of struggles between the various drives." The outcome of the struggle is that one group of ideas causes "the isolation and state of unconsciousness" of the other. The "process owing to which it has met with this fate is known as 'repression'" (p. 213). Hence the process of repression is a "struggle" in which one of the two drives achieves victory over the other—in other words, it is a dynamic process in which one of the drives together with its associated ideational patterns prevails "quantitatively" over the other and obtains or retains the latter's ideational patterns. *Repression is thus simply the activity of the relevant antagonistic drive in each case.* That emerges perfectly clearly, beyond any possibility of misunderstanding, from this short paper. As he was to write as late as in 1925, Freud manifestly always had precisely *this* concept of repression in the back of his mind—namely, that

> the psycho-analytic theory of the drives had *always been strictly dualistic* and had *at no time* failed to recognize, alongside the sexual drives, *others* to which it actually ascribed *force enough to suppress the sexual drives*. (These mutually opposing forces were described to begin with as the sexual drives and the ego drives. A later theoretical development changed them into Eros and the drive of death or destruction.) [Freud 1925e [1924], p. 218, my emphasis]

Although this conception is firmly anchored in Freud's fundamental theoretical ideas, and is thus actually—indeed always—*present*, it is nevertheless *not present* (on the "conscious surface" of his theoretical reflections) in many of his writings. The much-debated psychoanalytic issue of the nature of repression—of the entity to which the force needed to repress a drive can be ascribed[2]—is here answered by Freud clearly and simply within the logic of his model: if there are to be only two basic drives (dualism), of which one has the power to suppress— that is, to repress—the other, then repression must be seen as a *drive* process, with the logical consequence that *activation of the sexual drive activates the ego drive as repression, while activation of the ego drive activates the sexual drive as repression.*[3] From now on, therefore, when the term *repression* is used here *in a metapsychological sense*, it is to be understood as meaning the *drive* opposed to whichever other drive is relevant in a given case. This conception contributes decisively to the clarification, unification, and formalization of the model: the *driverepression theory* thus appears in the simpler guise of a *dualistic (antagonistic) drive theory*, so that all that now remains within the model (of the psychical apparatus) are *drives as variables* and *structures as switches*.

Single and Double *D-P-M* Unities

Freud turns to repression again in his "Formulations on the Two Principles of Mental Functioning" (1911b). He notes that neurotics *tend to turn away* from unbearable reality, while psychotics even *deny* it; and on this point he declares: "By introducing the process of repression into the genesis of the neuroses we have been able to gain some insight into this connection" (p. 218). "Turning

---

2 Sulloway (1979) regards this as one of the principal unsolved problems of psychoanalytic theory.

3 Before 1920, considerations on repression of the ego drive are lacking; Freud later found it easier to speak of the repression of the drives of death or destruction. However, Fenichel (1935) recognized this fundamental position only for the "first drive theory": "An ego drive thus fends off a sexual drive" (p. 458, translated for this edition). The fact that the ego drives also require repression was noticed by Alexander (1921): "There is no doubt a total lack of empirical evidence for the repression of ego drives; . . . yet the ego drives must surely also have experienced restrictions and repressions!" (p. 276f., translated for this edition).

away" and "denial" are seen as processes of repression, from which it follows that repression—as in the case of the psychogenic disturbance of vision—is understood overall as a *deficiency* of, or *deduction* from, the perception of reality, or, as we might say, a drive activity (obeying as it does a neurotic wish) with a *minus* sign. In his next step, Freud links these considerations on repression to the "unconscious mental processes," the primary mode of functioning of the psychical apparatus, and finds: "The governing purpose obeyed by these primary processes is easy to recognize; it is described as the pleasure–unpleasure… principle, or more shortly the pleasure principle. These processes strive towards gaining pleasure; psychical activity draws back from any event which might arouse unpleasure. (Here we have repression.)" (p. 219).

This is an important point, because it after all means that repression directly serves the gaining of pleasure: it prevents overexcitation of the system, reducing tension (which gives rise to unpleasure); and furthermore, this also applies in the unconscious, in the primary processes. Freud (1900a) has thus described an automatic mechanism of psychic regulation (p. 574), in that a *reduction in tension* (a minus), if not brought about by satisfaction from outside, *is made possible from within through the process of repression.* Considered in this light, repression, while a fundamental variable of the model as constructed, must— like all drive processes—first be shaped and differentiated in the course of development (in the form of *D-P-M* associations—i.e., of memory traces).

To exemplify this, Freud (1911b) again turns to the experience of the satisfaction of hunger. Hunger disturbs the "state of psychical rest" (that is, the system's equilibrium), compelling the system to undertake measures of homeostatic regulation: "When this happened, whatever was thought of (wished for) was simply presented in a hallucinatory manner" (p. 219). Hallucination thus has the function of restoring system equilibrium. Hallucination is the idea of the reality of a satisfaction situation—in other words, the cathexis (activation) of a memory trace containing (signaling) a reduction in tension— and is therefore in the service of the pleasure principle—that is, of homeostasis.

We now have two different propositions. We originally stated that *repression* subserves the gaining of pleasure (i.e., homeostatic regulation); and we have now found that the *drive*-induced *hallucination* of the situation of satisfaction, too, is in the service of gaining pleasure (i.e., of homeostatic regulation). A further question needs to be answered in order to understand the relationship between these two statements—namely, what actually is a hallucination, in *formal* terms—or, in other words, what *metapsychologically* relevant process is Freud outlining in the paradigm of the need–satisfaction sequence? The situation is of the utmost simplicity: the baby is hungry (i.e., a self-preservative drive impulse arises); the baby cries and thus induces the mother to feed it (i.e., to satisfy its need for nourishment). However, satisfaction as such does not exist within the model; that is to say, from the formal point of view, the statement that nourishment *satisfies* the drive is equivalent to the statement that nourishment *represses* the drive. This is because, in metapsychological terms, satisfaction means a return to homeostasis (in effect, to zero tension); and if we attribute a *plus* sign to a drive and a *minus* sign to its repression—or, conversely, in Freud's example, a *minus* sign to hunger (as deficiency) and a *plus* sign to nourishment—the two, when added together, produce the desired initial or equilibrium state of zero (the zero principle). If these components are deemed to be constitutive of hallucination, then hallucination of the experience of satisfaction is made up of an initially unlimited (i.e., "psychotic") idea of the excessive first drive impulse—"hunger"—and an initially equally unlimited (i.e., "psychotic") idea of the excessive second, repressing, drive impulse ("breast"), so that we have the following general equation:

hallucination = "psychotic" idea (–) + "psychotic" idea (+)

or, in the example discussed here:

hallucination = "hunger" idea (–) + "breast" idea (+)

which is formally equivalent to the equation:

hallucination = self-preservative drive idea (–) + sexual drive idea (+)

This does not yet tell us anything about the *contents* of the "psychotic" components of the "hunger" or "breast" ideas, but merely links the postulate of drive-defined (vectorial) unlimitedness to a familiar psychopathological notion. However, the really interesting question now is what ultimately remains behind as hallucination if, in purely arithmetical terms, a "plus" and a "minus" idea are added together to yield a "zero" idea. According to the underlying assumptions of our model conception, *zero* stands for the equilibrium state (zero principle) of the psychical apparatus, and *the equilibrium state is the system's optimum functional state.* "Zero" in this calculation is thus not equivalent to nothing, but rather to a state of equilibrium—that is, the *matching of two patterns of excitation.*

Figure II–1 clearly shows that *matching* in effect means *amplification and connection*: in the area of overlap between the two patterns of excitation, a state of equilibrium in the sense of a system-optimized amplification and connection of the ideational or excitation patterns of drive and repression has been achieved, whereas the "overflowing," excessive components of the two drive ideas—the "psychotic" margins of the two patterns—are not amplified and therefore drop out or remain subliminal. Hence what remains in the case of the hungerinduced hallucination is the result of a computation involving a highly complex combination of excitation patterns of the two directionally opposed drives. To return to our concrete example, we can say that the (repeated) entry of the satisfying (i.e., repressing) object into this unsatisfied (i.e., pressing) process constitutes for the drive an *"arrivée"*— a boundary at which a given combination of patterns is emphasized and amplified, marking the "appearance" of a first "experience of reality," which forms a memory trace in the psychical apparatus.[4] *"Arrivée"* thus means the matching of a

---

4 Brierley (1944) presents some interesting reflections in this connection: "It is agreed that sensory-affective experience must precede either hallucination or imagination. But images are not revived in isolation, they are revived in relation to their original impulsive and affective concomitants. Hence, memory-traces are probably better thought of as experience-traces rather than as sensory traces. To describe the mental organizations as systems of memory-traces is inadequate unless the memorytrace is regarded, objectively, as a responseor process-trace... The so-called structure imparted to the psyche by organization is a predisposing pattern of

drive question with its satisfaction/repression response—of a specific question pattern with its response pattern.

Figure II–I.

This conception has now provided us with a more differentiated view of hallucination. In the "Project," and also still in Chapter 7 of *The Interpretation of Dreams*, Freud characterizes hallucination as a reproduction, triggered by a particular drive excitation, of the experience of satisfaction—that is, a *wish fulfillment.* Now we see that this hallucination is composed of *two* directionally opposed wishes. We can thus define the wish as a simple *D-P-M* association, whereas hallucination is always a twofold *D-P-M* association; in other words, hallucination is always composed of *two* wishes, a drive wish and a repression wish, so that it is a (±) wish.[5]

---

response... once a given process has been activated by a specific stimulus, it will be re-activated by every succeeding stimulus of the same type. Such an assumption makes it far easier to understand modification and the genetic continuity of mental life" (p. 100).

5 This definition of the *wish as a simple (still unlimited—i.e., "psychotic")* D-P-M *association* corresponds to what Bion (1962) would call a *beta element*, whereas the conception of *hallucination as a D-P-M association that is twofold because it combines the drive wish and the repression wish* would be equivalent to an *alpha element* in Bion's sense: the beta element comprises a drive component *D* (needs), a perception component *P* (sensory impressions), and a motor or affective component *M* (emotions/emotional experiences and projections). Hence the *D-P-M* associations of *both* drives, if presented in *isolation*, yield *beta elements*, while an alpha element results only from their *combination* into a drive-repression unity. The combination, the *homeostatic regulation or switching principle*, is represented in Bion by the "*alpha function*," which transforms these beta elements "into alpha elements, which cohere" (p. 17). The proliferation of such alpha elements then yields a contact barrier. Using the example of the hunger-satisfaction sequence, Bion shows that hunger (i.e., the absence of the breast) is felt as a need, "the need itself being a bad breast... or what I have called   a beta-element" (p. 59). Both the breast that is present (the "good" breast) and the absent ("bad") breast (so to speak, the "feeding" breast

This provides the basis for an understanding of the sequence of the first drive-repression interaction, which is represented in hallucination. In economic terms, an increment in drive excitation always gives rise to repression, the change in drive *direction* always serving to prevent overexcitation of the system as a whole. (What triggers the reversal or changeover is a switch in the system—that is, a structure—for a drive can, so to speak, only *drive*, but not *switch*.) The actual quantitative increase in the level of tension thereby arising depends first on (psychic) structure as genetically determined[6] (i.e., in formal terms, as *specified* as a minimum condition of the model); then on the structure *introduced*[7] by an external satisfying object; and finally on the structure as *acquired* (i.e., modified) on the basis of this interaction. The onset of hallucination thus constitutes a crucial step in development, namely, the establishment of a psychic structure, or, put differently, the modification of a switching law whereby a *D-P-M* association resulting from the two antagonistic drives is combined in a new way. Hallucination is the first manifestation of such an endopsychic boundary specified "from outside" for the (self-preservative) drive, and the first internal representation of external reality; it is possible only when the psychical apparatus has become capable of retaining this experience of a *subject–object-related drive limitation* structurally—that is, in the form of

---

and the "hunger" breast respectively) correspond—each considered by itself—to a beta element, and an alpha element comes into being only when they are combined. This bringing together of the "bad" and "good" breasts may be "regarded as a transformation, by alpha-function, of an emotional experience into alpha-elements" (ibid.). This yields the same equation as given by us above, namely: hallucination = "bad" breast (–) + "good" breast (+).

6 Cf. the formulation in Rapaport's "model of primitive psychic functioning": "According to this model, when drive tension arises and the need-satisfying object is absent, the result is not the discharge of tension... but instead a redistribution of the tension—i.e., of energies. We describe this new energy distribution by saying that the unsatisfiable drive is repressed. In the place of the drive discharge that is prevented initially by the absence of the object and later by repression, there arise... ideational images in the form of wish-fulfilling hallucinations" (Rapaport, quoted in Zelmanowits 1971, p. 407, translated for this edition). Zelmanowits's critique of this suggestion—that it is absurd because the baby would die a silent death if its unsatisfied hunger were repressed—constitutes a confusion of the level of (concrete) psychic phenomenology with that of metapsychology.

7 The conception of the relationship between "inside" and "outside" is discussed in detail in Part III.

a switching law—and, in the event of a fresh drive excitation at *this* boundary, automatically initiates the process of repression, whereby the overall excitation of the system is reduced.[8] *Hallucination arises at this boundary, is located precisely at the switchover point between drive and repression, and contains and connects the (subject and object) representations of both drives, the self-preservative and the sexual drive.* This yields the general proposition that *psychic structure arises precisely at the time and place where a drive tendency switches over into a repression tendency, and therefore always represents a particular reciprocal relationship between the two drives.*

Freud now takes a further step. He introduces a "new principle of mental functioning" (p. 219)—namely, the *reality principle.*

> The increased significance of external reality heightened the importance, too,
> of the sense-organs that are directed towards that external world.... A special
> function was instituted which had periodically to search the external world, in
> order that its data might be familiar already if an urgent internal need should

---

8 Freud's idea of a hallucinatory wish fulfillment has been criticized on various grounds. Dornes considers it untenable mainly because the capacity for *free* and *image-based* hallucination of an absent object is, according to the results of research on babies, not present before the age of 18 months, and suggests the alternative "that hunger activates not an image-based memory but the motor activity of sucking. Sucking then activates the positive affect associated with it in the original satisfying situ ation" (Dornes 1993, p. 249, translated for this edition). This author would thus like to solve the problem by replacing the *P* component of hallucination (which in my view he sees too one-sidedly as the merely visual aspect of the scene, so that its auditory, haptic, gustatory, olfactory, and kinesthetic *P* aspects are disregarded) by its *M* component (the action of sucking), whereas here, on the formal metapsychological level, the complete *D-P-M* unity is always meant. The issue is therefore not whether the baby can from the beginning concretely and voluntarily (i.e., freely) summon up hallucinations, or from what age it is capable of doing so (although discovering this is certainly one of the many interesting tasks for infant research based on direct observation). The relevant point for the psychoanalytic theory of development *in the context of metapsychology* is in fact the *structural* postulate inherent in Freud's argument, namely that these experiences described on the basis of the need–satisfaction sequence leave behind *memory traces* in the form of *D-P-M associations* that are reactivated upon the re-emergence of a need from the same source, even if they are initially below the threshold of perception and do not yet give rise to actual concrete hallucinations; they are nevertheless the building blocks of the first *free*, *image-based* hallucinations, which, after all, do not suddenly appear out of the void at the age of 18 months but are merely available from a given time on to be summoned up freely and consciously (as images as well as in other forms) after countless repetitions of the same passages of excitation (what Freud calls facilitation).

arise—the function of *attention*. Its activity meets the sense-impressions half way, instead of awaiting their appearance. At the same time, probably, a system of *notation* was introduced, whose task it was to lay down the results of this periodical activity of consciousness—a part of what we call *memory*. [p. 220f.]

Reality is transmitted to the psychical apparatus through the intermediary of the sense organs—via the φ or P system—and is manifested in *consciousness*, the ω system or system *Cs*. Within the model, the phenomenon (the quality) of consciousness is a *process*—that is, a function or activity of a system, of a switch at a higher hierarchical level, of a macro-structure consisting of memory traces organized at different levels of complexity—what Freud calls the "system of *notation*" or "*memory*." The memory of the organ of consciousness responsible for the perception of reality (the system *Cs.*) contains the memory traces of, in principle, all the perceptions transmitted from the sense organs, and specifically those that have received particular *attention*. Attention is a "special function . . . [called upon] periodically to *search* the external world," which "*meets* the sense-impressions *half way*" (ibid., my emphasis); in other words, it is a *directional* process, and on the formal level of the model directional processes are simply drive processes. This view of the macro-system *Cs.* as a structural complex made up of countless *D-P-M* associations is thus perfectly consistent with the foundations of our model as already laid. The question now arises as to the relationship between hallucination and the perception of reality. Freud offers two explanations for this process:

> With the introduction of the reality principle one species of thoughtactivity was split off; it was kept free from reality-testing and remained subordinated to the pleasure principle alone. This activity is *phantasying*, which begins already in children's play, and later, continued as *day-dreaming*, abandons dependence on real objects. [p. 222]
>
> The place of repression, which excluded from cathexis as productive of unpleasure some of the emerging ideas, was taken by an *impartial passing of judgement*, which had to decide whether a given idea was true or false—that is, whether it was in agreement with reality or not—the

decision being determined by making a comparison with the memory-traces of reality. [p. 221]

Fantasying and daydreaming are characterized by the fact that they do not depend on the presence of real objects or the reference to reality. The same applies to hallucination of the experience of satisfaction in the absence of a real satisfying object. Hallucination, fantasying, and dreaming (or daydreaming) take place on a structural level *split off* from the structural level (the memory traces) of reality.[9] How then is it possible for a *judgment* to be formed within the psychical apparatus on whether a perception is a hallucination or a perception of reality? Freud had already answered this question in the 'Project' with the explanation of the w system; the answer in this case is by "*comparison with the memory traces of reality.*" The establishment of a second structural level of reality above (or alongside) this first structural level of hallucination/fantasy permits a *comparison* of memory traces, a *referencing of pattern formations*, with the result that, once again, the patterns on the first and second levels must *match* in order to trigger the necessary amplification (of the excitation) that is "evaluated" within the psychical apparatus as an indication of reality—and "evaluation" here means initiating "discharge."[10]

The question now arises as to what happens if the hallucinated satisfying object is not present in reality, and the special pattern of excitation on the first level is not activated, or is activated only incompletely, on the second level. If the two levels are regarded as *association or pattern* complexes of memory traces, it is clear that not only random individual elements but entire *sequences*

---

9 A further argument against Freud's conception of hallucination is directed at the psychopathological meaning of the term *hallucination*. I think this invalid, because, by introducing the level of reality, Freud makes it clear that he is concerned not with the clinical, psychotic aspect (phenomenology), but with the metapsychological conception: hallucination is a process that contains the drive-repression ideas *prior to* the computation level of reality, or in which this level is *deactivated*. However, since terms cannot be deprived of a substantial element of meaning, I shall couple Freud's notion of *hallucination* with that of *fantasy*, in which the reality level is also (largely) excluded.

10 So there is no *homunculus* at work that "evaluates" something as reality or "knows when and what to repress." On the problems concerning a (secret) agent or homunculus in psychological models, see, for example, Arnold (1984, p. 83ff.).

are stored, and these are now *"tracked"* by the *searching movement* until *identity* of the wished-for image and the perceived image is achieved— that is, until the excitation patterns of the first and second levels (approximately) *match*. Moreover, matching again signifies completion and hence "discharge," or triggering of the specific action, and thus homeostatic regulation. The entire process between the wish-related excitation of the first level and the finding of the object of the search in reality—the second level—can be pictured as a multiple circling, a to-and-fro movement, a scanning of pattern formations, a repeated "comparison" of memory traces on the level of hallucination with the memory traces of the reality level activated by perception; and the end result is:

psychic reality =   perception of   + "reality"/
                     hallucination (+)   sensory perception (–)

Accordingly, we now have *the same principle* three times over, described on each occasion *on a different level of complexity*, as follows:

1. Drive (+) and repression (–) are the simple variables of the model: we had stated that, at a given level of excitation of one drive, the opposing other drive is excited, thus assuring the homeostatic regulation of the system.
2. The concept of the wish in effect constitutes the next higher level of complexity. The simple wish is already a *D-P-M* association; a hallucination/fantasy arises in the area of overlap of the patterns of excitation (ideas) originating from both drives; the hallucination/fantasy—or the complete wish—is thus composed of two wishes, a (+) wish and a (–) wish, together making up a (±) wish.
3. The "reality principle" introduces an even more complex level of organization of the psychical apparatus. We have found that reality arises through the combination, or referencing, of two complex structural levels, that of hallucination/fantasy and that of what we call the perception of reality; considered as a whole,

psychic *reality* results from the summation or matching of the more comprehensive ("psychotic") hallucination/fantasy (+) and the more comprehensive (partly irrelevant) "reality"/sensory perception (–). The *psychic reality* resulting, in the area of matching, from this computation is a structure formed once again in the service of homeostasis; as Freud explains, it "need do nothing but strive for what is *useful* and guard itself against damage" (p. 223).

This formally unifying conception again has three implications:

1. If we specify that psychic structure arises at the precise time and place where a drive tendency switches over into a repression tendency, a *structure* can also be described as a *drive-repression unity*; in other words, the structure is the switch (controller) that homeostatically regulates the antagonistic drives—that is, the entities that are combined (the variables).[11]

2. The *activation of a structure*, or (±) pattern, on whatever level of complexity, in turn *results* overall in an *excitation* (with a [+] or [–] sign) that can formally be construed by another structure (possibly on the same level of complexity) as a *drive*; in this way entire groups of ideas or even systems (e.g., *Ucs.* vs *Cs.*) can exert mutually antagonistic effects that behave (or can be computationally combined) in the same way as drive and repression.

---

11   In a meticulous study, Gill (1963) argues that the organization of drives, their repression, and their discharge should be conceptualized *together* (he also mentions "impulse-defense units"). This results in a unified conception of the model of the psyche, in which the id and the ego are conceived of as belonging to a continuum within a hierarchical organization: the id is located on the most primitive level of psychic organization, which, however, is a level that already includes structure and the rudiments of a secondary-process organization, while the ego is situated on the highest level of psychic organization. According to Gill, this view has the advantage that drive and repression are conceptualized on all hierarchical levels as functionally inseparable and as aspects of behavior that belong together (p. 144ff.).

3. What Freud calls the "reality *principle*" is not a new or different *principle*, but a new *level* of complexity or structure with a modified switching law; there is only *one principle* of regulation, namely the *homeostatic* principle (Freud's "pleasure principle")—and that is why Freud was also able to write: "Actually the substitution of the reality principle for the pleasure principle implies no deposing of the pleasure principle, but only a *safeguarding* of it" (p. 223, my emphasis).

The Subject–Object Track

We have now considered the two antagonistic drives and their interaction in the drive-repression process—an interaction which was found to be structure-forming. An initial approach to a concept of the ego can now ensue from this structuring interaction. Freud presents some reflections on this point. In particular, he suggests the use, for the group of ideas that effects repression (which in his opinion is the *group of ideas of the ego drive*), of the "collective concept of the 'ego'—a compound which is made up variously at different times" (p. 213). The ego is thus defined as a group of ideas controlled by the ego drive. Freud is here returning to his two ego conceptions of 1895 and 1900 respectively. However, we can now see more clearly the configuration he probably had in mind: the *ego* as a macro-structure arises when, after a series of identical experiences, certain ideas that originate from the ego drive and are constantly repeated become firmly associated with each other, thus forming a *constantly associated* (*cathected or cathectable*) *group of ideas*, which acts as an increasingly complex center of organization and repression.

If the *ego* is thus understood in this way as a fixed group of ideas controlled by the ego drive, the question immediately arises whether Freud, at this point in the formation of his theory, also proposes a comparable agency within the psychical apparatus for the sexual drive. After all, the excitation of the sexual drive, or of its component drives, too, is linked to the perception of a satisfying object and a specific satisfying action in the mnemic systems to form a *D-P-M* association; in other words, everything assignable as "experiences" (passages of excitation) to the sexual component drives ought then likewise to yield a group of associated ideas that represents a kind of organizational center within the psychical apparatus in the form of a macro-structure (corresponding to the ego). This agency now appears, as suggested in *The Interpretation of Dreams*, to be the system *Ucs.*, the dynamic unconscious, which Freud distinguishes as "the repressed" from the purely descriptive unconscious (1912g). The development of these ideas can be studied even more precisely in connection with Freud's introduction of the reality principle:

> For while this development is going on in the ego-drives, the sexual drives become detached from them in a very significant way. The sexual drives behave auto-erotically at first; they obtain their satisfaction in the subject's own body..., and when, later on, the process of finding an object begins, it is soon interrupted by the long period of latency, which delays sexual development until puberty. [Freud 1911b, p. 222]

The *structural development of the drives* that is hereby implied takes place in opposing directions: the movement toward reality proceeds for the introversive ego drive from outside (preservation through the object) to inside (self-preservation), and for the extroversive sexual drive from inside (autoerotism) to outside (object love). This seems to have led Freud to draw two theoretical conclusions: first, that the sexual drive is the actual *outward-pressing drive*, whereas the *inward*-directed ego drive, on the other hand, should be imagined as the *repressing* entity; and, second, that the *ego drive ideas* repressed outward form *the ego* (the system *Cs.*), whereas the *group of ideas of the sexual drives* repressed inward by the ego drive gives rise to *the repressed* (the system *Ucs.*). If the *genesis of the structures of both drives is seen in each case as a consequence of their increasingly complex interaction*, their topographical position is found to be a *mirror-image projection*—of the sexual drives pressing toward consciousness into the unconscious, on the one hand, and of the ego drives pressing toward the unconscious into consciousness, on the other.

What, then, is the ego? It can now no longer be described simply as a group of ideas controlled by the ego drive, if, after all, ideas are to be thought of only at the point where one drive tendency switches over into the other, which represses it—that is, if ideas always contain the *D-P-M* associations of *both* drives in their respective proportions. Let us begin by deciding on the consistent use of the denotation *self-preservative drive* for what Freud sometimes called a self-preservative drive and sometimes an ego drive;[12] in this way we shall be making a more precise terminological distinction between drive and structure, as we inevitably associate the ego macrostructure of 1923 with the term *ego*, so that the term "ego drive" could imply the existence of a particular drive originating from this ego macrostructure—which is explicitly not the view taken here.[13] If it is further assumed that, at the beginning of the structural

---

12 The term "self-preservative drive" is itself not completely problem-free, because the use of the word "self" effectively declares an object to be a component of the notion of a drive. However, since the objects of a drive are by definition variable (Freud 1915c, p. 122), a drive can intrinsically be directed toward both external objects and the subject's own self; Freud described this situation for both the object-directed and the narcissistic orientation and object choice of the sexual drive. From this point of view, the term "preservative drive" (which can be directed toward both the subject's own self and other objects) would be more apt. But since the term "self-preservative drive" is universally accepted, it will be retained here. Loewenstein (1940) suggested replacing the former ego drives by other drive forces, which could be described as drives "of selfpreservation" or, alternatively, distinguished from Freud's life drives as "vital" or "somatic" drives. The self-preservative drives, including also aggression, ought in his opinion once again to be accorded independent status. The characteristic feature of the vital drives is in his view that they operate "as a function of the soma in contradistinction to the germ plasm" (p. 393). He thus contrasts the "somatic" drives with the sexual drives.

13 Although Hartmann agrees with Bibring (1941) that "all the drives [should be] realized to be part of the system id" and that one should no longer speak of ego drives (Hartmann 1950, p. 90), he nevertheless believes that "we find differences among the id and the ego and the superego not only with respect to the organization but also with respect to this momentum" (1948, p. 379). Again, making what is to my mind a conceptually unclear distinction between drive and energy, Hartmann writes: "The question whether all energy at the disposal of the ego originates in the instinctual drives, I am not prepared to answer. It may be that some of it originates in what I described before as the autonomous ego. However, all these questions referring to the primordial origin of mental energy lead ultimately back to physiology... We return to *the ego*. Regardless of whether its energic aspect be wholly or only partly traceable to the instinctual drives, we assume that once it is formed it disposes *of independent psychic energy*, which is just to restate in other terms the character of the ego as a separate psychic system. This is not meant to imply that at any given time the process of transformation of instinctual into

development of the psychical apparatus, the ideational representatives of both drives, activated in the drive-repression process, are not yet distinguishable, or not yet sufficiently distinguishable—that is, that the group of ideas (associated *D-P-M* unities) of the self-preservative drives always occurs in conjunction with those of the sexual drives that cause them to be repressed, and vice versa—then the fact of their so-called attachment as a *developmentally induced intrication* becomes clear. For whereas the group of ideas of the *self*-preservative drives initially still includes the representations of the feeding, preserving *object* and only later withdraws its boundaries to the psychic and somatic dimensions of the subject's own person that is to be preserved, the sexual drive must first be directed via the stage of "autoerotism" away from the subject's own person—the *self*—on to the psychic representative of the *object*. It follows that, especially *at the beginning of structural development, the newly forming groups of ideas of the component self-preservative and sexual drives still as it were constitute two substantially overlapping quantities.* This also enables us to postulate as a first approximation that *the gradually developing ego*, if defined as a macro-structure, a psychic organizational center coordinating both the interests of the subject and its orientation toward the object, *originates from this intersection of self-preservative and sexual ideas.*

Freud refers to the "attachment" of the component sexual drives to the self-preservative drives and to their "detachment" from them. The metapsychological significance of the term "attachment" has now become clearer. We can now imagine the psychical apparatus to be so constructed that this "attachment" of the sexual drives to the self-preservative drives is always retained in a relatively *simple* version at the base, in the primary structure-forming process of the drive-repression sequence. This would mean that the primary process contains

---

neutralized energy comes to an end; this is a continuous process" (Hartmann 1950, p. 86f., my emphasis). If it is assumed in our formalized model that the activation of each structure gives rise to a directional excitation that acts on another in the form of a drive excitation, the "neutralized energy" of the ego can perfectly well be conceived of as such a resultant—but not some form of *non-drive* energy of a so-called autonomous ego, or of autonomous ego apparatuses (whose position within, outside, or relative to the psychical apparatus remains unclear).

the ideas of the self-preservative drive—not yet unequivocally centered around the relevant "drive" idea—with the corresponding proportions of the sexual ideas activated for its repression, as well as the ideas of the sexual drive with the corresponding proportions of the self-preservative ideas activated for its repression. On this basis, the primary process standing for the system *Ucs.* could be characterized as the activation of a relatively *simple antagonism* of introversive self-preservative and extroversive sexual drive impulses including their corresponding ideational representatives.

This simple antagonism might also apply to the so-called *root* (the beginnings of structure formation) of the ego, which was later to be described as not being sharply separated from the id but as merging into it (Freud 1923b, p. 24). However, *after* Freud's postulated "detachment" of the sexual drives from the self-preservative drives, this antagonism would exist as it were *in duplicate*, for two different processes would then have occurred: first, with regard to the self-preservative drive, the group of ideas serving the ends of self-preservation would have set itself clearly apart from the group of ideas pertaining to their sexual repression, while, second, the group of ideas originating from the sexual drive would have likewise set itself apart from the group of ideas pertaining to the self-preservative drives, responsible for their repression; and *setting apart* is tantamount to becoming dominant or assuming primacy—to acquiring "quantitative preponderance." "Detachment" at this point can mean only that the two main tendencies of the sexual drive and the self-preservative drive together with the groups of ideas formed by them attain a certain autonomy or independence from each other within the organization of the psychical apparatus, by in effect forming (by association) two branches, each of which is subject to the hegemony of one drive, to which the relevant antagonistic drive (the repression component) is recessively subordinated. Considered in these terms, the "detachment" at issue would take the form of a differentiation of the main drive directions and their ideas (duplicated *D-P-M* associations) into two separate branches, which I should like, for the sake of clear illustration, to call the *subject track* and the *object track*; and within each track, the ideas belonging to the relevant *drive* become dominant, whereas those corresponding to its repression become recessive. These theoretical notions are illustrated by Figure II–2.

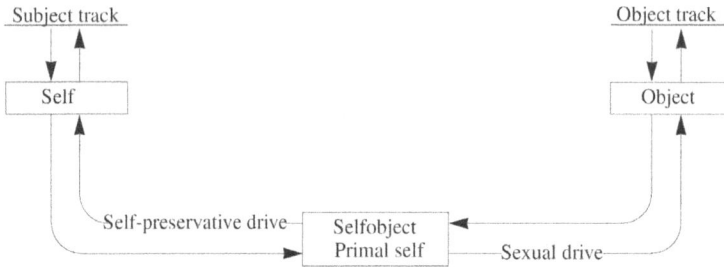

Figure II–2. The term *track* (subject track and object track) here introduced draws attention, in relation to the drive aspect, to the theoretical assumption of *directional* movements, which is perfectly consistent with Freud's idea of a *displacement* of libido. The base of the diagram represents the simplest form of drive-repression combination, an initial primitive structural level corresponding to Jacobson's (1964) *primal self* or Kohut's (1971) *self-object*. The subject and object tracks are then each assigned one structural complex: the *self* and the *object* respectively.

If such a differentiation is successfully achieved, it will be possible to identify on each track groups of ideas that form organized unities of differing complexity at different levels; in this connection a unity on the subject track will henceforth be described as the *self* and a corresponding unity on the object track as the *object*. Self and object are thus constant groups of ideas or representations organized on different levels with different degrees of complexity and made up of differing proportions, and both in turn exert antagonistic effects on each other within the ego.[14] However, if this detachment fails, the result, crudely

---

14 The term *self*—which had already been used by Freud (albeit not systematically)—was first employed by Hartmann (1950) with the specific purpose of *contrasting it with the object*. Although Hartmann thereby also meant the *concrete person of the subject*, both his suggestion and his recommendation of the terms self and object *representation* can also be interpreted in a purely metapsychological sense. Taking up Hartmann's notion of the self, Jacobson (1964) refers to an "undifferentiated 'psychosomatic' matrix . . . the *primal psychophysiological self*" (p. 6), or simply the "primal self" (p. 14). In her view, "the drives are actually turned *toward*, that is, aimed at discharge *on*, this primal self" (p. 6, my emphasis). If we regard the self as a structure (a structural

speaking, is a sexualization of the self and a functionalization of the object (in the service of self-preservation). This means that it is precisely the "detachment" of the sexual from the self-preservative drives that introduces and permits a further jump in level toward an increase in the complexity of drive-repression combination operations. We should then have a first approximation to a definition of the ego that contains the interaction of drive and repression in its structural concept, is open to the differentiated conceptions of object-relations theories, including the concepts of *intra*systemic conflict, and incorporates the conditions formulated by Freud for the secondary process in the idea of

---

complex), the drives are directed *toward* (not against) the self. What is *not compatible* with our ideas is Jacobson's initial hypothesis that drive energy is still in an *undifferentiated* state at the beginning of life and only gradually becomes differentiated through external influences into two different psychic drive forces. According to the proposal developed here, two antagonistic drives, as the two model variables of opposite sign, are constitutive of the system. However, if we *translate* Jacobson's assumptions into our formalized language, we can accommodate what she calls the undifferentiated drive stage, and with it also the "primal psychophysiologi cal self" or "primal self," at the base of the diagram (Figure II–2) (this would turn the undifferentiated state into one that could not, or could not readily, be differentiated on the *phenomenal* level), and her differentiation of the drives could then be understood as the structurally determined differentiation of the two *tracks*, each of which is by definition dominated by one of the two drives. Differing theoretical assumptions thus often prove to result from differences of linguistic perspective. Kernberg, who rightly sees Jacobson's developmental schemata as the embodiment of an "'intermediary language' between theoretical and clinical psychoanalysis" (1980, 1983, p. 95) and stresses their great relevance to *clinical theory*, suggests reserving "the term *self* for the *sum total of self representations* in intimate connection with the sum total of object representations. In other words, I propose defining the self as an *intrapsychic structure* that originates in the ego and is clearly *embedded in the ego*" (1984, p. 230, my emphasis except for the italicization of the first instance of "self"). The drive duality strictly observed in my book corresponds to Kernberg's conceptualization in so far as his proposed model even "conceives of the self as invested with both libidinal and aggressive drive derivatives integrated in the context of the integration of their component self representations" (ibid., p. 234). "It is, in short, an ego function and structure that evolves gradually from the integration of its component self representations into a supraordinate structure that [. . .] leads to the dual characteristics implied in Freud's *Ich*" (ibid.). However, my proposed formalized model is not consistent with Kernberg's view that the two directionally opposed drives must, from the beginning of life, develop and become differentiated only out of the affects of which they are composed (Kernberg, 1991a,b). Here, too, however, it seems to me that this difference in positions (apart from the postulate of the affects as the basic building blocks of the drives) is not due to theoretical incompatibility; in other words, Kernberg's hypothesis that the drives become differentiated only gradually is closer to phenomenological differenti*ability* and corresponds to the distinction postulated here between the two *tracks* of drive organization.

multiple structural condensation—these conditions being what we call high cathexis with bound energy coupled with low displacement or discharge.

This description of the ego and its introduction is correlated with Freud's introduction of the reality principle because he demonstrates by this principle how increasingly complex *groups of ideas* can be reciprocally *referenced*. The so-called reality principle introduces the referencing of the horizontal levels (wish and perception), while the introduction of the ego draws attention to the referencing of the vertical levels (the subject–object track). The point of these considerations is therefore to develop a conception of the rapid rate of increase in the complexity of psychic processes portrayed in metapsychological terms when the reality level and the subject and object tracks are introduced, even though the basic principle always remains the same.

DIFFERENTIATION AND INTEGRATION

Narcissism: The Drive Aspect and the Structural Aspect

We have now laid the foundations for reflecting on Freud's introduction of narcissism from a new perspective. To be precise, we have already done some preparatory work on this "legitimate... extension of the libido theory" (Freud 1914c, p. 75)—and indeed this is perfectly consistent with the chronology of his researches, because his first ideas on narcissism can be found in *Leonardo da Vinci and a Memory of His Childhood* (1910c), the case of Schreber (1911c [1910]), and *Totem and Taboo* (1912–1913a). In these works, Freud discusses the genesis of homosexuality in boys, the pathological megalomania of the schizophrenic, and the phenomenon of magical-animistic thought (a variety of megalomania and omnipotence) in imagined primal human beings and in children; these observations and reflections led him to the realization, reflected in his famous paper "On Narcissism: An Introduction" (1914c), that "individual features of the narcissistic attitude" and hence "an allocation of the libido such as deserved to be described as narcissism might be present far more extensively" than hitherto assumed, so that it "might claim a place in the *regular* course of human sexual development" (p. 73, my emphasis). This opens the way to a *metapsychological conception of narcissism* extending beyond the clinical level and representing a consistent continuation of his construction of the psychical apparatus. Let us begin with an overview:

> Recent investigations have directed our attention to *a stage in the development of the libido* which it passes through *on the way from autoerotism to object-love*. This stage has been given the name of narcissism. What happens is this. There comes a time in the development of the individual at which *he unifies his sexual drives* (which have hitherto been engaged in auto-erotic activities) in order to obtain a love-*object*; and he *begins by taking himself, his own body, as his loveobject*, and only subsequently proceeds from this to the choice of some person other than himself as his object. This half-way phase between auto-erotism and object-love may perhaps be *indispensable normally* What is of chief importance in the subject's *self* thus chosen as a love-object may already be the genitals. The line of development then leads on to the choice of an external object with similar genitals—that is, to homosexual object-choice—and thence to heterosexuality. [Freud 1911c [1910], p. 60f., my emphasis]

It is evident from this passage that the conception of narcissism once again includes a drive aspect and a structural aspect: the former concerns the libido—the sexual drive—and the latter the formation of complexes of ideas, whether self or object. Freud here explains that narcissism is a *regular* (transitional) stage in libidinal development on the way from autoerotism to the finding of an object. He had shown in the *Three Essays* that autoerotism is a phase in which the excitation of the component drives and the individual erotogenic zones still leads to separate (local) experiences of satisfaction. At a subsequent stage of development, the resulting memory traces, which at first form distinct groups of ideas pertaining to the sexual drives (part-objects in the sense of part-self and part-object unities), are, according to Freud, unified "in order to obtain a love-object." However, the first object resulting from such a unification (association) is not yet an "external" object, but the subject's "own body," or own "*self*" (Freud here uses precisely the term *self* that we had placed on the *subject track* in Figure II–2 to indicate a firmly associated group of ideas). This libidinal cathexis of the self unified in narcissism is supposed to be "indispensable normally" to continued development toward the "choice of some person other than [the subject] himself as his object." Again, since Freud always proceeds symmetrically in the development of his model, he adds the following in relation to the self-preservative drives: "Narcissism in this sense would not be a perversion, but the libidinal complement to the egoism of the drive of self-preservation, a measure of which may justifiably be attributed to every living creature" (1914c, p. 73f.). This situation is illustrated diagrammatically in Figure II–3.

Freud again asks: "What is the relation of... narcissism... to autoerotism, which we have described as an early state of the libido?" (1914c, p. 76). His answer turns out to be somewhat enigmatic: "... we are bound to suppose that a unity comparable to the ego cannot exist in the individual from the start; the ego has to be developed. The autoerotic drives, however, are there from the very first; so there must be something added to auto-erotism—a new psychical action—in order to bring about narcissism" (p. 76f.).

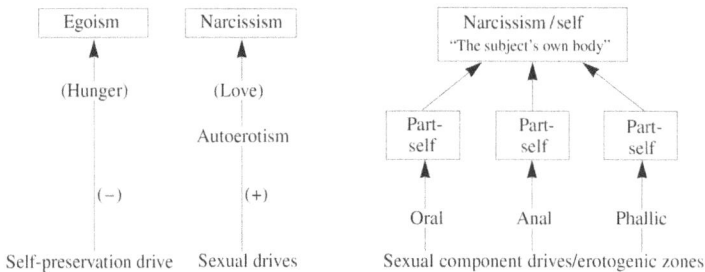

Figure II–3. The opposing directions of the drives (arrows) are here represented by the opposite signs; the boxes indicate groups of ideas (i.e., structures).

This indeterminate "new psychical action" that is supposed to bring about narcissism consists in the formation of associative links between the individual ideas of the component sexual drives. Freud is here unmistakably describing a process of *structure formation*, which he had already outlined for the self-preservative drive. In that case he had described the combination of a series of ideas of what he called the *ego* drive into a fixed group of ideas, which he termed the *ego*—and this is one of the main sources of confusion concerning his concept of narcissism:[15] references by Freud to the ego at this time do *not* denote the ego-as-macrostructure, as already discussed in the previous chapter, but only the associated group of ideas of the self-preservative drive—that is, what we have described as the *self* and accommodated on the *subject track*. In the present case, "ego" is equivalent to "self" or, if you will, a group of ideas on the subject track. Now the sexual drive is to bring about a unity comparable to the self—or, as Freud puts it, a "unity comparable to the *ego*." A unity comparable to the *self* is the *object*, which is equivalent to a group of ideas on the object track (see Figure II–2). The question is how such a group of ideas of the sexual drive—analogous to that of the "ego drive"—comes about. This is a matter of the development of structure: with the continued formation of memory traces, the initially isolated ideas combine into larger and larger groups, which become integrated on higher and higher hierarchical levels into unities organized with increasing complexity, and undergo further differentiation at each succeeding point in development. This *principle of integration and differentiation* is supposed to apply equally to the sexual drive and the self-preservative drive.[16] Freud develops the assumption that the ideas of the sexual drive (object ideas) unfold step by step from autoerotism (erotogenic zones as isolated *part*-objects) via so-called primary narcissism[17]

---

15 On this problem, see also Hartmann (1950).

16 Hartmann et al. (1946) distinguish between differentiation and integration in the formation of psychic structure. In their view, differentiation indicates the specialization of a function, while integration denotes the emergence of a new function out of previously not coherent sets of functions or reactions; differentiation and integration both flow from a principle (e.g., that of homeostasis) that regulates their interaction.

17 Various authors (e.g., M. Klein 1946, Jacobson 1964, Kernberg 1991b) have questioned or rejected the concepts of autoerotism and primary narcissism. Their retention in the formalized conception of metapsychology seems to me important because they paradigmatically explain the *principle of integration and differentiation*: from autoerotism as a phase in the formation of isolated groups of ideas (seen for example as "islands") to narcissism as an integration of these

(the subject's own "self," his own body, as a sexual object and selfobject in the sense of an integrated *whole* object) to the stage of object love (the "other" as a love object distinguished from the self).[18]

> Thus we form the idea of there being an original libidinal cathexis of the ego, from which some is later given off to objects, but which fundamentally persists and is related to the object-cathexes much as the body of an amoeba is related to the pseudopodia which it puts out. In our researches, taking, as they did, neurotic symptoms for their starting-point, this part of the allocation of libido necessarily remained hidden from us at the outset. All that we noticed were the emanations of this libido—the object-cathexes, which can be sent out and drawn back again. We see also, broadly speaking, an antithesis between ego-libido and object-libido. The more of the one is employed, the more the other becomes depleted.... Finally, as regards the differentiation of psychical energies, we are led to the conclusion that to begin with, during the state of narcissism, they exist together and that our analysis is too coarse to distinguish between them; not until there is object-cathexis is it possible to discriminate a sexual energy—the libido—from the energy of the ego-drives." [Freud 1914c, p. 75f.]

Freud's dictum of an "original *libidinal cathexis of the ego*" (i.e., of the *self*) can now be understood as the *libidinal cathexis of groups of ideas (structures) on*

---

islands into an initial complex unity, and thence to the differentiation of the subject and object tracks and the ultimate integration of both tracks into the ego-as-macrostructure.

18 The term *selfobject* was introduced by Kohut (1971, 1975, 1977) and in my view aptly denotes the early self and object representations which cannot, or cannot readily, be differentiated—that is, what belongs at the base of our diagram. It corresponds equally to the drive and structure aspects here postulated, in that (1) the object is perceived in the service of self-preservation (cf. the hunger-satisfaction sequence), and (2) the self is cathected as an object of the libido. On the basis of his clinical experience, Kohut deemed it necessary to split off his self complex from drive theory (this split is unnecessary from our present point of view), resulting ultimately in his radical assumption that he could replace drive theory throughout the domain of developmental psychology and pathology by his psychology of the self. On the current status of the self psychology originated by Kohut, see, for example, the compendia of Detrick and Detrick (1989) and Wolf et al. (1989).

the subject track—and these groups of ideas on the subject track are a *component* (so to speak, half) of the subsequent *ego*as-*macrostructure*. This is illustrated in Figure II–4, which is an expanded version of Figure II–2. Now, however, by virtue of his newly established "antithesis between ego-libido and object-libido," Freud has got into difficulties with his dualistic drive theory:

> ... if we grant the ego a primary cathexis of libido, why is there any necessity for further distinguishing a sexual libido from a non-sexual energy of the ego-drives? Would not the postulation of a single kind of psychical energy save us all the difficulties of differentiating an energy of the ego-drives from ego-libido, and ego-libido from object-libido? [p. 76]

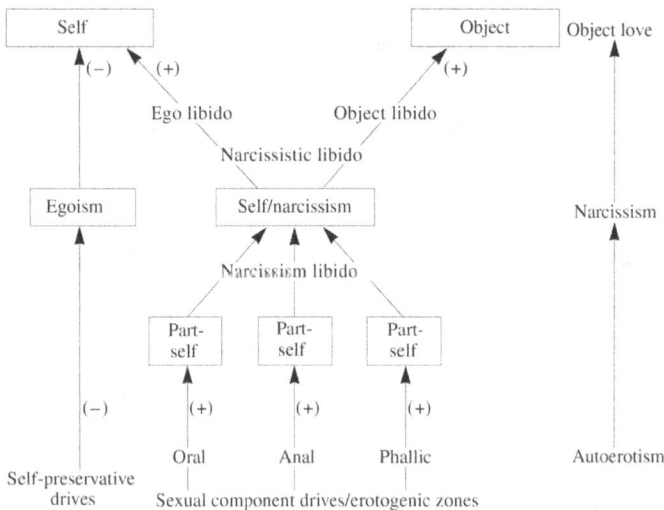

Figure II–4.

Any lack of clarity is mainly terminological. Freud does not for a moment question the dualism of the drives: "do not let us be deterred from pursuing the logical implications of the hypothesis we first adopted of an antithesis between ego-drives and sexual drives" (p. 79). However, he too evidently found the references to ego drives, their energy, the interest of the ego, and ego libido confusing—and, furthermore, regarding the psychic structures, he also seems to have sensed that confusion would arise between the ego as the group of ideas of the ego drives, the subsequent ego-as-macrostructure, which by this time had already taken on the outlines of an agency of consciousness and supervision for the entire psychic personality, and, finally, the ego as opposed to the external object—quite apart from how the representation of these entities within the psychical apparatus was to be conceived. It is fascinating to follow Freud as he overcomes every inconvenience in his unswerving pursuit of the correct theoretical construction of his metapsychological innovation, holding fast as he does to the *connection* he intuited between the fundamental antagonism of the drives and the differentiation of the separate sexual drive that he has just recognized:[19] "A differentiation of libido into a kind which is proper to the ego and one which is attached to objects is an unavoidable *corollary* to an original hypothesis which distinguished between sexual drives and ego-drives" (p. 77, my emphasis).

This quotation can be interpreted as meaning that the differentiation of libido into a kind applied to the subject track and another applied to the object track is an unavoidable corollary to an original hypothesis that distinguished between sexual drives and ego drives— because it followed from this hypothesis that every structure (group of ideas), whether on the subject track or the object track of the psychical apparatus, is constituted *by both drives*, is the result of a combining of both drives, and is located at the switchover point between one drive tendency and the other see (Figure II–5).

It may be wondered whether it is appropriate to distinguish between ego libido and narcissistic libido. From now on the following terminology will be used: the adjective *narcissistic* will be applied to libido in the phase of primary narcissism—that is, *before* the differentiation of the subject and object tracks (at the base of our diagram); while *narcissistic or ego libido* can denote the amount

---

19 This insistence on the antagonism of the sexual and ego drives in Freud's paper on narcissism has been called into question by Etchegoyen (1991) and Treurniet (1991). If Freud had dispensed with his fundamental notion of the antagonism of the drives, this would have had the consequence for the formalized version developed in this book of destroying the *formalizability* and hence the *logic* of the entire model.

of libido bound, once a differentiated psychic structure exists, to the groups of ideas controlled predominantly by the self-preservative drive as the repression component on the subject track. That is to say, it is preferable *not* to apply the term "ego libido" *globally* to the ego-as-macrostructure, but instead to use it *specifically* for the energy of the sexual drive postulated for the cathexis of the *groups of ideas organized on the subject track* within the ego-as-macrostructure (as well as the ego ideal). In other words, the energy of the sexual drive will always be designated by the term "libido"; and, depending on which structures are cathected by the sexual drive, we shall speak of narcissistic libido (at the base of the diagram), narcissistic or ego libido (on the subject track), or object libido (on the object track).[20]

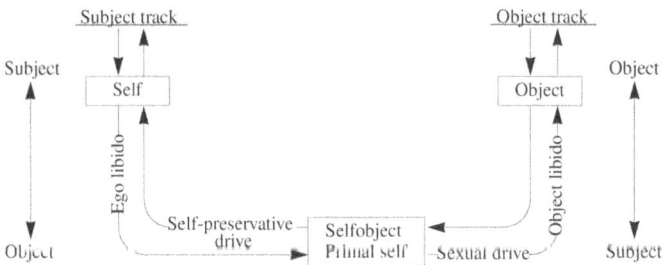

Figure II–5. This diagram illustrates the domains in which Freud refers to ego libido and object libido respectively. It shows, too, that the complex interwoven structures of memory traces and groups of ideas—the *self* and the *object* respectively—are always cathected, formed, or maintained by both drives. The dimensions of the orientation toward the subject itself or the object, which are directionally opposed on the two tracks, are also indicated on the right- and left-hand sides of the diagram.

---

20 The term *narcissism* thus signifies sexual-drive processes (or libidinal cathexes) (1) referred to a concrete phase of development and (2) directed toward specific structures, as well as (3) certain structures, or groups of ideas, dominated by these cathexes. (Green [1983] particularly emphasizes this structural aspect of narcissism.) Narcissism is thus always referred to the sexual drive. Grunberger's "psychoanalysis beyond drive theory" (1988a, b), on the other hand, implies a kind of "'pure narcissism,' a fundamental force or tendency *without instinctual base*" (Grunberger 1971, p. 166).

The Construction of Comprehensive Representations: The Ego Ideal

If (primary) narcissism is thus understood as a regular transitional stage in the line of development of the drives, the question immediately arises as to what subsequently happens to the memory traces, or ideational representatives, of this phase. That brings us to the issue of structure formation: no account has so far been given of *how* the division into two directionally opposed branches of structured drive activity arises.

For this purpose, let us be guided by our postulated axiom of the *antagonism* of the self-preservative and sexual drives and confine our investigation initially to subject-track processes. We can then state, with regard to the beginning of structural development, that the lower the degree of structural cross-linking (associations of *D-P-M* unities), the less inhibition will be experienced by passages of excitation and the more excessive the drive excursions will be, and with them the greater the activated quantities that will have to be put into balance. This situation can most conveniently be represented diagrammatically by a *spatial metaphor*, in which excessive outward-directed tendencies of the extroversive sexual drive mobilize excessive inward-directed tendencies of the introversive self-preservative drive, and vice versa. Their combination in a given instance establishes a relative and temporary equilibrium that ultimately tends toward *the relative midpoint* between two extremes. *Each drive-repression combination establishes a structure*, which furnishes a kind of orientation point for its successor. The more stable the associations between the various "accumulated" *D-P-M* unities and the more integrated the functioning of such complexes, the greater the influence they will have on the organization of the drive processes. For this reason, both the individual (micro)structure and the more comprehensive (substructure and macrostructure) complexes are "attractors"[21] for subsequent structure formation, albeit to different degrees owing to their relative positions in the hierarchy. See Figure II–6.

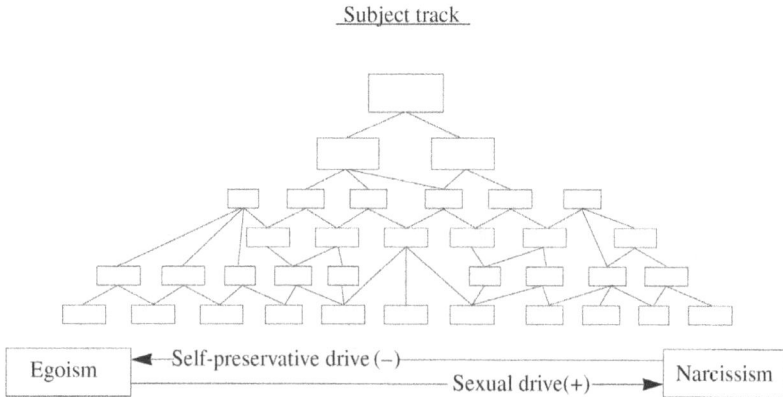

Figure II–6.

Let us clarify this assumption by turning again to Freud—because we are by no means simply transplanting a modern but alien concept (the "attractor") into metapsychology as a spurious explanation. It is fascinating to discover that Freud in fact already described the *principle* of the attractor in the "Project" in 1895. Here (1950c/1950a [1895], p. 323f.), in the context of his conception of the processes of (neuronal) structure formation, he shows that (1) a passage of excitation leads to the *facilitation* of the neuronal contact barriers, (2) this results in *cathexis* of ψ-nuclear neurones, and (3) such cathected neurones effect an *inhibition* for subsequent passages of excitation—because the cathexis acts like a temporary *higher-order* facilitation, thus modifying the passage in such a way that an excitation that would otherwise have been distributed along the facilitated neurones is now *directed toward the cathected neurone*. The cathected

---

21 The term *attractor* originates from chaos theory. "Attractors are geometric structures that characterize long-term behavior in phase space. Crudely speaking, an attractor is everything toward which a system tends or by which it is attracted" (Crutchfield et al. 1989, p. 12, translated for this edition).

neurone of the "Project" corresponds to our notion of structure as a drive-repression unity—so that the establishment and cathexis of such a structure exerts an *attraction* on subsequent passages of excitation; in other words, *the establishment of such a structure constitutes an attractor for subsequent passages of excitation, and at the same time a modifying factor of inhibition.*

Having given this account of the development of the subject track, at the base of which the first structures of the so-called primitive self are established (and at whose top the structures of the "mature" self will subsequently be located), we must now show how, with a slight time lag, the object track forms. There are two possibilities. The first is that, the denser the structure on the subject side of the psychical apparatus becomes, the stronger the inhibition "inward" for the introversive self-preservative drive will be there, and the further "outward" the tendencies of the extroversive sexual drive will "extend", thus successively displacing outward the equilibrium point of homeostasis (in the sense of a *dynamic* stability). In systemic terms, therefore, it is structurally determined displacements of equilibrium, and hence in turn temporary instabilities, that give rise to a new homeostatic regulation process, which initiates a new cycle of structure formation under the aegis of a new "ordering entity."[22] As an alternative, second possibility, the "attractive force" of an attractor on the subject track decreases with increasing density of the structures surrounding it, resulting, at a given point in structure formation, in a kind of "jump" on to the object side of the psychical apparatus (an excessive sexual drive excitation extends so to speak far beyond the structures of the not yet fully formed subject track); on the object side, an initial structure (i.e., an attractor) is then laid down, as a basis for the gradual establishment, accretion, and accumulation of further structures similarly constituted in terms of their drive composition (i.e., ones in which the sexual drive predominates), and from these structures the object track progressively develops.

---

22 The notion of the *ordering entity* or ordering parameter is used by Haken and Haken-Krell (1989) in their theory of synergetics to explain the *self-organization* of open systems in the case of *instability* and the formation of macroscopic structures in biology.

Let us end these reflections for the time being by assuming that both tracks of drive organization are to function increasingly in the form of structural complexes *connected in parallel*, as substructures of the ego-as-macrostructure.

Freud calls structures, formed and associated during the phase of primary narcissism, the "ego ideal":

> This *ideal* ego is now the target of the self-love which was enjoyed in childhood by the actual ego. The subject's narcissism makes its appearance displaced on to this new *ideal ego*, which, like the infantile ego, finds itself possessed of every perfection that is of value. As always where the libido is concerned, man has here again shown himself incapable of giving up a satisfaction he had once enjoyed. He is not willing to forgo the narcissistic perfection of his childhood; and when, as he grows up, he is disturbed by the admonitions of others and by the awakening of his own critical judgement, so that he can no longer retain that perfection, he seeks to recover it in the new form of an *ego ideal*. What he projects before him as his ideal is the substitute for the lost narcissism of his childhood in which he was his own ideal. [Freud 1914c, p. 94, my emphasis]

In the phase of primary narcissism, the "ego" (equivalent to the self) is its own ideal and coincides with it; more precisely, the *ideal* as it were has its libidinally cathected obverse in the representatives formed during the primary narcissistic phase, whereas egoism, as the group of representatives of the self-preservative drives, is located on its reverse or shadow side (Freud 1916–1917f [1915], p. 223). In this phase of development, therefore, ideas and, with them, structures are formed which, when connected in fixed association, give rise to an organizational unity at the base of the subject track, which, as the *ego ideal*, becomes the starting point of a new structural complex: the narcissistically cathected self from the phase of primary narcissism as it were forms the nucleus or attractor for the development of a new structural functional unity (a "column"). This striving back toward narcissism is nothing other than the activity (the consequence of the excitation) of the sexual drive, and the "object" of this narcissistic tendency is the abandoned narcissistic position from the beginnings of structural development—namely, the ego ideal. Put differently, both entities— the *mature self* (real self) and the *ego ideal* (organized around the ideal self)—act as *antagonistic attractors* on the drive and structure-formation processes on the subject track.

> We are naturally led to examine the relation between this forming of an ideal and sublimation. *Sublimation* is a *process that concerns object-libido* and consists in the drive's directing itself towards an aim other than, and remote from, that of sexual satisfaction; in this process the accent falls upon deflection from sexuality. *Idealization* is a *process that concerns the object*;[23] by it that object, without any alteration in its nature, is aggrandized and exalted in the subject's mind. For example, the sexual overvaluation of an object is an idealization of it. *In so far as sublimation describes something that has to do with the drive and idealization something to do with the object, the two concepts are to be distinguished from each other.* [p. 94, my emphasis]

This passage clearly shows that Freud, who always sees the "drive" as primarily sexual, initially regards sublimation as a process of drive direction occurring solely on the object track: not narcissistic or ego libido but only object libido is capable of sublimation, of deflection from pure sexuality. However, he goes on to specify by definition that sublimation is "something that has to do with the drive." Since the question of the *directing of drives* (e.g., sublimation) is theoretically a question of the *organization of the system* and cannot be linked to the (+/–) directionality of only one of the two drives, we can immediately add that *sublimation of narcissistic or ego libido and of the self-preservative drive* may also be assumed to occur.[24] Freud's considerations on the formation of the ideal—that is, on the ego and sexual ideals—although

---

23 [Translator's note: This word is in italics in the original.]

24 Pasche (1993) addresses this point in his reflections on the "ego drives." He doubts that it is correct to confine the role of the "ego drives" to the preservation of the individual; emphasizing also their *shaping* function, he goes on to inquire: "Are they not also involved in the construction of the ego ideal; in a word, *Can they not be sublimated like the sexual drives?* I do not know, but the question is worth asking" (p. 5, my emphasis [translated for this edition]).

based exclusively on the libidinal drive, nevertheless apply on both tracks of drive activity (see Figure II–7). His brilliant discovery of the formation of the ideal in connection with his investigation of narcissism may be said to have

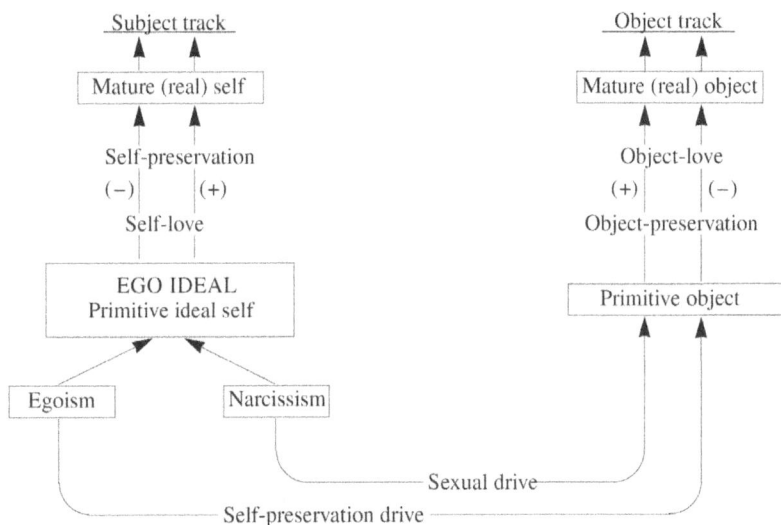

Figure II–7. The ego ideal arises as the *integration product of egoistic and narcissistic* tendencies; the equation of egoism and narcissism implies that egoism is already a product of the integration of part-ideas of the self-preservative drive (not mentioned in Freud but analogous to the part-objects of the sexual drive). Egoism and narcissism are then the first *products of differentiation* of the two drive ideas, which are *integrated* again in the ego ideal. We also clearly observe the antagonism of the *mature (real) self* and the *ideal self* (as a part of the ego ideal), and the analogous antagonism on the object track of the mature (real) object (which can be "elevated" to the status of the *sexual ideal*) and the early *primitive object*. By analogy with *self-love*, a function of the sexual drive on the subject track, the notion *"preservation of object"* included on the object track stands for the function of the self-preservative drive that limits the sexual drive on that track; this will be discussed in greater detail in connection with the genesis of the superego.

established the *libidinal frame of reference for both the subject and the object tracks* between the ego ideal and the sexual ideal. Again, although Freud's account concentrates in each case on one drive (usually the sexual drive), the relevant disregarded drive component (as a rule the self-preservative drive) manifestly coexists with it on the reverse of his theoretical imagining—and it is therefore clear that, if this drive-theory counterpart of his concepts were not made consciously explicit, the logic of his metapsychology would inevitably be pervaded with faults or discontinuities.

MICROANALYSIS OF DRIVE PROCESSES

Extension of the *D-P-M* System and Introduction of the Biogenic Zones

Once Freud had introduced narcissism and thereby arrived at a more differentiated view of the sexual drive—that is, in fact, of the structural development thereby initiated—he seems to have found it necessary, on the level of metapsychology, to put forward a *differentiation of his general concept of the drive*, which, together with some complementary assumptions, we shall incorporate in a model that will facilitate in-depth reflection on what is covered by Freud's notion of the vicissitudes of the drives. Let us begin with his celebrated 1915 definition of the drive:

> If we now apply ourselves to considering mental life from a *biological* point of view, a "*drive*" appears to us as *a notion*[25] *on the frontier between the mental and the somatic*, as the psychical representative of the stimuli originating from within the organism and reaching the mind, as a measure of the demand made upon the mind for work in consequence of its connection with the body. [1915c, p. 121f., my emphasis except for the italicization of "biological"]

---

25 [Translator's note: Strachey's word "concept" has here been changed to "notion" for the reason explained in footnote 26.]

This conception of the *notion of the drive* runs through the whole of Freud's oeuvre in this or similar fashion. Its crucial aspects are as follows: the drive is a *frontier notion*, embracing both the somatic and the psychic, "representing" *psychically* the specific physiological stimulus and *physiologically* that which must be tackled psychically (i.e., the measure of the demand for work). There is no need to dispute whether the notion of the drive, as thus defined, should be assigned more to the psychic or to the physiological side, as Freud gives *equal weight* to both components. Let us instead concentrate on the terminological differentiation within Freud's *drive concept*.[26]

The Two Primal Drives

Let us begin at the base of our model, with what we have here called the *D* system. Freud admits that any number of drives could be supposed to exist—a drive of play, of destruction, of gregariousness, and so on—but wonders whether "drive motives like these, which are so highly specialized..., do not admit of further *dissection* [my emphasis] in accordance with the *sources* of the drive" (ibid, p. 124), so that it is appropriate to take only the "primal drives—those which cannot be further dissected" as basic axioms of a scientific theory. He states, "I have proposed that two groups of such primal drives should be distinguished: the *ego*, or *self-preservative*, drives and the *sexual* drives" (ibid.).

Freud describes this postulate of two primal drives as "merely a working hypothesis" (ibid.)—that is, as something that does not "really" exist. Although it is appropriate, in terms of the functions to be assigned to the two primal drives, that he called them the self-preservative drive and the sexual drive, the essential point for the system is that there are *two* drives that stand in an

---

26 I distinguish between the *notion of the drive* (in the narrower sense), which is defined as a *variable* within our model, and the (more comprehensive) *drive concept*, which includes all the components that will now be enumerated in succession and that, in its complete version, irrespective of level, is always represented by a *D-P-M unity*. The *drive concept*, when examined closely, thus proves to be a drive structure concept.

antagonistic relationship to each other—for this is a "necessary postulate" for the "biological purpose of the mental apparatus," its homeostatic regulation. Freud develops these ideas as follows:

> Are we to suppose that the different drives which originate in the body and operate on the mind are also distinguished by *different qualities*, and that that is why they behave in qualitatively different ways in mental life? This supposition does *not* seem to be *justified*; we are much more likely to find the simpler assumption sufficient—that the *drives are all qualitatively alike* and *owe the effect they make only to the amount of excitation they carry, or perhaps, in addition, to certain functions of that quantity*. [p. 123, my emphasis except for the italicization of "qualities"]

Within our model, we had assigned the drives a direction—that is, a (+/−) sign—and drive energy a value—that is, an "amount of excitation," or quantity. Freud now makes precisely the same demand for his drives: in formal terms, they are "*qualitatively* alike," and owe their differing effects "only to the *amount* of excitation they carry," as well as "perhaps, in addition, to certain functions of that quantity." The amounts are "qualitatively" alike and the "certain functions" result from the opposite signs. We had (arbitrarily) endowed the amounts of excitation of the sexual drive with a (+) sign and those of the self-preservative drive with a (−) sign, thereby ensuring the distinction between the two drives in terms of their effects from the D system on, given an exclusively quantitative notion of energy. Another new term here makes its appearance, namely *pressure* (which is firstly intended to correspond to the motor expression of the drive [*M*], and secondly represents an elucidation of the general, abstract notion of the drive); it too is consistent with our sign-based distinction between the drives:

> By the pressure [*Drang*] of a drive we understand its motor factor, the amount of force or the measure of the demand for work which it represents. The characteristic of exercising pressure is common to all drives; it is in fact their very essence. Every drive is a piece of activity; if we speak loosely of passive drives, we can only mean drives whose *aim* is passive. [p. 122]

The "amount of force" or "measure of the demand for work" is represented by the amount of excitation or *quantity* of energy. As a general property of drives, pressure is simply the activating entity, whether for "active" (+) or for "passive" (–) drives.

Drive Sources

In the section on the *Three Essays*, we assigned the D system a higher level in the hierarchy—comparable to a master switching center—and accommodated the drive sources (e.g., the erotogenic zones) in the P system in accordance with the fundamental assumptions of the "Project," because they convey the decisive *sensory* impressions from the periphery of the psychical apparatus. In 1915 Freud preserves the distinction between the drives and their sources: "By the source [*Quelle*] of a drive is meant the somatic process which occurs in an organ or part of the body and whose stimulus is represented in mental life by a drive..., sometimes its source may be inferred from its aim" (p. 123).

The source of a drive is a process in an organ that triggers a stimulus—a drive stimulus or, more precisely, a component-drive stimulus— which becomes known to us through a pressure it exerts, or, if you will, by its aims, namely the performance of a specific satisfying action. In the case of the sexual drive, this means that a component drive that presses toward a satisfying action is excited at the source of the drive, an erotogenic zone (which may be oral, anal, or genital). Let us take the self-preservative drive as a counterexample. If it is to be the case that the "source may be inferred from its aim," it follows that one aim of the self-preservative drive—that is, the ingestion of nourishment—is indicative of its source, the stomach; and here again it should be noted that the drive source (the stomach), together with its component drive (hunger), is distinct from the higher-level primal drive, the self-preservative drive. In other words, just as, in the concrete somatic domain, there is a *combined action* of neurophysiological processes in the brain and ones in the internal organs (stomach, intestine, etc.)—whose overall resultant is what we experience as hunger—so, in terms of the model, there is an interaction, association, or combination of a central excitation of the self-preservative drive in the *D* system with component-drive excitations in the *P* system, which as a whole evoke the drive aim of the ingestion of nourishment. The centrally positioned self-preservative drive is the more comprehensive, hierarchically supraordinate entity, which controls and coordinates the component drives assigned to it. In accordance with the wider definition of the term *self-preservation*, we can already formulate a series of drive aims of this kind: not only the ingestion of nourishment and liquids but also the excretion of digestion products, respiration, maintenance of body temperature, and so forth. In this way we can add in the *sources of the self-preservative drive* omitted by Freud or at least not explicitly described by him as such: the stomach, intestines, kidneys, liver, lungs, and so on—that is, the *internal organs*, which I shall henceforth (by analogy with the use of the term *erotogenic zones* as the sources of the sexual drive) call the *biogenic zones of the self-preservative drive*. This is consistent with the schematic structure we have been using (as appropriate for a formalized model), in which the sexual drive is the one directed *outward*, and therefore essentially activates the *external* organs—the classical triad of mouth, anus, and genitals—as well as the outwardly oriented sense organs (eyes, ears, nose, and skin) as drive sources or *erotogenic zones*, whereas the self-preservative drive is the one directed *inward* and thus activates the *internal* organs, which should also be deemed to include the inward-oriented sense organs, as drive sources or *biogenic zones*. The point of this terminological supplementation is, first, to reestablish the symmetry of the model structure (so far there have been specific zones only for the sexual drive), and, second, to allow for the fact that, on the metapsychological level, we cannot of course speak of the stomach but certainly can of a biogenic zone.[27]

---

27 The contributions of Simmel (1924, 1933), whose titles translate as "The psychophysical significance of the intestinal organ for primal repression" and "Pregenital primacy and the intestinal stage of libido organization" respectively, are interesting in this regard.

Drive Aims

These were mentioned in the quotation reproduced earlier. Freud goes on: "The aim [*Ziel*] of a drive is in every instance satisfaction, which can only be obtained by removing the state of stimulation at the source of the drive" (p. 122). This definition is directed toward the restoration of homeostasis, or, more precisely, toward the act necessary for this purpose—for Freud had shown in the *Three Essays* that the *aim* is the *appropriate action*. We had assigned this, as the satisfying *action*, to the *M* system. In this way the *D*, *P*, and *M* systems are again combined in Freud's drive concept, and for this reason the notion of the drive *aim* receives the additional significance of a *completion* of the general pattern of every psychic process, as follows. The combination of the excitations of these three systems—of a drive excitation in the *D* system, which leads to the activation of a component drive in the *P* system, and triggers a drive action in the *M* system (drive aim)— constitutes a complete psychic unity (a *D-P-M* unity) that contains all the elements of Freud's drive concept. The thesis is that *all* psychic processes take place via these three systems and involve each of them. Here, we may say, the *D* system is assigned supraordinate coordinating and initiating functions, the *P* system has receptive and specifying functions, while the *M* system acts as an effector. However, it should not be forgotten that simultaneously, as it were on the reverse of this unity, a corresponding process of opposite sign is taking place—that is to say, in our present conceptualization, the correlative repression process is added to the simple drive process, so that in each case we have *binary D-P-M unities*. Put differently, in formal terms "removing the state of stimulation" is the same as "repression" of this drive stimulus, which returns the system to the equilibrium state. The drive aim, considered *formally* or, if you will, purely mathematically, is then the triggering of this "repression" with a view to initiating the removal of the stimulus. All processes in the *D*, *P*, and *M* systems are thus always twofold, comprising a drive component and a repression component. It follows in effect that the equilibrium of the system lies in the completeness of its processes, and that, where they are not so completed, a *tendency toward completion* persists.

We have thus laid the structural foundations of our model, as follows. At the base of the hierarchically supraordinate D system we find the two antagonistic drives, the self-preservative drive and the sexual drive; at the base of the P system we have accommodated the drive sources (the biogenic and erotogenic zones with the component drives issuing from them); while at the base of the M system are the motor images, as they are called in the "Project"— that is, the patterns of the specific action, or action representations. We can now build on these foundations.

The Object

The object had been an important element of Freud's drive concept since the "Project." Since the "image of the object" is conveyed to the psychical apparatus via the sense organs (the φ system), we had assigned it to the P system, where it is now accommodated in the model above the biogenic and erotogenic zones.

> The object [*Objekt*] of a drive is the thing in regard to which or through which the drive is able to achieve its aim. It is what is most variable about a drive and is not originally connected with it, but becomes assigned to it only in consequence of being peculiarly fitted to make satisfaction possible. The object is not necessarily something extraneous: it may equally well be a part of the subject's own body. It may be changed any number of times in the course of the vicissitudes which the drive undergoes during its existence; and highly important parts are played by this displacement of the drive. [p. 122]

Considered in terms of a genetic line, the situation is as follows. At first, the object of the drive is still a part of the subject's own body— for example, an erotogenic zone. Freud calls this phase *autoerotism*. At this stage of development, the following is stated to apply to the "components of the later sexual function": "their object is negligible in comparison with the organ which is their source, and as a rule coincides with that organ" (p. 132). In autoerotism, a drive (*D*) is satisfied directly at the drive source, its first object (*P*), by means of masturbation, the specific action (*M*). In this way the drive aim is attained and the process completed. How object development commences on this basis is described by Freud as follows:

> Originally, the action [of masturbation] was a purely autoerotic procedure for the purpose of obtaining pleasure from some particular part of the body, which could be described as erotogenic. Later, this action became merged with a wishful idea from the sphere of object-love and served as a partial realization of the situation in which the phantasy culminated. [1908a, p. 161]

The autoerotic action "merges"—is linked, or associated—with a "wishful idea from the sphere of object-love" (describable as hierarchically supraordinate), which is established *above* the erotogenic zone. The genesis of the idea of the object thus appears as a step in maturation and development, revealing a line from the "*somatic*" *object* (whose drive source is the biogenic and erotogenic zones) via the part*selfobject* and the primitive *whole selfobject* (narcissism) to the *mature self* and the *mature object*—so that the *object representation* can be accommodated within the *P* system so to speak on the second tier above the drive source.[28]

Affect

Freud takes the parallel step in development for the *M* system immediately afterward in his paper "Repression" (1915d), where he introduces a differentiation of his drive concept of particular importance to his theory of defense, namely the separation of "idea" (self or object) and "affect":

---

28 The position of the object representation "above" the biogenic and erotogenic zones—that is, at a higher hierarchical level within the *P* system—corresponds to Schur's (1966) concept of desomatization and to Freud's "hypochondriacal speech or 'organ-speech'" (1915e, p. 199).

In our discussion so far we have dealt with the repression of a drive representative, and by the latter we have understood an idea or group of ideas which is cathected with a definite quota of psychical energy (libido or interest) coming from a drive. Clinical observation now obliges us to divide up what we have hitherto regarded as a single entity; for it shows us that besides the idea, some other element representing the drive has to be taken into account, and that this other element undergoes vicissitudes of repression which may be quite different from those undergone by the idea. For this other element of the psychical representative the term *quota of affect* has been generally adopted. It corresponds to the drive in so far as the latter has become detached from the idea and finds expression, proportionate to its quantity, in processes which are sensed as affects. From this point on, in describing a case of repression, we shall have to follow up separately what, as the result of repression, becomes of the *idea* and what becomes of the drive energy linked to it. [p. 152]

In terms of our model, this means that the "idea or group of ideas"— more generally, the *object* representation—with or upon which a drive is sensed corresponds to the psychic *perception* of the drive, and is therefore a component of the P system, whereas the strength of the drive (its energy) finds "*expression proportionate to its quantity*" in the affects, which, as "processes of discharge," are to be accommodated in the M system (1915e, p. 178). When Freud now subdivides the drive idea, which had originally been conceived as a unity, into (P) idea and (M) affect, the affect then also corresponds in the M system precisely to the level of development possessed by the object representation in the P system, so that the affect representation should likewise be accommodated in the M system on the second tier *above* the action representation. The affect as it were supersedes the action and is to that extent the *sensation* of a drive action. A *drive excitation* in the D system thus has repercussions on an *object representation* in the P system and activates an *affect representation* in the M system. The complete description of this process is as follows: a drive-repression unity issuing from the D system is fully represented psychically by a self and object representation and an affect.[29]

Thing Presentation and Word Presentation

In the study "The Unconscious" (1915e), composed a short time later, Freud goes on to subdivide the "idea of the object" further into *"thing presentation"* and *"word presentation"*[30]: "What we have permissibly called the conscious presentation of the object can now be split up into the presentation of the *word* and the presentation of the *thing*; the latter consists in the cathexis, if not of the direct memory-images of the thing, at least of remoter memory-traces derived from these" (p. 201).

In our model, thing presentations, which are at least in part attributable to direct sensory perceptions, are once again a component of the P system—and since Freud distinguishes them from ideas of the object and allows them to originate also from "remoter memory-traces" that are merely *"derived"* from the direct memory images (so that thing presentations can also arise through processes of generalization, combination, and so on), the *thing representations* (in accordance with the meaning content of this term—i.e., *thing*) will now, as the most abstract ideational units, so to speak most remote from the personal object reference, be placed on the third tier above the object representations in the P system. Already in the "Project," Freud had assigned word presentations— or, in this case, "motor word-images"—a place in the M system owing to their connection with the "path of discharge" (1950c/ 1950a [1895], pp. 365, 366).

---

29 This is consistent with Kernberg's (1980) notion of the *unity of self, object and affect*, which constitutes a *P-M* connection in our model. He sees "units of self and object representations (and the affect dispositions linking them) [as] the building blocks on which further developments of internalized object and self-representations, and later on, the overall tripartite structure (ego, superego, and id) rest" (p. 17).

30 [Translator's note: The same German word, *Vorstellung*, is translated by Strachey as "idea" in the case of the object and as "presentation" in the terms "thing presentation" and "word presentation." See Strachey's footnote in *Standard Edition* 14, p. 201.]

Like thing representations, word representations also belong on the third tier *above* affect representations in the *M* system: expression by speech can thus be seen as the equivalent of an affect in the same way as a drive action; in this sense, after all, Freud saw thinking too as *trial action.*

This account of the successive stages in the terminological differentiation of Freud's drive concept in the wider sense yields a model structure (see Figure II–8) that initially clarifies two points. First, it emphasizes the line of development of the individual functions (from the bottom up in the progressive direction), thereby also making clear their reciprocal relationship and dependence on each other; and, second, it illustrates the fact that, in accordance with Freud's expanded conception of the drive, each psychic unity, from the simplest to the most complex, always takes the *composite* form of a *D-P-M* unity—that is, it involves in each case at least one component of these three systems— and, furthermore, the complete psychic process cycle, constituting a drive-repression unity, corresponds to a binary *D-P-M* unity.

In this *D-P-M* model, we have subsumed the *self* and the *object*—it is always their representations that are meant—under the general term *object representation* (*P2*), and have used the same terms within our subject–object track (e.g., Figures II–5 and II–7). This term thus appears in two different frames of reference, and we must now be more specific. The self and object representations within the *P* system correspond rather to the complex sensory perceptual pattern—that is, the self and object representations within the *D-P-M* model relate to the self and the object as differentiated from any affect representations, action representations, word or other representations that can be associated with them—whereas the self and object representations of the subject–object track constitute more complex pattern formations, configurations of self and object that include components from all three domains of the *D-P-M* model. In other words, an object representation within the *D-P-M* model is the psychic representation of its complex sensory "pure imago," whereas an object representation on the object track is a pattern of associations on a higher level of integration, containing as it does drive and component-drive aspects specifically brought into line with the present situation in each case, as well as the affects, thing presentations, and word presentations connected with them, and is directed toward a particular drive aim; and it is perfectly possible for one or other constituent part from the three *P-M* tiers to be lacking. This means that, in the conception developed here, the specific processes taking place within the *D-P-M* model in each case are again represented, *in terms of their result*, in the self and object representations of the subject–object track.

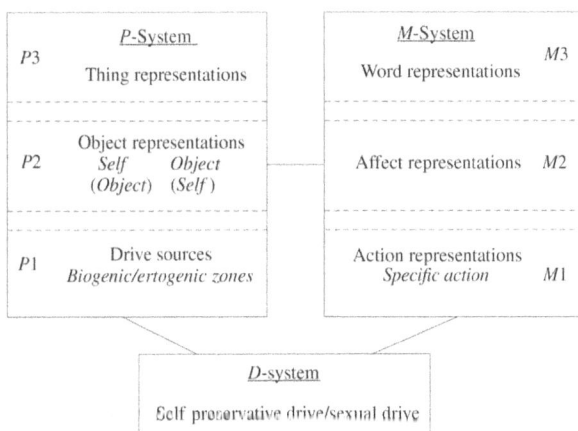

Figure II–8. Figure II–8 contains all the components of the fully differentiated drive concept, subdivided in accordance with the three systems to which they belong, which together represent a complete psychic process cycle, a *D-P-M* unity. The *D* system contains only one item, the self-preservative drive and the sexual drive. The *P* and *M* systems are each shown as possessing three levels of development of increasing abstraction from bottom to top; the line of development *action—feeling—thinking* is clearly discernible within the *M* system.[31]

---

31 On this basis, Rapaport's (1960) postulate of three primary and three secondary models of action, feeling, and thinking, with which he sought to construct an expanded economic model, would be confined to the *M* system. Roy Schafer's (1976) suggested replacement of metapsychology by an action language (as closer to the practical situation) would be tantamount to an even more far-reaching restriction and dedifferentiation of metapsychology back down to the lowest tier of the *M* system.

Principles of Combinatorial Switching

Our *D-P-M* model, as now fully differentiated, will help us to understand better what Freud was seeking to conceptualize by the term *drive vicissitude.* In calling his paper "Drives and their Vicissitudes,"[32] he was signifying his concern not only to elucidate and subdivide his drive concept but also to give an account of the "vicissitudes"—or "fate"—of the drives. What are we to make of the splendid name "drive vicissitude"? Vicissitudes are something like the *pathways, turning points,* and *nodal points* experienced by drives "in the process of development and in the course of life" (1915c, p. 126). However, we specified earlier that a drive is a unidirectional entity whose direction is indicated by either a (+) or a (–) sign; that is to say, although the drive, as the fundamental variable of our formalized model, can by itself assume "pathways" (in one direction), it cannot negotiate turns or exhibit nodal points. The simple drive must therefore be complemented by something else. As Freud puts this, "Bearing in mind that there are *motive forces* which *work against a drive's being carried through in an unmodified form,* we may also regard these *vicissitudes* as modes of *defence* against the drives" (p. 126f., my emphasis except for the word "defence").

On the formal level of metapsychology, "motive forces" are simply drives— or the ideas associated with them. That which "works against a drive's being carried through in an unmodified form" can only be the antagonistic other drive—that is, repression. We thus once again have the formalized drive-repression concept, in which repression is defined metapsychologically as the activity of the relevant antagonistic drive. A drive vicissitude is so to speak the *combination* (nodal point) of a *drive* (pathway) with a *repression* (turning point). For Freud, too, the drive vicissitudes are nothing but "modes of defence"—or, in metapsychological terms, processes of repression.

Freud adduces four different possible drive vicissitudes, in the following order: *reversal into the opposite* (which can be subdivided into a "change from

---

32 [Translator's note: Usually known, of course, as "Instincts and their Vicissitudes."]

activity to passivity" and a "reversal of [the] content" of the drive aim, such as the transformation of love into hate [1915c, p. 127]); *turning round on the subject's own self* (i.e., "change of the object"); *repression*; and *sublimation*. The drive vicissitudes considered by Freud (based on the example of sadism-masochism) draw our attention to questions such as: *Where* in our model structure does such a drive process take place? *How* does it take *what turn*? *Where* is the energy of the drive displaced, directed, or diverted to? In other words, on the metapsychological level, the term *drive vicissitude* makes statements about the interchanging of activity and passivity, of subject and object, of loving and hating—in a word, about the interchanging of the drives (*D*), the object (*P*), and the affects (*M*). Using the example of the pair of opposites "sadism-masochism," Freud describes only the extreme (pathological) version of a general drive-repression vicissitude, which lends itself particularly well to illustrating how a process of this kind leads to an "interchange" of pattern cathexes in every single one of the three systems (*D*, *P*, and *M*). This reveals a further advantage of our model structure (Figure II–8): it affords an overall impression, and allows an initial ordering, of the various "drive vicissitudes" in all their diversity. Let us therefore turn our formalization and the model structure derived from it to account by drawing some conclusions from it about the drive-repression process. We had postulated that each psychic unity contains at least one component of the *D*, *P*, and *M* systems, and that the complete psychic process cycle constitutes a drive-repression unity and hence a binary *D-P-M* unity; and that is intended to imply, too, that a drive process and a repression process take effect in each of the three systems. What possible combinations can be derived from this assumption, or, if you will, what are its implications for our understanding of drive vicissitudes?

In the case of the *D* system, the answer is simple: either the self-preservative drive represses the sexual drive or the sexual drive represses the self-preservative drive. No other possibilities are so far discernible. The situation is different with the *P* system: here the *drive* may cathect a source, an object representation, and/or a thing representation—and likewise *repression* (the antagonistic drive) may cathect a source, an object representation, and/or a thing representation. The situation in its simplest form might be where, for example, drive and repression cathect the same object; in this case the questions of matching could be answered relatively easily and in accordance with the quantities activated in the particular case. Things are less simple if the drive cathexis of an erotogenic zone has the consequence of the repression cathexis of a biogenic zone, as this would mean that the drive conflict occurs not on the same "object" (structure) but is played out between two different "objects," albeit still on the same tier. However, one could also conceive of a cathectic process including a jump from one tier to another—for example, the drive might cathect a drive *source* and the repression a repression *object*. Alternatively, within the sphere of object representations (second tier), further complication could be introduced into the process according to whether the repression process operates on the same track of the drive organization or the opposite track. The most variable level within the P system, which has the most manifold possibilities of cathexis, is unmistakably the third tier, with its potentially infinite number of thing representations that can be interchanged with each other x times over. All this results in a virtually infinite number of possibilities. After all, since both drive and repression cathect *ideational patterns* that in each case possess complex organization, the drive can in principle cathect all three tiers of the P system simultaneously and many times over, in each case in different positions on the subject and object tracks. The same applies to repression; in other words, the patterns recruit their constituent elements from all three tiers, thus ultimately resulting—particularly if we assume not an individual idea but sequences (e.g., scenic successions of such ideas)—in a mathematically unlimited number of possibilities of variation for the activation of pattern formations within the P system by a drive-repression process. The same can moreover be assumed in the case of the M system: here again, all possible combinations of drive-repression cathexes are conceivable simultaneously, in multiple form, and in different weightings on all three tiers, the number of potential variations again being greatest on the third tier, the plane of word representations. However, the application of our postulate of an exchange of drive and repression on the level of affect representations—for example, in the cathexis of combinations of two or (more) different affect representations, one of which is activated by the drive and the other by the repression—also admits of the conception of a wide range of affective "mixing ratios" and hence of the fine modulation of emotional nuances. In addition to all this, there are the infinite diversity of subtly differentiable action processes likewise to be conceptualized as driverepression combinations within the lowest tier of the M system.

The spectrum of possibilities becomes greater still if it is realized that the repression process can treat the cathexes within the P and M systems in different ways. Freud presented a number of relevant examples. For instance, in obsessional neurosis, the *object* (P) *may change* while the *drive aim* (M) *remains the same*; or, conversely, *an idea* (P) may be *preserved*, while the associated *affect* (M) is *repressed* or *converted*; and so on. An understanding of this diversity of possible combinations within the drive-repression process, of which only a rough outline is given here, will be facilitated by reference to the subdivisions of our D-P-M system model (Figure II–8). This enables us to make hypotheses about the sites at which, and the manner in which, the drive-repression process can arise and become active, and which components may then be modified or exchanged. We can begin within the D system (from which the P and M systems are excited), with the drives; we can go on to the P system, with the drive sources, object representations, and thing representations; and we can turn finally to the M system, with action representations, affect representations, and word representations. It then becomes clear that what can be represented in this way as a *drive vicissitude* is based on the use of our simple formula deemed to apply from the first psychic configuration on—namely, hallucination = (+) idea/wish + (–) idea/wish—now differentiated and supplemented by the individual component parts of the elaborated drive concept, according to which the drive-repression process always operates on all components and on every tier of the D, P and M systems, all in an enormous variety of combinations.

So far, the drive-repression process has been portrayed as a binary one effectively proceeding in a single cycle, in which varying amounts of excitation from both antagonistic drives are used to cathect pattern complexes (representations) on all three levels of the *P* and *M* systems. However, Freud's conceptualization in fact turns out to be much more complex (and this is precisely where the use of the *D-P-M* model structure can help us to preserve an overall view). The statement that *a drive triggers* a repression on the one hand refers to the fundamental organizational principle of the psychical apparatus (or of all processes within it), but on the other, when related to an individual psychic process cycle, should be seen as either a *convenient simplification* or the *end result* of an enormously complex process preceded by a large number of different combinatorial operations (comparable with, say, the thousands of neuronal switching operations that take place in our central nervous system within fractions of a second). Behind the fundamental organizational principle contained in the simple equation:

$$\text{resultant idea} = (+)\ \text{idea} + (-)\ \text{idea}$$

that is applicable to *all* constituent parts of the drive concept on all tiers of the *D-P-M* system—for example, also:

$$\text{resultant affect} = (+)\ \text{affect} + (-)\ \text{affect}$$

—there may therefore, in certain circumstances or according to the relevant possibilities, lie concealed an extremely intricate *drive vicissitude*, of which, on the phenomenal level, we ultimately perceive only the end result. Freud recognized this precisely: his metapsychology of repression led him to the conclusion that the "process of repression is not to be regarded as an event which takes place *once*, the results of which are permanent, as when some living thing has been killed and from that time onward is dead" (1915d, p. 151); repression, for Freud, is rather a *dynamic process*, which can be broken down into a number of *individual steps*. In the treatment of drive vicissitudes, we could of course confine ourselves in each case to determining, or asking, on which tier within the three systems (*D*, *P*, and *M*) a drive-repression process can be demonstrated; we should then already have much to do, and also have gained much. Nevertheless, this conception would still be too simple and would also fail to clarify the details of some processes, a closer analysis of which cannot in my view be dispensed with. If we therefore put together Freud's reflections on the drive vicissitudes specific to individual neuroses in accordance with the criterion of their *directionality* (for drives here are *directional entities*), it follows on the formal level from his description of the vicissitudes of the drives—*reversal into the opposite, turning round upon the subject's own person, re-flection*, and *displacement*—that a drive excitation may be conducted on to, or combined in a switching operation with, *the antagonist*, or conveyed *forward* or *laterally* or *back*. I therefore suggest—explicitly on the basis of the organizational principles of neuronal switching operations (i.e., as a continuation of Freud's approach in the "Project"), but also to complete our description in terms of systems theory—that for the time being we assume the following combinatorial possibilities to exist for both drives:

Antagonistic excitation and antagonistic inhibition
Feedback excitation and feedback inhibition
Feedforward excitation and feedforward inhibition[33]
Lateral excitation and lateral inhibition

---

33 Pribram (1989) shows that feedback loops serve for error processing and to maintain constancy, whereas feedforward is used for the more creative aspects of information processing: "There are two very different mechanisms to be distinguished: mechanisms that maintain constancy through error processing and mechanisms that process alternatives, i.e. 'good' information. There is, therefore, a distinction to be made between error processing and information processing. Error processing depends on feedback, closed-loop mechanism; information processing depends on a higher order feedforward open loop (helical) mechanism that subsumes *alternative* feedback loops *connected in parallel* and thus transcends (brings under 'voluntary' control) the operation of any single feedback" (p. 149). In this connection Pribram interestingly refers (ibid., p. 150) to Ashby (1960), who showed that "simply multilinking feedback units with one another leads to hyperstability and thus to almost total resistance to change (i.e. the system cannot learn)." Since learning, considered from a higher-order perspective, also has the long-term function of safeguarding the system's equilibrium in its changing environment, feedback and feedforward measures prove to be different ways of preserving the homeostasis of a system in the event of a "disturbing" influence exerted by free input variables (any drive excitation may be deemed "disturbing" for our purposes).

In all these cases, the principles of *divergence, convergence*, and *summation* (facilitation in time and space) may also become operative. In the enumeration of these eight different possibilities, it is initially wholly immaterial whether they should all be assumed to be appropriate or whether some of them must be eliminated (as mathematically untenable or clinically not demonstrable), and whether, as is probably the case, other, additional ones should be formulated. There are in fact two important points. First, the assumption of combinatorial modalities of these (and similar) kinds allows a formalized portrayal of the *composite nature* of drive representations within patterns; and, second, we are concerned here with the *quantitative element* of drive activity, which is (purely mathematically) relevant in these combinations. For example, in the case of a feedback excitation, there must be a quantitative increase in (amplification of) the excitation due to repeated or multiple cathexis of the same representation, thus, say, giving rise to a facilitation in time in regard to this representation or reinforcing the principle of divergence; or, with a feed-forward inhibition, the result may be the exclusion (non-activation) of an entire sequence of representations that are subject to the quantitatively dominant cathexis of a drive—in which case the amounts of excitation that would otherwise be conducted on from these cathexes to other representations also cease to be operative. The crucial point is that these combination possibilities, which are initially to be considered in purely mathematical terms, determine all processes in all three systems (*D, P,* and *M*). Figures II–9a through II–9g will clarify these assumptions.

Such reflections, whereby Freud's *drive vicissitudes* appear, for the purposes of the formalized version of the model of the psychical apparatus, as different fundamental forms of combinatorial switching applicable to both drives, clearly show that *drive vicissitudes are driver-epression combinations within the D, P, and M systems with different modalities and differing consequences for the amounts (quantities) of energy proceeding from the relevant combination and activated on a given representation (or configuration of representations).*

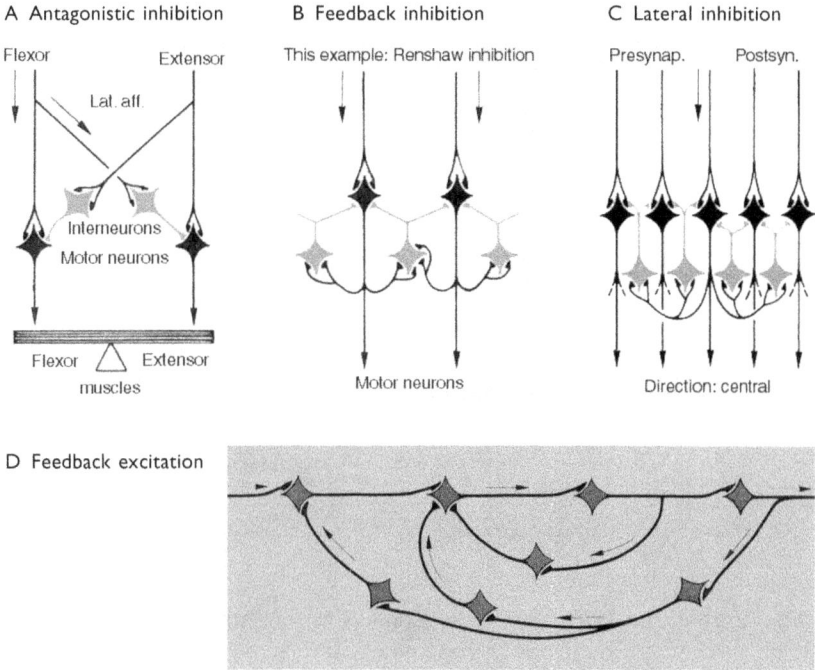

A Antagonistic inhibition

Flexor   Extensor

Lat. aff.

Interneurons
Motor neurons

Flexor △ Extensor
muscles

B Feedback inhibition

This example: Renshaw inhibition

Motor neurons

C Lateral inhibition

Presynap.   Postsyn.

Direction: central

D Feedback excitation

Figures II–9. (A–G) show some of the simpler possibilities of combination as established schematically for the physiology of small neuronal complexes, with comments relevant to our model. Parts A–C show "typical inhibiting circuits," the inhibiting interneurones being indicated in light-gray. (All diagrams and quotations are taken from Schmidt 1983, pp. 106–113, translated for this edition.) The interneurones can be replaced within our model by what Freud calls "intermediate links," which would involve a cathexis of representations as a means of achieving the combinatorial modalities of, for example, *antagonistic inhibition, feedback inhibition,* and *lateral inhibition.* Part D shows a *feedback excitation:* the "neuronal combination of an exciting feedback. This hypothetical combination could, given appropriate scaling, result in a circulation of excitation." Whether or not circuits with positive feedback can be shown to exist in the CNS, we can adopt feedback excitation as a *theoretical postulate,* as, for instance, representations derived from an associative complex would then take the place of the interneurones, and the circulating excitation would in this way amplify the cathexis of this complex.

E Divergence

F Convergence

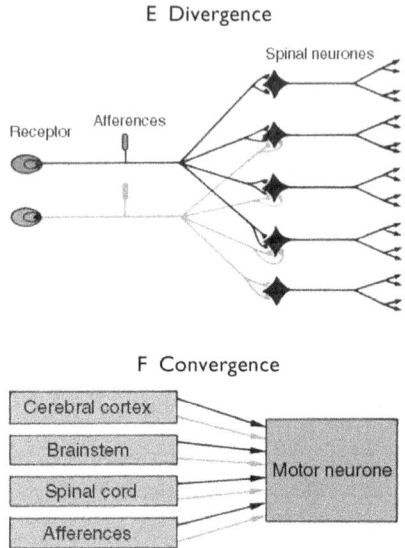

Part E illustrates the "schematic divergence of two dorsal root fibers (afferences) to spinal neurones. The axons of these neurones are ramified in turn into a large number of collaterals." *Divergence* may be assumed to exist, for example, in the case of the ramifications of the excitations from the *D* system to the various tiers of the *P* and *M* systems, or for the libidinal cathexes passing from the structural level of narcissism in the direction of the subject and object tracks. **Part F** of the diagram illustrates a *convergence*—more precisely, "excitatory and inhibitory afferences converging on a motor neurone" (the inhibition is indicated in lightgray). Convergence applies, for example, to the multiple cathexis of a representation by both antagonistic drives (whose afferences can in turn originate from a wide variety of representations), all values being subjected to combinatorial computation; convergence also corresponds precisely to Freud's description of the dream mechanism of "condensation."

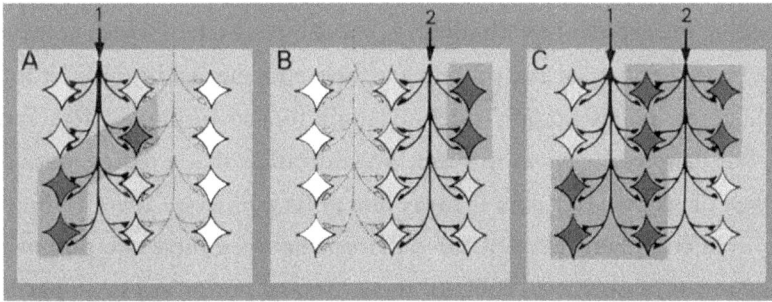

In **Part G** Freud dealt at length with *facilitation* in the "Project." Part G is an example showing the effect of the simultaneous excitation of two afferences: in the case of *facilitation in space*, afferences 1 and 2 diverge "in each case to eight of the total of twelve neurones, both afferences converging on to the central row of four neurones. (A) Activation of afference 1 results in subliminal EPSPs [excitatory postsynaptic potentials] in five neurones (light-gray) and to supraliminal EPSPs in three neurones (shaded dark-gray). (B) Activation of afference 2: six neurones are excited subliminally and two supraliminally. (C) Simultaneous activation of afferences 1 and 2 excites all the central-row neurones supraliminally. The number of supraliminally excited neurones thus exceeds the sum of those excited by individual stimulation: 8 > 3 + 2" (ibid., p. 109). *Facilitation* in space could, for example, instantaneously explain why the interpretation of splitting processes—i.e., confrontation with non-associated or only subliminally associated representations (the simultaneous mention of 1 and 2 in a manner that connects them)—leads to the amalgamation of two representations previously kept separate from each other into a complete pattern, in the sense of an experiential unity. In addition to this *facilitation in space*, there is also *facilitation in time*, which is not illustrated diagrammatically here, and in which subliminal EPSPs triggered in quick succession are added in their excitatory effect on a neurone and lead to the onward conduction of an action potential if the threshold is attained. "Facilitation in time is of great physiological significance, as many nervous processes, such as receptor discharges, proceed repetitively, so that their summation can give rise to supraliminal excitations on synapses" (ibid., p. 107).

This innovation and further differentiation, undertaken by Freud under the heading of *drive vicissitudes*, of course has implications for our view of the component parts of his drive concept. For if we now see more clearly than before that what we previously subsumed (regardless of its tier in the *P* and *M* systems) within the unified notion of a *representation* is in fact a complex process involving a vast number of drive-repression combinations proceeding in accordance with differing modalities, each of which contributes to the further course of the process and hence to the "end result," it follows that the term "representation" does not stand for something in effect static or fixed, but denotes a *dynamic process*. We said earlier that a representation is a structure or switch, but now it turns out to be a process. There is, however, no contradiction here, because the difference between these two propositions is only one of perspective. After all, the structural notion stresses a particular constellation at a particular time (transverse section), whereas the process view relates to a dynamic change over a certain period (longitudinal section), and thus tracks the particular combination of individual elements that generates a specific functionality of the structure.[34] This explains both the stable and the flexible component of the structural notion, which we use mostly in the (transverse-section) sense of a switch (containing a particular law and operating in accordance with a specific modality for the maintenance of homeostasis); however, if we focus on the variability of structures (e.g., adaptation to current demands, or learning), this calls for a dynamic view, in which the notion of structure is seen in process terms, as already indicated by Freud.

What does this now imply for the components of the *D*, *P*, and *M* systems? On the assumption that this definition applies to *all* tiers of both the *P* system and the *M* system, Freud's remarks on drive vicissitudes are found to explain on the *conceptual* level how such a wide range of different *ideas* and *affects* can be developed from only two basic drives and can be portrayed as organized in accordance with uniform principles.[35]

---

34 The earliest study of this subject, which still makes interesting reading today, was published by Brierley under the title "Notes on Metapsychology as Process Theory" (1944). Freud's "Project" already includes precursors of this modern structure theory: "Thus the ego is to be defined as the totality of the *y* cathexes, at the given time, in which a *permanent* component is distinguished from a *changing* one" (1950c/1950a [1895], p. 323, my emphasis).

35 Overviews of the psychoanalytic theory of the affects are given by, for example, Löfgren 1968, Kernberg 1976, Lester 1982, and Shapiro and Emde 1992. A high proportion of the discussions within affect theory centers on the issue of whether affect is a *phenomenon of discharge or of tension*; Jacobson (1971) strongly criticizes both the tension and the discharge theory and suggests a combination of the two. Brenner (1974a,b, 1982) takes the view that ideas on the one hand and sensations of pleasure and unpleasure on the other together constitute an affect

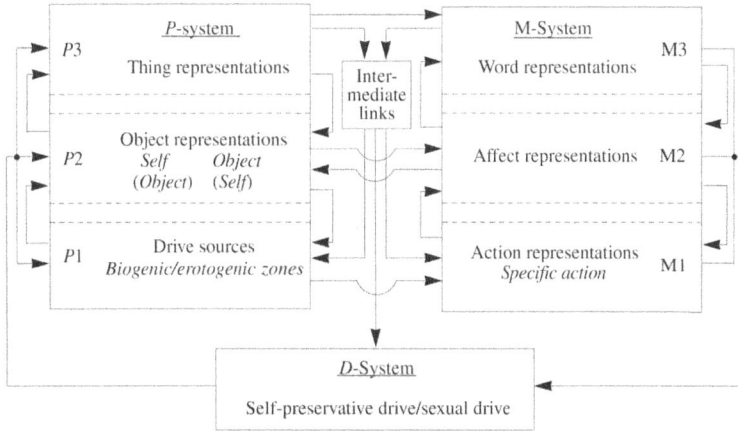

Figure II–10.

The advantage of this systems-theory version of our model is as follows. If we regard the various tiers (in the model as a whole) as different switches within coupled control circuits, our postulate of the various combinatorial modalities (antagonistic, feedback, feed-forward, and lateral excitation and inhibition respectively) can be applied to these (macro)switches in exactly the same way as, previously, to an individual representation (the principle is again valid for and applicable to all levels within our model). For example, feed-forward inhibition can affect *an entire tier* and thereby *inactivate* it (e.g., in catatonic stupor [*M*1], the anesthesias [*P*1], affective atrophy [*M*2], or mutism [*M*3]), or an associated group within a tier (e.g., in frigidity [*P*1] or hysterical paralysis of an arm [*M*1]); conversely, a feedback excitation may result in the overexcitation of an entire tier (e.g., in catatonic excitation [*M*1], the hyperesthesias [*P*1], affective flooding [*M*2], or logorrhea [*M*3]); or the principle of convergence (say, of all amounts in the *P* and *M* systems) can reveal the *synthetic function of the ego*; and so on. Ultimately, then, *all* combinations

as a psychological phenomenon. Kernberg (1976, 1991a) inverts Freud's postulated relationship between drive and affect: in his theory the affects are the building blocks of the two major drives.

of excitation and inhibition of all components of the D, P, and M systems can be represented in this way—including the seemingly "impossible" ones[36] accommodated by Freud under the higher-order heading of *false connection*, whose domain of application can be extended to all organizational levels of the psychical apparatus. Hence the assumption of different combinatorial modalities of these and similar kinds on the one hand allows us to *conceptualize* the various clinical pictures on the *formal level* (i.e., without the need for statements that seek to explain a given pathology by a "*fear of*"—for fear as a feeling state does not, after all, exist within a formalized model, although it does in a clinical theory), while, on the other, perhaps also affording the clinician criteria for an initial crude orientation within the infinite diversity of pathological pictures. What Freud sought to formulate in his essay on drive vicissitudes is thus of fundamental importance to an understanding of the psychical apparatus, its structure, and its functioning. From this point of view, his model of the psyche—which is ultimately built upon nothing but the two drives (variables) and the hierarchically arranged structures (switches)—is an impressive embodiment of the principle of parsimony in scientific explanations.

The Mind–Body Question and the Introduction of the *Pucs.*

With his essays "Instincts and their Vicissitudes" and "Repression," Freud moves closer to the metapsychological conceptualization of the nub of psychoanalysis, the *unconscious*; indeed, all his ideas on the vicissitudes of the drives and on repression may—once the aspects of *where* and *how* have been clarified—in fact be said to converge on the issue of *what* elements of a psychic process are or become conscious and unconscious respectively. There is an obvious temptation here to relate the *what* of the unconscious to its contents—

---

36 M. Klein (1948) and her followers have researched and described many forms of such "impossible" combinations and their significance for early disturbances—e.g., the "devouring breast" (mother) and the "devouring penis" (father).

and thereby to exchange the level of metapsychology for the much more colorful one of clinical theory—but Freud's reflections are rational and systematic: he speaks of mechanisms, of functional changes of state, of activation, and so forth, thus abiding strictly by his criteria for a metapsychological presentation, namely, "describing a psychical process in its *dynamic, topographical* and *economic* aspects" (1915e, p. 181, my emphasis). Since Freud uses the terms conscious and unconscious on the one hand for psychic *states* as manifested in varying present-day forms, and on the other for two *organizational unities* or *systems* (*Ucs.* and *Cs.*), which operate in different ways, two questions arise. First, what are the formal criteria whereby a psychic process can be described as conscious or unconscious (that is, in phenomenological terms, whereby it appears as such); and, second, what characterizes the operation of the unconscious (system *Ucs.*) as opposed to the conscious (system *Cs.*)? For Freud (1915e) it is initially a result of psychoanalytic research

> that in general a psychical act goes through two phases as regards its state, between which is interposed a kind of testing (censorship). In the first phase the psychical act is unconscious and belongs to the system *Ucs.*; if, on testing, It Is rejected by the censorship, it is not allowed to pass into the second phase; it is then said to be "repressed" and must remain unconscious. If, however, it passes the testing, it enters the second phase and thenceforth belongs to the second system, which we will call the system *Cs.* [p. 173]

Freud has thus described the path followed by a drive impulse from the unconscious to the conscious: a "psychical act," which is at first "in general" unconscious, undergoes a "kind of testing (censorship)," and, if it passes the test, meets the conditions for becoming conscious. However, we can also say that the *treatment* by the "censorship" has the consequence that a psychic process is *transferred* to a state that corresponds to either the conditions of the conscious mind or those of the unconscious. We previously equated the censorship with *repression* (or with a complex of measures of repression— i.e., drive vicissitudes); so that the censorship treats the drive impulse with a measure of repression; it therefore follows that *the unconscious drive impulse*

*is linked to a repression impulse at the point of transition from the system Ucs.
to the system Cs., giving rise to a complete drive-repression unity, which*—again
subject to certain conditions—*meets the conditions for it to become conscious.*
This thesis in principle corresponds precisely to our previous conclusions
on hallucination, according to which a (+) drive pattern + a (–) repression
pattern yield a hallucination only *together* (by matching). This postulate can
now be extrapolated without problems to a higher level in the hierarchy. In
this case, the following assumptions are found to be contained in the above
thesis concerning the transition of a psychic process from the system *Ucs.* to
the system *Cs.*:

1. The system *Ucs.* must include representations (drive ideas),
    or chains of representations (patterns), that are (when seen in
    functional terms or as organizational unities) *cathected from only one
    drive*, and may be described as *unifilar* (single *D-P-M* unities that
    may be linked either individually or in relatively large numbers);
    these, in other words, do not constitute complete drive-repression
    unities, the condition for whose existence is completion by the
    censorship.

2. It follows that there could then also be unifilar representations (or
    chains of representations) that do not constitute complete *D-P-M*
    unities. For example, the *P* or the *M* component might be lacking,
    in which case we should have *fragments* of unifilar unities, which,
    precisely for that reason, could not be linked to form complete
    drive-repression unities at the point of transition to the system *Cs.*
    These fragments would include, for instance, all the "psychotic"
    margins that could not be "matched" in the combination of two
    antagonistic drive ideas, and have therefore been "eliminated" and
    not undergone further (combinatorial) processing.

3. Although the treatment of such fragments by the censorship
    (repression) would result in a doubling—that is, a binary drive-
    repression unity—the ensuing *D-P-M* unity would be incomplete:

such "*bifilar fragments*" would (owing to the lack of a *P* or an *M* component) not be sufficiently homeostatically regulated and, precisely for that reason, would be incapable of becoming conscious; but, having already been treated and repressed by the censorship, they would also belong to the domain of the dynamically repressed.

4. In order for a "psychical act" to be capable of consciousness, it must therefore satisfy the criterion of constituting a complete drive-repression unity passing through all three systems (*D*, *P*, and *M*) for both drives; such complete unities, already possessing a relatively complex organization, may, being homeostatically regulated in the sense of possessing dynamic stability, be deemed capable of consciousness: they "pass the testing" of the censorship.

An important point now arises. According to our view, there can be no consciousness or unconsciousness as such in a formalized model; nor, consequently, can there be any place for a somatic or a psychic field within such a theory. What is therefore to be used to represent the somatic and the psychic within our deliberately narrowly defined boundaries? This question unexpectedly places us on the threshold of a fundamental issue, the mind–body question: What relation does the somatic bear to the psychic and, conversely, the psychic to the somatic? On this point, here is Freud's (1891b) much quoted position from the study of aphasia, formulated in accordance with the ideas of Hughlings-Jackson:

> The physiological events do not cease as soon as the psychical ones begin; on the contrary, the physiological chain continues. What happens is simply that, after a certain point of time, each (or some) of its links has a psychical phenomenon corresponding to it. Accordingly, the psychical is a process parallel to the physiological—"a dependent concomitant." [p. 207]

Freud thus does not set an upper limit: all psychic processes, however differentiated and elaborate, presuppose, and are *dependent concomitant phenomena* of, physiological processes. He does, however, lay down a lower limit in stating that, "after a certain point of time," each physiological process "has a psychical phenomenon corresponding to it." This assumption is not essential; indeed, it disrupts the logical stringency of the model. We could say that psychic processes (whether conscious or unconscious) that we can recognize *as such* exist only from a certain point in time—which does not rule out the possibility of regarding the psychic as such a parallel process of the physiological even *before* this boundary—that is, down to the cellular and molecular level. If, then, we eliminate the lower boundary, our thesis will be that there is nothing physiological without a psychic element, so that, conversely, the psychic is never of course conceivable independently of the physiological.

From the point of view of our chosen perspective, therefore, we could say only that the pattern formations on the microlevel or nanolevel constitute *conceptually* the first, basic building blocks of the psychic—that is, that they have the consequence of nanopsychic events outside our capacity for perception (including unconscious perception)—and that it is only their integration into larger unities, say at primary-process level, that becomes tangible to us as something psychic; that is to say, *all* pattern formations, from the nanoto the macro-domain of global excitations of the nervous system, by definition have what we qualify as psychic within this formalized model. These patterns, *as patterns*, are no longer something material, nor are they yet, *as patterns*, something psychic (because we use the term psychic to denote feelings, thoughts, memories, wishes, etc.): *these patterns and pattern formations will here be deemed the field of metapsychology and of its conceptualizations of both the psychic and the somatic.* This has two consequences. First, the psychic is not *reduced* to the somatic and the mental to the material, although both are *conceptualized* as directly dependent on each other; and, second, the field of validity of metapsychology is not *confined* either to the psychic or to the somatic, but is *situated in the boundary area between the psychic and the somatic.*[37]

Let us now, on the basis of the above division, assume the existence of four subsystems—that is, four different functional or organizational levels of psychic processes. Since we may postulate both a *continuum* of processes and the *switchover* of the processes of a subsystem from one level of organization or complexity to the next, we must now turn to the *boundary areas* between the various subsystems. We had considered at the beginning of this section that there might be *"unifilar" representations, or "unifilar" chains of representations,* of both drives in the unconscious, and mentioned single *D-P-M* unities as an example. However, we had stipulated that each complete psychic unity was to be a "bifilar" (drive-repression) unity. We now see how an additional domain can be opened up for the idea of the unifilar representations (or chains of representations): *we shall deem unifilar all the representations, or chains of representations, of both drives that arise, operate, or are situated as it were solitarily in the boundary zone of two different subsystems*—or, more precisely, *whose drive component is located on an organizational level different from (higher or lower than) the repression component.*

---

37 Freud tried to describe such a position between mind and brain: "I shall entirely disregard the fact that the mental apparatus with which we are here concerned is also known to us in the form of an anatomical preparation, and I shall carefully avoid the temptation to determine psychical locality in any anatomical fashion. I shall remain upon psychological ground, and I propose simply to follow the suggestion that we should picture the instrument which carries out our mental functions as resembling a compound microscope or a photographic apparatus, or something of the kind. On that basis, psychical locality will correspond to a point inside the apparatus at which one of the preliminary stages of an image comes into being. In the microscope and telescope, as we know, these occur in part at ideal points, regions in which no tangible component of the apparatus is situated." (Freud, 1900, p. 536) See also Schmidt-Hellerau, 2002.

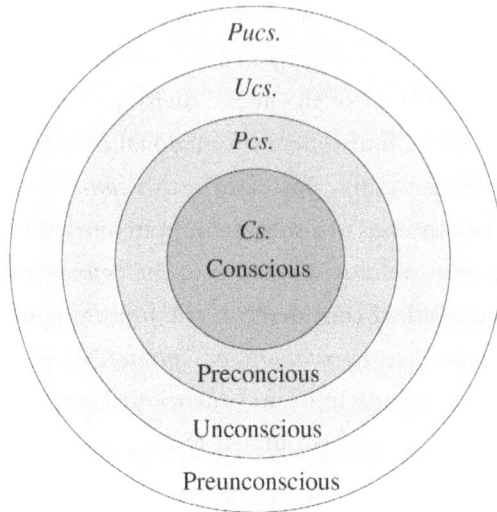

Figure II–11 shows the division of the overall system of the psyche into four different subsystems, to each of which functional patterns of specific complexity (level of organization) are to correspond. The differential shading of the individual circles is meant to indicate differences in the structural density, or homeostatic regulation, of the processes in the subsystems; the number of combinatorial switching operations and hence also the degree of differentiation of homeostasis (restricted zones) are considered to increase in the direction of the conscious.

Let us now take a further look at Freud's comments on the (pre)conscious. Processes in the system *Pcs.* are distinguished from those of the *Ucs.* by

an *inhibition* of the tendency of cathected ideas towards discharge. When a process passes from one idea to another, the first idea *retains* a part of its cathexis and only a small portion undergoes displacement. *Displacements* and *condensations* such as happen in the primary process are excluded or very much *restricted*. This circumstance caused Breuer to assume the existence of two different states of cathectic energy in mental life: one in which the energy is *tonically "bound"* and the other in which it is freely mobile and presses towards discharge. Further, it devolves upon the system *Pcs.* to makes communication possible between the different ideational contents so that they can influence one another, to give them an order in time, and to set up a *censorship or several censorships*; "reality-testing" too, and the reality-principle, are in its province. [1915e, p. 188, my emphasis]

This may be summarized, for the secondary process, in the wellknown formula of *high cathexis* coupled with *bound energy* and *low displacement*. The inhibition is structurally determined and increases in proportion to the number of structures or structural complexes involved in the particular process cycle; an example of a structural condensation for the process cycle is the insertion of reality testing, in the sense of comparison with a reference level. However, the use of the term "inhibition" should not mislead us into assuming that the processes thus *inhibited* in the Cs. proceed as it were *more slowly* than the uninhibited ones in the Ucs. The notion of inhibition in Freud relates not only to the course of an excitation along certain facilitated pathways and the structures situated on these pathways (switches), but mainly to what he calls "discharge," which is the aim of the drive excitation.

Let us now perform a hypothetical calculation. Let us stipulate that, in a drive excitation, a given *quantum* (+/–) of energy is released for the cathected process within one or all of the system's subsystems— for example, (+/–) 10 [*Q*]. Let us further specify that the passage of excitation, from its presumed commencement to its end point, takes 1 *unit time* [*t*]; in a given unit time, the same quantum of energy then passes through, say, 10 *switches* or *structures* [*S*] in the less structured primary process and, for example, 100 [*S*] in the highly structured secondary process (the number of switches stands for path length). On this presupposition, *speed* in secondary-process cycles is much higher (100/1) than in their primary-process counterparts (10/1). Now let the *intensity factor* [*I*] of a psychic process cycle correspond to the quotient obtained by dividing the quantity of drive energy released [*Q*] by the speed of the process cycle (the path-time dimension, or *S/t*), i.e.:

$$I = Q \div (S/t)$$

This yields the following intensity quotients:

$$\text{for the } Ucs.: [I] = 10 [Q] \div (10 [S]/I[t]) = 1$$
$$\text{for the } Cs.: [I] = 10 [Q] \div (100 [S]/I[t]) = 0.1$$

Hence, although the processes of the *Ucs.* are slower, their lower structural density (number of switching points) means that they have a higher intensity quotient than the secondary processes, which take place at much higher speed although the intensity of the process cycles is less. From these assumptions that each structure (i.e., switching point) contributes to homeostatic regulation and that the secondary process is characterized by structural condensation, it may be concluded that higher process-cycle speed coupled with lower intensity values is an important precondition for the comparatively more differentiated computing of complex pattern formations in the *Pcs./Cs.*

In terms of our general understanding of the division of the psyche into various subsystems, this implies that a given degree of organization within the computing of pattern formations is specific to and optimal for each individual subsystem, and that with effect from a given degree of complexity within this organization the psychic process cycle in each case as it were switches over to a new organizational level. Whether this switchover takes place is ultimately a question   of matching within cathectic processes: if a complex of representations on the boundary between subsystems can be matched with another in a combinatorial switching operation, it will attain the next higher level of organization. Freud calls the relevant decision the "censorship".

Turning back toward the system *Cs.*, we find that consciousness, as a rule, presupposes the involvement of the *M* system—hence Freud's explanation "that the system *Cs.* normally controls affectivity as well as access to motility" (p. 179). More precisely, then, the conscious is associated with the condition of a *simultaneous or successive cathexis of the P and M systems* issuing from the *D* system, while the *secondary process* is dependent on a *coordinated activity of the three systems (D, P, and M)*. The reader clearly notices how, having arrived at this point in the development of his theory, Freud becomes aware that he has made a discovery:

> We now seem to know all at once what the difference is between a conscious and an unconscious presentation [*Vorstellung*].... The system *Ucs.* contains the thing-cathexes of the objects, the first and true object-cathexes; the system *Pcs.* comes about by this thingpresentation being hypercathected through being linked with the word-presentation corresponding to it. It is these hypercathexes, we may suppose, that bring about a higher psychical organization and make it possible for the primary process to be succeeded by the secondary process which is dominant in the *Pcs.* [p. 201f.]

The "linking" of the thing presentation with the word presentation corresponding to it, this "hypercathexis" that brings about "a higher psychical organization" and causes "the primary process to be succeeded by the secondary process which is dominant in the *Pcs.*," is a *functional change of state of the cathexes.* In this way, the example of a coincidence of thing and word (P3–M3) can be extrapolated to the linking of object and affect (P2–M2) and of drive source and drive action (P1–M1): all three cases involve nothing but the establishment of a more complex psychic organization, a more differentiated homeostatic regulation, by the completion of a psychic process cycle to form an integrated *D-P-M* unity—which, in the optimum case, involves the cathexis of all three tiers of the *P* and *M* systems in the system *Cs.* and of as large as possible a number of structures and structural complexes within them.

III

THE SHAPE OF THE MODEL

(analysis of Freud's writings
from 1920 to 1925)

THE FINAL VERSION OF THE DRIVE THEORY

Pleasure and Unpleasure in Relation to Tension and Excitation

Freud's metapsychological papers all center on the drive theory (the classification and determination of the drives) and the structure theory (the principles of regulation of the psychical apparatus). In our endeavor to establish a formalized and logically consistent version of psychoanalytic theory, we have confined ourselves to these two axioms, considering the drives as the variables and the structures as the switches within a dynamically stable system. In so doing, we have found again and again that, whereas the two axioms cannot be conceptualized independently of each other, they must nevertheless be carefully distinguished in our thinking. Many of the logical contradictions in Freud's theoretical thought result from shortcomings in this differentiation, as regards the *assignment* of the individual theorems (derived in part from clinical phenomena) to either the drive aspect or the structural aspect of his model. This problem has already arisen in connection with the introduction of narcissism, and now becomes particularly evident in the development of his concept of the death drive. From this point of view, it is worth noting that Freud begins both the major contributions devoted to the revision of his *drive theory—Beyond the Pleasure Principle* (1920g) and "The economic problem of masochism" (1924c)— with a discussion of *structure theory*.

> In the theory of psycho-analysis we have no hesitation in assuming that the course taken by mental events is automatically regulated by the pleasure principle. We believe, that is to say, that the course of those events is invariably

171

set in motion by an unpleasurable tension, and that it takes a direction such that its final outcome coincides with a lowering of that tension—that is, with an avoidance of unpleasure or a production of pleasure. [1920g, p. 7]

Let us take a closer look at Freud's assumptions. First, we can agree with Freud that the *experience of pleasure* arises when tension is reduced, for this reduction is so to speak the metapsychologically defined condition for, or foundation of, that experience. However, an experience cannot be said to regulate an apparatus or to constitute a principle. It is therefore appropriate to separate the experiential (phenomenological) plane of consideration from that of formal logic and to confine ourselves to the latter for the purpose of constructing our model. We are then left with the proposition that (drive) processes within the psychical apparatus are regulated by the principle that tensions arising are reduced. But what is tension? By definition, it is a state that comes into being between two *directionally* opposed poles. Whenever Freud refers to "excitation" leading to tension and unpleasure, he always means the excitation of a drive—that is, of a *directional* value—so that it is an obvious assumption that the other, *directionally* opposed, pole is represented by repression, the antagonistic drive. In other words, tension is the consequence of an excitation, of whatever kind, of the two directionally opposed drives. The question then still remains as to where tensions are actually "perceived"—that is, registered—in our model. The answer is clear: whereas a drive can generate a tension, it cannot register it; registration of the tension and the adoption of tension-reducing measures are the function of structure. In relation both to the general principle of regulation of the psychical apparatus and to the nano-level of the model (a hypothetically isolated elementary switch), we can therefore formulate Freud's postulate as follows: the excitation of a drive (the input variable) is registered by the structure (controller) as "tension" (deviation from a set ratio of the excitation values of the two drives) and leads to a compensating measure, which is the specific activation of whichever drive is the antagonist in the individual case (the output variable).

Our conception of structure was that of a switch incorporating a specific law. This law determines and regulates the permissible (quantitative) excitation ratio of the two antagonistic drives—that is, the tension between the two directionally opposed poles—and thereby defines what is in each case to constitute *homeostasis*. In formal terms, we can denote the tension that stands, according to a specific law, for homeostasis by the imaginary value "0", but "1" or any other value could equally well be chosen. The choice of value is completely arbitrary; in other words, if Freud invokes a *zero principle*, we need not *concretistically* assume that he means a tension with an absolute value of zero, for any value could be taken for the sake of simplicity as "zero." At this point, Freud is in any case not referring to his early principle   of inertia, or zero principle, but to the *principle of constancy*, as modified by the "exigencies of life." The principle of constancy ensures that a given "store of $Q\acute{\eta}$"—that is, endogenous (excitation) quantity—and hence a constant tension, is constantly maintained within a system; that is why Freud regards it as a special case of Fechner's principle of the "tendency towards stability." For the regulating principles of the psychical apparatus, we therefore have a series extending from *zero* via *constancy* to *stability*—to which we have here added the more modern notions of *homeostasis* and *dynamic stability*. If equilibrium or stability is now to be determined not concretely by an absolute tension level of "zero," but by any value enshrined in the law of a switch, then there is no reason why any conceivable excitation ratio of the two drives should not constitute stability. In simple terms, the ratio might be, say, 1:1, 1:2, 2:3, 3:4, or the like. Furthermore, such a law could include the additional term ±c, where c is a constant representing the permissible deviation in favor of the predominance of one drive or the other within the dynamic stability of the relevant system. In other words, the entity that expresses the switch's law, whatever that entity may be, is the range of a given *tension* between the two drives that is defined as *equilibrium*. This tension, which is defined differently for each structure (or, as the case may be, each complex of structures)—let us call it *switch tension*—constitutes the precondition for the system's being in an optimal functional state of dynamic stability, because in the absence of such a tension it would be impossible to conceptualize any "flow of energy" and hence any cathectic processes or pattern formation.

This immediately leads us on to a consideration of excitation states of the system beyond the range of the switch tension—that is to say, states that represent a substantial departure from the differentially defined stability values (irrespective of their hierarchical level or level of integration) in the various structures. Drive excitations of this kind also lead to tension—to distinguish it from the former variety, let us term it *system tension*—and here we can stipulate, as Freud does, that this tension, or deviation from the equilibrium values enshrined in the structure, gives rise (on the phenomenological level) to unpleasure, whereas the restoration of homeostasis produces pleasure. What generates pleasure is therefore the decrease in system tension and not in switch tension: if switch tension were to fall below a specific value embodied in the structures, this would correspond to a departure from its optimum tension value—so that the tension would become system tension—and would thereby give rise to unpleasure (and not to something "beyond" pleasure). Hence a decrease in system tension is not identical to a decrease in switch tension, but corresponds to an approximation to the switch tension, and is for that reason deemed to be a condition for pleasure. In other words, system equilibrium is a state not of zero tension but of optimum (switch) tension—which positively calls for a certain *quantity of excitation*. As Freud reflects, "if the work of the mental apparatus is directed towards keeping the quantity of excitation low, then anything that is calculated to increase that quantity is bound to be felt as adverse to the functioning of the apparatus, that is as unpleasurable. The pleasure principle follows from the principle of constancy" (ibid., p. 9).

The *switch tension* is a quantity that has to do with the excitation ratio of the two drives, and this ratio is supposed to be kept "constant," while the *system tension* represents the deviation from this ratio—that is, the deviation from the switch tension law—and this deviation is to be "as low as possible." Clearly, however, in describing any increase in the "quantity of excitation" as "adverse to the functioning of the apparatus" and postulating that the apparatus "endeavours to keep the quantity of excitation present in it as low as possible or at least to keep it *constant*" (ibid.), Freud manifestly has in mind a different kind of quantity from that of a simple drive excitation—or, let us say, a different, higher level of organization of the system:

> What we are implying by this is not a simple relation between the strength of the feelings of pleasure and unpleasure and the corresponding modifications in the quantity of excitation; least of all—in view of all we have been taught by psycho-physiology—are we suggesting any directly proportional ratio: the factor that determines the feeling is probably *the amount of increase or diminution in the quantity of excitation in a given period of time*. [ibid., p. 8, my emphasis except for the words "in a given a period of time"]

In Part II we introduced a value, or "quantity," that includes this *time factor*, namely *intensity*. We said that the intensity of a psychic process cycle corresponds to the ratio of the *quantities* of drive excitation activated in the particular instance to the *speed* of the process cycle (the number of combinatorial switching operations per unit time). We represented this by the equation $I = Q \div S/t$. Using this equation, we calculated (on the macro level of the model) a lower intensity factor for the more densely structured *system Cs.* than for the *system Ucs.* If we now relate Freud's "quantity of excitation" to this *intensity* value, we obtain, for the passage of a psychic process cycle from *Ucs.* to *Cs.*, the familiar proposition that every movement in the direction of the *system Cs.* is accompanied by a *diminution* in the intensity of the psychic process cycles (secondary process). Since the direction of psychic processes is deemed to be from *Ucs.* to *Cs.*, we here again observe the general tendency of the pleasure principle, namely, that of reducing quantities of excitation or keeping them low. Hence, conversely, any increase in intensity would be "adverse to the functioning of the apparatus." From this point of view, Freud's postulate that "quantities of excitation" tend to decline relates to a general tendency within this model conception, and runs as follows: *the structural tendency within the psychical apparatus conforms to the pleasure principle—namely, a progressive diminution of the "quantities" of excitation or, if you will, intensity, to be processed.* Let us now consider this *genetic* aspect in more detail.

We have divided the overall system constituted by the psyche into the four subsystems *Pucs.*, *Ucs.*, *Pcs.*, and *Cs.*, each characterized by a different, successively higher organizational level resulting from the increasing number of combinatorial switching operations. In this way, each structural complex, operating on its own level of functional integration—each nanosystem, microsystem, subsystem, and macrosystem— has its own equilibrium state, its own specifically defined range of dynamic stability. What is right—that is, constitutes equilibrium—for one system (say, the *Ucs.*) may perfectly well not be appropriate for another (the *Cs.*), for which it would constitute a departure from equilibrium. Precisely this point is now emphasized by Freud when he turns to (neurotic) conflict as an "occasion of the release of unpleasure" (p. 10): the opposing poles in this case are "the coherent ego and the *repressed*" (p. 19), and it is clear that the satisfaction of repressed drive impulses "must cause the ego unpleasure, . . . That, however, is unpleasure of a kind we have already considered and does not contradict the pleasure principle: *unpleasure for one system and simultaneously satisfaction for the other*" (ibid., my emphasis).

Conflict is a central aspect of psychoanalytic theory, and in this quotation, Freud is formulating his fundamental metapsychological principle that pleasure (tendency toward equilibrium) for one system is equivalent to unpleasure (increasing disequilibrium) for the other. The question now is how a *resolution* of the conflict can be conceptualized. We are familiar with Freud's clinical answer: by making the unconscious conscious. However, that is precisely the problem: when the unconscious is made conscious, this must lead, where the "coherent ego" is concerned, to a system tension, because the "coherent ego" (system *Cs.*) is characterized by a different switch tension from the "repressed" (system *Ucs.*). Can this system tension, then, be converted into switch tension, and, if so, how might the switching laws be modified? Already in the "Project," Freud had developed the idea that the passage of certain quantities of excitation through the neuronal pathways led to facilitations and cathexes that *modify* future passages of excitation (a frequently activated structure is subject to more extensive modification than one that is seldom activated); that is to say, the process of conduction itself is structure-forming, or, in other words, the passage of the drive excitation modifies the switching law of a structure, while, conversely, the switching law of a structure modifies the passage of a drive excitation. This idea is not, therefore, new, but it is precisely this interdependence of drive processes and structural processes that makes the model conception so confusing at certain points. However, *learning* and *adaptation* would not otherwise be possible in the context of the development of structure.

This is in fact precisely Freud's concern in his ensuing discussion of some examples that seemingly contradict the pleasure principle: patients with traumatic neuroses who repeat the unpleasure-producing trauma in their anxiety dreams; the child repeating the painful departure of the mother with the reel of string; and the analysand who repeats painful childhood experiences in the transference. These are instances of unpleasure-generating psychic activities, and ought consequently to conflict with the pleasure principle. However, in all these cases Freud recognizes "that, even under the dominance of the pleasure principle, there are ways and means enough of making what is in itself unpleasurable into a subject to be recollected and *worked over in the mind*," that these "cases and situations, which have a yield of pleasure as their final outcome," actually presuppose the "existence and dominance of the pleasure principle," and "give *no* evidence of the operation of tendencies *beyond* the pleasure principle" (p. 17, my emphasis except for the word "beyond"). What is in fact involved in this "working over in the mind" can be demonstrated from the example of trauma. Trauma results from the breaking through of powerful excitations (p. 29) to which the system responds with an " 'anticathexis' on a grand scale," for which it summons cathectic energy from all sides (p. 30). If this higher level of cathectic energy had been present at the time of the traumatic event, the breach would not have had a traumatizing effect. The development of anxiety constitutes just such an anticipatory anticathexis, intended to protect the system from a traumatic irruption. That is the reason for the repetition of the unpleasurable situation: the dreams of accident victims who have become neurotic "are endeavouring to master the stimulus retrospectively, by developing the anxiety whose omission was the cause of the traumatic neurosis" (p. 32). The idea is that an *appropriately proportioned* increase in quantities of excitation from within (which gives rise to tension and hence anxiety, or anxiety dreams) results in a gradual raising of the permissible tension levels (modification of the switch's law), and that this modification of its switch tension makes the system better able in the future to preserve its (relative) equilibrium. This involves the same "exigencies of life" that had, in the "Project," already modified the zero principle by the "storage" of certain "quantities" (values) and thereby converted it into the principle of constancy. The process that Freud here calls the "working over in the mind" of the trauma thus progressively converts system tension into switch tension: the range of permissible values of excitation and tension that can be homeostatically regulated within a switch increases and the dynamic stability of the system is consolidated.

So far we have said that each activation of an excitation of this kind in the mnemic systems corresponds to a combinatorial switching operation (or a large number of such operations) and hence to a partial and ultimately increasing homeostatic regulation. We can now be more specific, and state that the quantities of excitation activated in the repeated cathexis of these memory traces (experiential patterns) lead to the formation of new structures and, overall, to a concomitant modification of (macro) switch tension. These two aspects of one and the same process also constitute the formal basis, fully formulated in metapsychological terms, of Freud's conception of the resolution of conflict, namely, the transformation of unconscious into conscious—or of what Freud was later to express in the famous sentence: "Where id was, there ego shall be" (1933a [1932], p. 80). In *Beyond*, he explains his conception of this process of structure-forming and structure-modifying conversion of system tension into switch tension again, as follows:

> We have found that one of the earliest and most important functions of the mental apparatus is to bind the drive impulses which impinge on it, to replace the primary process prevailing in them by the secondary process and convert their freely mobile cathectic energy into a mainly quiescent (tonic) cathexis.

While this transformation is taking place no attention can be paid to the development of unpleasure; but this does not imply the suspension of the pleasure principle. On the contrary, the transformation occurs on *behalf* of the pleasure principle; the binding is a preparatory act which introduces and assures the dominance of the pleasure principle. [1920g, p. 62].

The *binding* of drive excitations consists in the *conversion* of freely mobile *energy* into quiescent *tonic cathexis* (tonus = tension!)—that is, in the formation of new structures and in the modification of the switch tension laid down in the structural complexes. The higher the permissible tensions, the less incoming quantities of (drive) excitation can cause the system to become overexcited. In other words, the "adaptation" or "learning capacity" of the psychical apparatus consists in the storage of the switch tension generated and specifically modified by the passage of excitation in the structures responsible for the various psychic functions. We here assume that the structures are responsible more for persistence—for *inertia and constancy*—whereas the functional flexibility and variability of the psychical apparatus are more the preserve of the drives. The drives work, so to speak, to change the structure, but structural modification— the permanent alteration of states of equilibrium (switch tension)—is a process that takes place only gradually, and is, moreover, additionally "retarded" by the hierarchical construction of the system as a whole.

Lethe: The Introduction of a New Notion of Energy

These detailed reflections on how tension and excitation are related to pleasure and unpleasure are necessary because this relationship is the stated reason for the revision of drive theory that now ensued. In pondering over the fact that patients on the one hand put up so much resistance to the analytic treatment while on the other *repeating* instead of merely remembering so many painful infantile situations in the transference, Freud recognizes that "the patient's resistance arises from his ego, and we then at once perceive that the compulsion to repeat must be ascribed to the unconscious repressed" (ibid., p. 20).

The fact that the resistance arises from the ego is self-evident: the economic explanation is that the ego wishes to spare itself the unpleasure that would result from the liberation of the repressed. But why should the repetition compulsion therefore be ascribable solely to the unconscious repressed? Is the "coherent ego," which always deploys the same arsenal of repression responses to the constantly repeated pressure of the unconscious, not also unmistakably under the sway of a compulsion to repeat? *Is this entire process of pressure and repression not therefore also subject to a repetition compulsion?* Does this reproduction of scenes, relational configurations, and indeed entire life destinies not result from the activation of complex patterns and pattern sequences? We have, after all, deemed such patterns to be drive-repression unities and hence structures. From all our reflections so far, it therefore follows that *the repetition compulsion is a structural phenomenon*, or, if you will, should be conceptualized as a consequence of the activity of structure: psychic processes always follow the same pathways—the best "facilitated" ones—so that the repetition compulsion cannot be limited to the repressed, but is a structural property inherent in all systems.[1]

---

1 Freud always distinguished clearly between the terms *Instinkt* [instinct] and *Trieb* [drive] (Nagera 1977). Instinct for him is analogous to an "inherited mental formation" (Freud, 1915e, p. 195), and such a formation, whether purely inherited or partly inherited and partly acquired, is a complex structural phenomenon. It is a general implication of the ideas developed in this book that all complex processes are represented by a specific structure within the system. Lorenz (1981) subsumed such processes (for example, the famous egg-rolling movement of the greylag goose) within the graphic term *fixed action pattern*. In psychoanalytic language, this would mean that, in relation to certain releasing mechanisms, animals are subject to a "repetition compulsion," performing certain actions in always identical sequence until the entire process is completely at an end. Tinbergen (1951) places particular emphasis on the *structured* nature of such behavior, defining an instinct as "*a hierarchically organized nervous mechanism which is susceptible to certain priming, releasing and directing impulses of internal as well as of external origin, and which responds to these impulses by coordinated movements that contribute to the maintenance of the individual and the species*" (p. 112). The concepts of drive and structure are therefore being confused if Freud's term *Trieb* is translated by the equivalent of *Instinkt*—for instance, by *instinct* rather than *drive* in English, by *istinto* instead of *pulsione* in Italian, or *only* by *instinto*

Freud's unilateral assignment of the repetition compulsion to the unconscious repressed has consequences. From the "new and remarkable" fact that the compulsion to repeat also brings up so many unpleasurable experiences, he concludes "that there really does exist in the mind a compulsion to repeat which *over-rides the pleasure principle*," and thereby testifies to the existence of something *beyond* pleasure (p. 22, my emphasis).[2]

With regard to the repetition compulsion, however, Freud is concerned not so much with the pleasure principle as with a new, general *definition of the drive* and the introduction of the *death drive*: he calls the compulsion to repeat a "*manifestation of the power* of the repressed" (p. 20), deems it "more primitive, more elementary, *more rooted in the drives* than the pleasure principle which it over-rides" (p. 23, my emphasis), recognizes that it exhibits "to a high degree the character of a *drive*, [giving] the appearance of some 'daemonic' force at work" (p. 35, my emphasis), and, after some wide-ranging, bold but not uninteresting speculations, comes to the following conclusion:

> But how is the predicate of being "rooted in the drives" related to the compulsion to repeat? At this point we cannot escape a suspicion that we may have come upon the track of a universal attribute of drives and perhaps of organic life in general which has not hitherto been clearly recognized or at least not explicitly stressed. *It seems, then, that a drive is an urge inherent in organic life to restore an earlier state of things* which the living entity has been obliged to abandon under the pressure of external disturbing forces; that is, it is a kind of organic elasticity, or, to put it another way, the expression of the inertia inherent in organic life. [p. 36].

in Spanish (Laplanche and Pontalis 1967, p. 214) [translator's note: *pulsión* is in fact now common in Spanish].

2 Bibring (1941) unequivocally considers the repetition compulsion to be a principle of regulation (a structure): "It is a general regulative principle and serves to bind energies, i.e. to bring them from a state of 'flow' to one of 'rest.' That a regulative trend of this sort does exist seems beyond doubt. The way in which the ego works, too, presupposes this possibility of binding, and of arresting tensions—of making them static. In the same way the repetition compulsion seems to be a sine qua non of all the other regulative trends" (ibid., p. 127, note 4).

Freud himself considers this conception of the drives "*strange*" because, seen in this way, the drives are no longer "a factor impelling towards change and development" but instead an "expression of the *conservative* nature of living substance" (ibid.). That, indeed, is precisely the point: in our formalized version of metapsychology, a drive is merely a directional value (a vector) within the model of the psychical apparatus. For this reason, it proceeds, in virtually unlimited fashion, in one direction only. Whereas it may be diverted from this direction (by a drive vicissitude), a directional value of this kind can never return to an "earlier state," as it were turning itself back in the opposite direction (feedback excitation, too, is always progressive; it is "retrogressive" for structural reasons only). For this reason, in the conception developed here, a drive cannot consist in an "*urge . . . to restore an earlier state of things.*"

Furthermore, this new definition of the drive is formulated in *teleological* terms and is for that reason alone irreconcilable with the strict (parsimonious) fundamental conditions of our formalized model. After all, if drives are ascribed an "intention" of achieving a specific objective—"to restore an earlier state of things" (p. 36)—they then become *intelligent* entities that *know* what they want, and *remember* what has been. This, however, is inconsistent with the conception of the drives expressed by Freud two pages earlier, as belonging to the type "of *freely mobile* [nervous] processes which press towards discharge" (p. 34). Whereas a "nervous process" may assume a direction and take a certain course, it cannot seek "to reach [a] goal" (p. 38). The fallacy in his argument is as follows. The point in time *when* the earlier state of things is achieved, and the *nature* of this state—that is, the point at which the drive ought, as it were, to cease to exert a driving force—is determined by the law of the structure (the switch tension), and not by the drive: *a system's memory consists in its structures, and not in its drives.*

At this point in his reflections, Freud appears to be as confused as he is fascinated, and, although he notices that, with the definitive introduction of this new general description of the drives, he will be raising a number of far-reaching theoretical questions, he nevertheless succumbs to the temptation "to pursue to its logical conclusion the hypothesis that all drives tend towards the restoration of an earlier state of things" (p. 37). Going back from earlier and earlier states to, in effect, the primordial or initial state inevitably leads to cosmological speculations, or, as we might put it today, to the big-bang theory.

> If we are to take it as a truth that knows no exception that every thing living dies for *internal* reasons—becomes inorganic once again— then we shall be compelled to say that "*the aim of all life is death*" and, looking backwards, that "*inanimate things existed before living ones.*"
>
> The attributes of life were at some time evoked in inanimate matter by the action of a force of whose nature we can form no conception. The tension which then arose in what had hitherto been an inanimate substance endeavoured to cancel itself out. In this way the first drive came into being: the drive to return to the inanimate state. [p. 38]

It is a logical consequence of these ideas that Freud called the drive that seeks to restore a primal state of this kind a *death drive*. The death drive is thus the first of all the drives and, strictly speaking—since the inanimate existed before the animate—the only one directed toward *repetition*. However, a Freudian drive always needs an antagonist, and the antagonist of a death drive can only be a *life drive*. In this way the two new drives are set to work.

Freud now adduces the behavior of germ cells that "*work against* the death of the living substance" (p. 40, my emphasis) as a paradigm of his postulated life drive, and then immediately applies the idea expressed by this concrete biological example (that reproduction generates life) to the group of the *sexual drives*, in respect of which he now writes:

> They are the true *life* drives. They operate *against* the purpose of the other drives, which leads, by reason of their function, to *death*; and this fact indicates that there is an opposition between them and the other drives, an opposition whose importance was long ago recognized by the theory of the neuroses. It is as though the life of the organism moves with a *vacillating rhythm*. One group of drives *rushes forward* so as to reach the final aim of life as swiftly as possible; but when a particular stage in the advance has been reached, the

other group *jerks back* to a certain point to make a fresh start and so prolong the journey. And even though it is certain that sexuality and the distinction between the sexes did not exist when life began, the possibility remains that the *drives which were later to be described as sexual* may have been in operation *from the very first*, and it may not be true that it was only at a later time that they started upon their *work of opposing* the activities of the *"ego-drives."* [p. 40f., my emphasis]

Freud is thus assuming the existence of two antagonistic drives (1) that, when combined in a switch on a structure, ensure the dynamic stability of the system (2). These are the two constants that permeate Freud's entire theoretical thought, and constitute the linchpin of his theoretical model's consistency. Now it is not difficult to link the *oppositions* of *life* and *death*, of *sexual drives* and *"ego drives,"* this *vacillating rhythm* of *rushing forward* and *jerking back*, with our own conception. For if we concentrate on the formal aspect of directionality, our postulate of a (+) drive and a (–) drive can readily be linked to the new nomenclature in the form of a (+) life drive and a (–) death drive (and indeed the minus sign seems to be even more appropriate for a death drive than for a self-preservative drive). From this point of view, Freud's new names for his drives are seen to be merely a prolongation of their directional aspect and a widening of their application from the individual domain ((+) *sexuality* and (–) *self-preservation*) to the general sphere ((+) *life* and (–) *death*). This results in his new "opposition between the ego or death drives and the sexual or life drives" (p. 44). However, Freud considers such a continuation of the old drive order into its successor unsatisfactory because, death being so difficult to conceive as an extension of self-preservation, he is led astray by the semantics of his new notions: "The hypothesis of self-preservative drives, such as we attribute to all living beings, stands in marked opposition to the idea that the life of the drives as a whole serves to bring about death" (p. 39).

This difficulty would not have arisen on the formal plane, because life, sexuality, self-preservation, and death *as such* do not exist within a model of this kind, but only (±) drive excitations and pattern formations of differing complexity (levels of organization). The question of life and death would thus have been posed in other terms by the adoption of this approach. Freud dispels his confusion by now placing *both* the sexual *and* the self-preservative drives under the umbrella of the life drive and postulating, alongside these, an as yet unknown group of death drives, for whose existence he must now present evidence. It is worth re-examining in detail these arguments, which introduce *sadism* (and in its wake *masochism* and consequently also *aggression* and *destruction*) as *representatives of the death drive*:

> In the obscurity that reigns at present in the theory of the drives, it would be unwise to reject any idea that promises to throw light on it. We started out from the great opposition between the life and death drives. Now object-love itself presents us with a second example of a similar polarity—that between love (or affection) and hate (or aggressiveness). From the very first we recognized the presence of a sadistic component in the sexual drive. *But how can the sadistic drive, whose aim it is to injure the object, be derived from Eros, the preserver of life?* Is it not plausible to suppose that *this sadism is in fact a death drive* which, under the influence of the narcissistic libido, has been forced away from the ego and has consequently only emerged in relation to the object? It now enters the service of the sexual function. During the oral stage of organization of the libido, the act of obtaining erotic mastery over an object coincides with that object's *destruction*; later, the sadistic drive separates off, and finally, at the stage of genital primacy it takes on, for the purposes of reproduction, the function of overpowering the sexual object to the extent necessary for carrying out the sexual act. It might indeed be said that the sadism which has been forced out of the ego has pointed the way for the libidinal components of the sexual drive, and that these follow after it to the object. Wherever the original sadism has undergone no mitigation or intermixture, we find the familiar ambivalence of love and hate in erotic life. [p. 53f., my emphasis]

In his endeavor to find an example of the death drive, Freud again turns to two oppositions, the seemingly antithetical *affect representations* (*M2*) of love and hate, and two (also affectively represented) *action representations* (*M*1), tenderness and aggression. In our present conception, however, both affect representations and action representations are deemed to be *patterns*—that is, drive-repression unities—so that they always incorporate the cathexes of *both* drives, combined in varying modalities and degrees of dominance. But then, an individual drive—the death drive—cannot be directly derived from an affect (a drive-repression unity, namely *hate* or *aggression*). Once Freud has resolved to pursue this "idea," though, the subsequent steps in the argument quickly follow: hate and aggression seek to "injure" and in the extreme case even to kill the object, and thus oppose "Eros, the preserver of life." Drawing attention to the long familiar "sadistic component in the sexual drive," Freud asks: "But how can the *sadistic drive*, whose aim it is to *injure the object*, be derived from *Eros, the preserver of life*?" Sadism, being a sexual perversion, is in fact *not* of course primarily aiming "to *injure* the object," but instead seeking sexual pleasure, *sexual satisfaction* on the object—but by way of a specific action (a drive action), originating, in this case, from a perverse structural level. Yet, once again, we are concerned here not to analyze a complex *clinical* concept such as sadism (and later masochism), but with the metapsychological argument. The main reason why the passage quoted above is so important is that, by his "idea" of *sadism as the representative of the death drive*, Freud here paves the way for his final, teleological drive concept. The confusion of the roles of drive and structure is again a problem here. If death is deemed to be the primal, initial state to be restored, and if sadism, with its intent to injure, is the representative of the death drive, then *death is defined as the injuring or destruction of life*. Putting this in everyday language for the sake of clarity, we then do *not* have a simple vectorial definition of the drive involving an antagonism roughly as follows: *the* (–) *death drive wants to die, and the* (+) *life drive wants to live*. The definition arrived at by Freud is, instead: *the death drive does not want the life drive to live*, or *the death drive wants the life drive not to live* (which amounts to the same thing); as Freud put it, the death drive wants "to lead *what is living* into an inorganic state" (1940a [1938], p. 148). In other words, the death drive is here defined by way of the life drive—as a "negation" of the life drive—and hence, strictly speaking, not as a drive but as a *drive vicissitude*, or drive-repression combination involving a structure.

Freud turns back, in his account of sadism, to the oral stage of organization, in which the "act of obtaining erotic mastery over an object coincides with that object's *destruction*": the *aim of injuring* results from the *destruction*. However, Freud could equally well have used the following formulation: the act of obtaining erotic mastery still coincides, at the oral stage, with the incorporation of the object, thus merely indicating a wholly *inward-directed process*, whereas destruction, and the aim of injuring, is a process *directed outward*. In this way the choice of a single term can steer all subsequent reflections in a particular direction. In this case, this is not a mere stylistic decision, but underlies the next problem arising with the new conception of the drive. It is that we now, for the time being, have *two outward-directed drives*—the sexual drive (as the representative of the life drive), which aims for the "external" object, and sadism (as the representative of the death drive), which, with its intent to injure, is also aimed at the "external" object. Given Freud's absolute attunement to the fundamental logical structures of his theoretical imagining, he was of course perfectly aware that his system of two drives operating in the same direction would no longer be capable of homeostatic regulation. He therefore hastens to apply a correction, whereby the antagonist of the outward-directed life drive is now deemed to be an originally inward-directed death drive, for which a primary masochism can be taken as the representative (1920g, p. 55). By this *change from sadism to masochism* as the actual representative of the death drive, Freud corrects the orientation of that drive—from a sadism directed outward, toward the object, to *masochism, directed inward*, on to the subject's own "ego." What goes uncorrected here is the death drive's "aim to injure"—also called "primal sadism" (1924c, p. 164):

> In (multicellular) organisms the libido meets the *drive of death*, or *destruction*, which is dominant in them and which seeks to *disintegrate* the cellular organism and to conduct each separate unicellular organism [composing it] into a state of inorganic stability (relative though this may be). The libido has

the task of making the *destroying drive* innocuous, and it fulfills the task by diverting that drive to a great extent *outwards*—soon with the help of a special organic system, the muscular apparatus—*towards objects in the external world. The drive is then called the destructive drive*, the drive for mastery, or the will to power. *A portion* of the drive is placed directly *in the service of the sexual function*, where it has an important part to play. *This is sadism proper.* Another portion does not share in this transposition outwards; it remains inside the organism and, with the help of the accompanying sexual excitation described above, becomes *libidinally bound* there. It is in this portion that we have to recognize the *original, erotogenic masochism.* [ibid., p. 163f., my emphasis]

This can initially be expressed in our terms as follows. The two fundamental drives, which originate from the *D system*, are now called the life drive and the death drive. The libido of the life drive, directed outward "towards objects," meets the death drive, which is directed inward against the subject's own self. The two drives undergo combinatorial switching, or, in Freud's terms, mixing; a portion of this mixture is "placed directly in the service of the sexual function," and is directed, in the form of sadism, outward toward the (love) object, whereas another portion remains inside as "*original, erotogenic masochism,*" and continues to be directed toward the subject's own self. This, then, is how sadism and masochism arise. Now, since Freud holds that what "distinguishes from one another the mental effects produced by the various drives may be traced to the difference in their *sources*" (1915c, p. 123, my emphasis), and the above-mentioned mixture of the life and death drives takes on a *sexual* tinge in both cases (those of sadism and erotogenic masochism alike), it may be concluded that within our *D-P-M* model the combining of the life and death drives takes place at the drive sources (*P*1); the transposition outwards via the motor system (*M*1)—the "muscular apparatus"—mentioned at this point also conforms readily to this conception. In other words, in his account of the interaction of the life and death drives—from which a representative of the death drive is supposed to originate—Freud is describing a complete *D-P-M* cycle involving *both* drives (the death drive and the sexual or life drive). We thus always encounter the *representatives* of the two fundamental drives already in the form of "a very extensive fusion and amalgamation, in varying proportions, of the two classes of drives," which is effected only in the *P* system, and it is for this reason that Freud also acknowledges that, on the concrete level of clinical phenomenology, "we never have to deal with pure life drives or pure death drives but only with mixtures of them in different amounts" (1924c, p. 164). This justifies us in reserving the life drive and the death drive in their "pure" form, as the two *fundamental drives* of the model, wholly for the *D system*. Conversely, the *"representatives"* of the two drives arise only by way of combinatorial switching at the base of the *P system*. This can be expressed as follows. The *erotogenic zones* are the places of formation of the *sexual drive* with its two components, sadism and masochism (their relative dominance varying according to their "mixing", or combination, ratio), whereas the *biogenic zones* are the sites of formation of the *self-preservative drive* with its various components. Considered in these terms, the new dualism of the life and death drives would not supplant the old dualism of the sexual and self- preservative drives, but would in effect extend it downward to the *D* system. Moreover, the nomenclature "life drive" and "death drive" would, by virtue of the concomitant detachment from the specific functions of the drives within the organism (sexuality and self-preservation), correspond more to a generalized, or indeed also formalized, (+/−) version of the drive.

In the above quotation, Freud refers to a *"drive of death, or destruction,"* that seeks to *disintegrate* the cellular organism," as a result of which the life drive is then assigned the task of making this *"destroying drive innocuous."* This it does by transposing it outward on to objects, and, as Freud then recognizes, it "is *then* called the destructive drive." This means that we ought really to speak *first of a death drive* and *then of a destroying drive*. On the basis of the foregoing considerations, we can state that the *death drive* and the *destroying drive* are *not* wholly *identical*. The destroying drive—like sadism-masochism, and like hate and aggression—already proceeds from a "mixture of drives"; it results from the combining of the two antagonistic drives, from a *drive-repression unity*, which at the same time involves a complete *D-P-M unity* (e.g., the object [*P*2], aggression [*M*1/2], and hate [*M*2]). Freud failed to recognize clearly this distinction between the death drive and the destroying drive—a distinction that concerns the *organizational level* of the drive process. Since I consider that clearly defined terminology can greatly facilitate conceptual clarification, I should like to propose the following:

1. The two fundamental drives originating from the *D* system will henceforth be referred to solely as the (+) *life drive* and the (−) *death drive*.

2. When these are combined with the drive sources of the *P* system, two specific formations ("mixing proportions") result. The first, which proceeds via the erotogenic zones and their component drives, will be called the *sexual drive* or *Eros*, and the other, which incorporates the biogenic zones and their component drives, will be referred to as the *self-preservative drive*.

3. It is only at the next stage of combination of the sexual and self-preservative drives that what Freud calls the *destroying drive* or *aggressive drive* comes into being; it arises as erotogenic *masochism* or *sadism* on the side of the sexual drive and as, for example, *egoism* on that of the self-preservative drive.[3]

At this point I wonder whether it is appropriate, within the conception developed here, to postulate the existence of an aggressive *drive*,[4] or whether

---

3 This hierarchical arrangement is consistent with Kernberg's (1976, 1991b) concept of the *composite* nature of the drives—of both the *sexual drives* and the *aggressive drives*—which are deemed to be made up of the "building blocks" of perceptual and behavioral patterns, various affective dispositions, and so on.—I now conceptualize aggression as the intensification of one or both primal drives (see footnote 5 and the Epilogue of this book).

4 Bibring (1941, p. 115f.) distinguishes between "*primary*" and "*secondary destructiveness*," and therefore finds the assumption of an *independent aggressive drive indispensable*. Rank (1949) emphasizes the *adaptive value* of aggression in regard to, for example, internal or external *frustrations* (see also Dollard et al. 1939). Brun (1953) attributes both the sexual component drives and aggression to a *fusion* or *confluence* of drives resulting from the self-preservative aim and does not recognize a "primary aggressive drive." Gillespie (1971) considers it a spurious conceptual solution to deem aggression to be one of the two fundamental drives. For A. Freud

it might be more correct to speak instead of *aggression* in the sense of an affective action (*M*1/2) or of an affect (*M*2), having precisely the purpose of *self-preservation* or operating in the service of *sexuality*. This conceptualization would constitute a return to Freud's original view of aggression, in which he rejected the idea of assuming "the existence of a special aggressive drive *alongside* of the familiar drives of self-preservation and of sex, and *on an equal footing with them*" (1909b, p. 140, my emphasis), preferring instead "to adhere to the usual view, which leaves each drive *its own power of becoming aggressive*" (p. 141, my emphasis). It would also subsume Freud's second concept of aggression, according to which aggression and its equivalent in feeling, hate, "always remains in an intimate relation with the self-preservative drives" (1915c, p. 139). Freud's indication at this point that hate, "as a relation to objects, is older than love" (ibid.) could in fact make us aware of the need to take more account of the *question of structure* in our attempts to clarify the concept of aggression—for example, in the sense that aggressive drive actions always proceed from a more regressive ("less mature") structural level, or indeed solely from a structural complex on the subject track (the track of the "ego drive"). The logic of this assumption would be that any exclusion of structures—and in particular the exclusion of all structures on the object track—corresponds to a diminution of the combining operations previously undergone by a drive process ("inhibitions" or instances of homeostatic regulation), in which

---

(1972), aggression does not have a drive aim of its own, nor is its source known; however, it appears as an economic factor in the service of a variety of psychic aims, helping to achieving these when obstacles arise. Parens (1973) declares *the self-preservative drive to be superfluous* and urges that the *aggressive drive be substituted for it*. He makes a general distinction between destructive and non-destructive energy, regarding the neutral ego energies as derivatives of non-destructive aggression. Stern (1974) recognizes "primary defenses" or "*primary agitations*" (Mahler's "affectomotor storm") as the matrix of aggression. Compton (1981) thinks that the *life* and *death drives* should be abandoned in favor of the sexual and aggressive drives. For Winnicott (1984), aggression is one of the two sources of psychic energy; it is not primarily hostile or destructive, but serves the purposes of self-assertion, exploration of the world, and demarcation from the object. Rizzuto et al. (1993) see aggression as a "biologically rooted drive capacity," which is summoned up when an obstacle needs to be overcome; their model is not one of drive discharge, and they focus instead on the achievement of a *motivational* aim. In their view, aggression always occurs in the form of an action, albeit accompanied by widely differing affects.

aggression (*aggredi*—"to go toward") still arises from a higher structural (or combinatorial) level than destruction (to "de-story," or ruin the structure of something).[5]

Now we must turn to two further assumptions by Freud that stem from the idea of the "destructive aspect" of the death drive. His postulate that the aim of the destructive drive is "to undo connections and so to destroy things"—which is why it is called the death drive—leads him to the opposite function of the life drive, "to establish ever greater unities and to preserve them thus—in short, to *bind* together" (1940a [1938], p. 148, my emphasis). The term "binding" relates, from the "Project" on, to a process in which so-called freely mobile cathectic energy (primary process) is converted into "quiescent (tonic) cathexis" (secondary process) (1920g, p. 62). As already established in the first section of Part III, the *binding* of drive energy or drive excitation consists in a modification of the switch tension set up in the *structures*. For this reason, we need only recall briefly here that, in accordance with our vectorial

---

5 My views (Schmidt-Hellerau 2000) are based on the idea that an important role in aggression (*aggredi* = to go toward) is played not only by the *time factor* (the speed or intensity of the psychic process cycle), but also by a *spatial distance factor*, namely the desired or presumed *distance between self and object*. This would mean that, in the event of an attack—that is, if the distance between subject and object falls below the optimum—the aggressive reaction has the aim of reestablishing this optimum distance. However, if the distance of the object is perceived as excessive, as, for example, in neurotically distorted perception, the aggression would merely have the aim of reaching the object; in this case we should have a kind of neurotic "miscalculation" within the psychical apparatus. Aggression as a rule involves the action representations (*aggredi* [*M*1]) and the affect representations (*M*2), the affects appropriate to aggression being, for example, rage and hate (structurally early "global" affects), or annoyance and anger (structurally mature, "specifically directed" or "limited" affects). I would draw a conceptual analogy between aggression and a grasping movement with a specific goal; it would then have *something to do with assessment of the object's distance*. In this conception, destruction would differ from aggression in that the object would no longer be perceived as external (separate from the self), but as (having already penetrated) *inside* the subject's own self, so that (as in the case of selfpreservation) the only possible course is to destroy it. Aggression is seen here as one of the many *anticipations* to be constantly undertaken by the psychical apparatus. It is not by chance that Freud, in his last theory of anxiety (1926d [1925]), declared the anticipation of danger to be the trigger of the signal of anxiety; we can likewise deem the *anticipation of distance* to be the trigger of "aggression." *Aggression* ought, on this basis, to be conceptualized in *structural terms* rather than as a *drive*: relatively immature structures (or regressive states) as a rule show more aggression than more mature ones.

conception, a drive can only "drive," and, moreover, can do so in only one direction; the "binding" of drive energy, conversely, like "mixing" or indeed also "neutralization," results from a *switching* operation that *combines* both drives on the structure, so that it is a *structural process*. Within our model, therefore, *the binding and unbinding of drive energy are to be a function of structure and not to form part of a definition of the drive.*

Finally, there remain the specific mechanisms of action of the death drive, derived from the intent to injure. These mechanisms are *aggression* and *destruction* (a characterization to which Freud always remained faithful), and it is this aggressive drive (or, less frequently, destructive drive) to which psychoanalysis as a whole became committed, whereas most analysts reject the death drive as a concept. On the one hand, Freud was surely content with the revision of his final drive theory, because, as we know, aggression as a metapsychological concept in its own right was until then lacking. On the other, Freud subsequently wondered, quite justifiably, why it took him so long to decide "to recognize an aggressive drive" (1933a [1932], p. 103), considering that aggression was a ubiquitous form of human behavior which he too could not of course have overlooked. He presumes that his hesitation, as well as the rejection met with by his final drive theory, was due to wishful thinking as manifested in the belief in the natural morality and good nature of man. In my view, this explanation is wrong. The rejection by Freud's analyst colleagues of the 1920 drive theory concerned the death drive only, and not an "immoral" or "wicked" aggressive drive, which had immediately been accepted as a long overdue complement to psychoanalytic theory; moreover, Freud himself, in the development of his theories, had never allowed himself to be put off by moral reservations, as, for example, his unprejudiced exploration of the sexual drive shows. His questioning thus draws attention to a sore point in his last, definitive drive theory.

If the antagonism of the drives is expressed by the opposing signs (+) and (–), and if their activation from the structures in accordance with the principle of regulation applicable in each case is assumed to underlie the dynamic stability of the psyche as a system, the characterization of love and hate, or, as the case may be, aggression, initially seems to fit in very well with a (+) life drive and a (–) death drive, love being seen as a positive, "*good*" drive activity, and hate or aggression as a negative, "*bad*" one. However, there are no such things as "good" and "bad" within our formalized model: in the *quantitative* conception, there is only *more* or *less*. Are we then to assume that the original (–) activity of the aggressive drive reduces the (+) activity of Eros, for example in such a way that the (actually inward-directed) aggressive drive ensures that the Eros directed toward the loved object does not go too far (outward)? This, however, would be inconsistent with Freud's insight that a "surplus of sexual aggressiveness will turn a lover into a sex-murderer, while a sharp diminution in the aggressive factor will make him bashful or impotent" (1940a [1938], p. 149). Aggression here performs not a (–) function, for instance to inhibit, limit, or repress Eros, but a (+) function: (+) Eros and (+) aggression make a man a lover or indeed a sex murderer, whereas too little (+) aggression makes him bashful and impotent, preventing Eros from coming out far enough toward the object. Aggression is thus once again used to perform an outward-directed function, so that our vectorial calculation in the sense of a balance between the two drives (+) and (–) no longer works out. Something is therefore wrong with this construction, which turns the death drive into an aggressive drive.

However, it was not only the (self-)injuring, aggressive side of the death drive that Freud recognized; some completely different notes are also struck in his reflections:

> Another striking fact is that the life drives... [emerge] as breakers of the peace... while *the death drives seem to do their work unobtrusively.* [1920g, p. 63, my emphasis]
>
> [We] are driven to conclude that *the death drives are by their nature mute* and that the clamour of life proceeds for the most part from Eros. [1923b, p. 46, my emphasis]
>
> It would be possible to picture the id as under the domination of *the mute but powerful death drives* which *desire to be at peace* and (prompted

by the pleasure principle) *to put* Eros, the mischief-maker, *to rest.* [ibid., p. 59, my emphasis]

The manifestations of Eros were conspicuous and noisy enough. It might be assumed that *the death drive operated silently within the organism towards its dissolution*, but that, of course, was no proof. [1930a [1929], p. 119]

A careful reading shows that the death drive is now *silent* and *mute*, doing its work *unobtrusively within*, and wishes to *"cancel out"* (1920g, p. 38) the tension that arose in the remote past, for the purpose of *"returning* to inorganic existence" (p. 39); it desires to be at *peace* and to put everything to rest—in accordance with the aims of the *"Nirvana principle, belonging as it does to the death drive"* (1924c, p. 160, my emphasis):

The dominating tendency of mental life, and perhaps of nervous life in general, is the effort to reduce, to keep constant or to remove internal tension due to stimuli (the "Nirvana principle," to borrow a term from Barbara Low... —a tendency which finds expression in the pleasure principle; and our recognition of that fact is one of our strongest reasons for believing in the existence of death drives. [1920g, p. 55f.]

In this way we obtain a small but interesting set of connections. The *Nirvana* principle expresses the trend of the death drive; the *pleasure* principle represents the demands of the libido. [1924c, p. 160]

The above quotations highlight a completely different dimension of the death drive, whose metaphorical reclothing in the comprehensive idea of *Nirvana* expresses a tendency diametrically opposed to that of the descriptions so far. Conceived in effect as the shadow (the "negative")[6] of a phenomenally active, extroversive defensive measure (aggression), the death drive now reveals itself in its *passive, introversive features*—especially in the passages that describe the death drive as a *slipping into death*, and recognize *masochism*, whose action

---

6 Green (1983, 1986, 1993) has explored this aspect of *"le négatif"* in the death drive in a large number of contributions extending over many years.

is essentially *mute*, as its primal representative. Freud was perfectly aware of this more concealed, silent, introversive tendency, and thereby points the way to a conceptualization of the death drive that is quite consistent with our formalized version of his metapsychology so far, as we shall now see.

We at first described one of the two fundamental drives, the selfpreservative drive, as *directed inward, toward the subject's own person and the unconscious*, and assigned passivity to it on the phenomenal level. We have now found *introversive, passivity-inducing* tendencies of this kind in the characterization of the death drive too. Concentrating on these aspects in our reflections on the death drive, we see that, by his postulate of a death drive, Freud introduced a *quietistic agent*, which makes its silent, unobtrusive contribution to the organism's internal equilibrium, performing a repressing function in relation to the clamorous pressure of the life drive. Just as the death drive ensures that the life drive does not exhaust itself in the infinite expanse of the outside world, so, conversely, the life drive prevents the death drive from losing itself in the silent inner worlds of a Nirvana. The underlying significance of the poetic formulation is clear. More directly and in a manner less open to misunderstanding than his idea of the death drive's primary inward-directed aggression and injuring intent, Freud's notion of the *quietive of the death drive*, virtually preformulated as if in a dream, reveals the simple, unvarying configuration of his model of the psychical apparatus: a (+) life drive, a (−) death drive, and their combination on a structure together guarantee the dynamic stability of the system as a whole.

The above approach makes it clear why Freud always had difficulty with his assignment of (self-)aggression to the death drive, which, for him sometimes and for most today, leads to the equating of the death drive with the aggressive or destructive drive. He failed to heed the "voice of reason," his inner *logos*, and did not follow the quiet, correct promptings of his thought, but instead became confused by the clamor of aggression. That is why Freud did not recognize what he had actually known about all along: the *quietistic tendency of the death drive*. We can now understand, too, why he was never able to find a suitable name for the *energy* of the death drive.

We may picture an initial state as one in which the total available energy of Eros, which henceforward we shall speak of as "libido," is present in the still undifferentiated ego-id and serves to neutralize the destructive tendencies which are simultaneously present. (We are without a term analogous to "libido" for describing the energy of the destructive drive.) At a later stage it becomes relatively easy for us to follow the vicissitudes of the libido, but this is more difficult with the destructive drive. So long as that drive operates internally, as a death drive, it remains silent; it only comes to our notice when it is diverted outwards as a drive of destruction. [1940a [1938], p. 149f.]

Whereas the energy of, at first, the sexual drives, and later, more fundamentally, of the life drives, under the name *libido* borrowed from Moll (1897), has accompanied and enriched the theoretical debate almost from the very beginnings of psychoanalysis, there has never been a genuine counterpart for *the energy of the drive antagonist*, whether this be the self-preservative drive (or ego drive) or the death drive.[7] *Ego interest* as a term to denote the energy of the self-preservative drives was always an expedient that manifestly never fully convinced even Freud; at any rate, neither he nor his successors were particularly keen on its use. Whereas we refer to libidinal cathexes, we cannot speak of "interested" or "interesting" or "interest" cathexes: here language directly draws our attention to the faulty construction of this notion of energy. However, the introduction of an aggressively defined death drive seemed to offer a way out of the old dilemma: there was now no objection to the idea of a "cathexis with libido and/or aggression" or of a "libidinal" and/or "aggressive" cathexis. In this way aggression came to stand for the energy of the death drive—or, more precisely, the energy of the aggressive drive. For the conceptual reasons mentioned above, I regard this decision as misleading, because it directs our attention outward to the activating tendencies on the phenomenal level

---

7 Federn (1930) suggests the term "mortido" to denote the energy of the death drive; Weiss (1935) recommends "destrudo." According to Hartmann et al. (1949), the energy of the aggressive impulse should be called "aggression." Green (1983, p. 107) uses the phrase "'libido 'mortifiée'" ["'mortified' libido"] for a mixture of "libido d'Eros et celle des pulsions de destruction" ["libido of Eros and libido of the destructive drives"].

instead of inward to the silent, passivity-inducing trends, and bespeaks a higher level of drive organization than a simple, basic drive. But if we bid farewell to aggression as the notion representing the energy of the death drive, we reopen the old crack. Where do we go from here? The absence of a term for the energy of the death drive is a serious problem, because, without a conception of this energy, we cannot readily reflect on what the cathectic processes emanating from the death drive are actually supposed to bring about.

In view of the quietistic tendencies of the death drive to which I have drawn attention in the last few paragraphs, I therefore suggest that the energy ascribable to it be referred to by the name *lethe*, borrowed from Greek mythology. *Lethe means forgetfulness; a river in Hades or on the boundary of the Realm of the Dead bears the name Lethe.* Greek mythology, to which Freud so often had recourse in the choice of his theoretical terms, can thus once again come to our aid, as *lethe* seems to me to satisfy in every respect the requirements laid down by Freud for a term to denote the energy of the death drive, as I shall now show.

Lethe is a term both analogous and equivalent to *libido*; the fact that the term *lethe* means forgetfulness (repression) is consistent with our constant emphasis on the inward direction of the (–) drive, toward the unconscious; the term *lethe*, through the image of a river, evokes the idea of a *flow of energy directed by the drive*, and since the river Lethe flows from the world of the living to that of the dead, the name *lethe* also takes account of the ultimate aim of Freud's postulated death drive; on the relevant *plane of meaning*, the term *lethe* expresses precisely what we have determined and established from the beginning on the *formal level of metapsychology*, namely the "energetic" (–) tendency of the one drive, which it has now also been possible to demonstrate in the quietistic tendencies of the death drive in the final version of the drive theory; the term *lethe* is consistent with the language of metapsychology, as there is no objection to speaking of a *lethic cathexis* (as the antithesis of a libidinal cathexis) or a *lethic tendency*; and, last but not least, *lethe* is used in everyday language in precisely our sense: we call someone's behavior *lethargic*, and we speak of *lethargy*, of a *deleterious* condition, and of a *lethal*[8] dose of a particular substance, such as a drug.

In this way we have at the same time redefined the orientation of our affective points of reference: whereas Freud based the development of his final drive theory on the antithetical feelings of *love* and *hate*, the pair of notions formulated here, libido and lethe, points more to oppositions such as *vivacious—listless, vigorous—*languid, cheerful— *melancholic* or *happy—sad*.[9] However, these merely indicate tendencies concerning the relative dominance of the drives, and not direct, exclusive affect equivalents, because feelings (mental states) are still conceived as drive-repression unities.

Now, as we saw in the introduction, the critics of metapsychology are positively unanimous in dismissing the metapsychological *notion of energy*. Their main objection is that it is a vitalistic concept or vectorial entity, and therefore irreconcilable with the energy notion of the natural sciences, which is supposed to be a nondirectional scalar determined only by its quantitative value. We countered this argument by distinguishing between the drive itself (a vector) and energy, or drive energy (which is a scalar), and this remains our position. The notion of energy in our formalized version of metapsychology is, in the first place, in no way defined in terms of *substance*; "energy," like the "drive," is not deemed to be an entity that exists "in reality," but is merely an ideational construct that enables us to formulate certain connections.[10] Second,

---

8 The etymological connection between the last two of these words and the Greek *lethe* is disputed.

9 See also Braitenberg (1994): "The 'theater of the passions,' as depicted for instance in old engravings, possesses two basic forces, *sadness* and *happiness*, with a group of female figures representing hate, despair, hope, and love circling round them. The system is multidimensional, with *two basic forces, plus and minus, dominating the brain*. Nowadays these ladies are called testosterone, dopamine, endorphins, etc.— the internal hormonal system. The complexity here is very low compared with that of the neurones" (p. 10, my emphasis; translated for this edition).

10 In a discussion of the terms *energy* and *entropy* as used in research in the natural sciences and the humanities, Pribram (1989) advocates a "dematerialized" conception of the notion of energy: "To do this we must first agree *that energy per se is neither material nor mental but can readily be transformed into 'matter' and 'mind' and that the transfer functions that describe the transformations can be precisely stated*. We must also agree to the scientific definition of energy as a measure of a potential or actual performance of work" (p. 144, my emphasis).

this notion of energy is intended to be susceptible to (mathematical) treatment as a scalar, an "amount of energy." The drive, defined as a vectorial entity, then adds direction—here represented by a plus or a minus sign—to this amount of energy. This distinction is to remain valid, even if it is no longer so clearly expressed in the choice and definition of the terms libido and lethe, because libido stands for (+) energy and lethe for (–) energy. This exposes us to the charge that the notion of energy advocated here has ultimately after all been tacitly reinterpreted as a directional (vectorial) entity.

The reasons why I have persisted with this approach despite the possibility of such an objection are purely pragmatic. Strictly speaking, if we are to abide rigorously by the vectorial conception of the drive and the scalar conception of energy, we ought always to speak of life-drive cathexes, sexual-drive cathexes, death-drive cathexes, and self-preservative-drive cathexes (or tendencies). However, one need only read these lines to realize how ponderous ("self-preservative-drive tendencies") and to some extent also strange ("death-drive cathexis") this form of expression is—and such formulations are even less suitable for oral use. The conciseness of a term such as *libidinal* or *lethic cathexis* or *tendency* stands in sharp contrast to these. The economy of our thought cannot but opt for these brief phrases, which contain everything that might thereby be meant—namely, the following. If we always keep in mind the (+/–) orientation of both drives, this orientation will automatically apply on all levels of drive organization, to the basic life and death drives, the more highly structured sexual and self-preservative drives, or the later drive and component-drive formations: at all these levels, either the (+) or the (–) portion of a process will ultimately predominate in every case. Although we shall not always be in a position to specify the exact level of organization or complexity on which a postulated process belongs, we shall be able to say whether we have in mind the dominance of a (+) or a (–) tendency. Hence *the terms libido and lethe are intended to apply generally to both (+/–) drive antagonists*—equally to the life and death drives, to the sexual and self-preservative drives, and to other drives. In other words, at every level of their hierarchical organization, we can use the stylistic device of an elliptical *pars pro toto* formulation to make statements about the orientation and action of the drives, and, instead of referring to the individual drives by name, on occasion refer only to libido and lethe, or, as appropriate, to libidinal and lethic cathectic processes.

Moreover, life, death, sexuality, and self-preservation are highly complex notions with a rich penumbra of connotations, which arouse in each of us certain individually tinged chains of associations molded by our life experiences, and these in turn influence our thinking to a greater or lesser extent. That is to say, these terms lack the degree of abstraction desirable for rational, formal discussion and debate in the domain of metapsychology (as opposed to that of clinical theory). The terms libido and lethe do not possess this individualized aspect of meaning, because they do not belong to the language of our childhood, and no early infantile fantasies emanate from them. Even if the term libido has now become a media cliché, and even if we have benefited from a humanistic education that has familiarized us with Greek mythology, our acquaintance with these two terms is of recent date, so that they are incomparably less burdened with unconscious baggage than "life," "death," "sexuality," and "self-preservation." Although they are more abstract than the terms for the drives, the idea of a libidinal or lethic cathexis does not sound as arid and sterile as that of mere "(+/–) cathexes"—that is to say, *libido and lethe are notions on the boundary between (+/–) tendency and meaning*, and therefore seem to me particularly appropriate for stimulating our thought without exerting an excessive seductive influence on the unconscious level of our fantasy.

Let us end this section by summarizing the results of our reflections so far in a simplified tabulation (based on the dominant tendencies):

Sign	(+)	(−)
Direction:	"Outward"	"Inward"
Drives (Level 1) (D system):	Life drive	Death drive
Drives (Level 2) (D-P systems):	Sexual drive	Self-preservative drive
Drive sources:	Erotogenic zones	Biogenic zones
Energy:	Libido	Lethe
Tendency:	Pleasure	Nirvana
Drive object:	(External) object	Self
Drive aim:	Activity	Passivity
Consciousness:	Increasing	Decreasing

Figure and Ground: A Change of Perspective

Our entire discussion of Freud's *Beyond the Pleasure Principle* (1920g) so far has concentrated on distinguishing as clearly as possible whether a notion or process relates to a property of a drive (a variable) or to a property of a structure (a switch) in our formalized model. We found that in this essay Freud again and again lumps together the functions that we have specifically assigned separately to the drives on the one hand and the structures on the other. We first encounter this with his introduction of the *repetition compulsion*; it continues with the new general *definition of the drives*; and it applies also not only to the postulated *intent to injure of the death drive* (*aggression*) but also to its two representatives (*sadism* and *masochism*), and to the specific tasks of the life and death drives, *binding* and *unbinding* respectively. We must now enquire what is involved in this mixing of two fundamental axioms—what it is that is seeking expression in this *condensation* of the notions of drive and structure. To pursue this question is tantamount to exploring what lies *beyond* the pleasure principle—for so far we have remained entirely within its bounds. What, then, is the nature of this *beyond*?

Freud formulates the problem as follows at the end of his difficult contribution: "We have still to solve the problem of the relation of the drive-based processes of repetition to the dominance of the pleasure principle" (p. 62). The issue thus concerns the relations between drive and structure, and perhaps even an expanded dimension in the understanding of the living (i.e., dynamic) organization of our system; this, we may add, would concern its chronology, the course of its history. Let us once again carefully read the passage in which Freud attempts to prepare the soil for his idea:

> We have found that one of the earliest and most important functions of the mental apparatus is to bind the drive impulses which impinge on it, to replace the primary process prevailing in them by the secondary process and convert their freely mobile cathectic energy into a mainly quiescent (tonic) cathexis. While this transformation is taking place no attention can be paid to the development of unpleasure; but this does not imply the suspension of the pleasure principle. On the contrary, the transformation occurs on *behalf* of the pleasure principle; the binding is a preparatory act which introduces and assures the dominance of the pleasure principle.
>
> Let us make a sharp distinction that we have hitherto made between *function* and *tendency*. The *pleasure principle*, then, is a *tendency* operating in the service of a *function* whose business it is to *free* the mental apparatus *entirely from excitation* or to keep the amount of excitation in it constant or to keep it as low as possible. We cannot yet decide with certainty in favour of any of these ways of putting it; but it is clear that the *function* thus described would be *concerned with* the most universal *endeavour* of all living substance—namely to return to the *quiescence of the inorganic world*. [p. 62, my emphasis except for the word "behalf"]

We have already considered the first paragraph of this passage: as described by Freud, *binding* is a process in which what he calls "freely mobile" drive energy is *converted* into "quiescent (tonic) cathexis." Cathexis occurs in no other place than on the structures; it *is* nothing but the activation or generation of such structures. In this process, the permissible aggregate homeostatic value (tension) is increased (successively) in the switches of the relevant structures, so that subsequent excitations of the same magnitude no longer fall outside but again lie within the range of the structurally based regulation of equilibrium. Binding is thus a process of conversion of system tension (above a certain threshold, so that it generates unpleasure) into switch tension (defined as equilibrium) by a modification of the relevant laws in the newly constellated groups of structures.

These reflections have answered the question as to *how processes are converted into structures*. The opposite question then of course immediately arises: *Is there evidence that structure formation has the character of a process?* I believe that this is the question posed by Freud in   the second paragraph of the above quotation. His argument is not easy to follow. Let us try to do so by expressing his notions in our own terms—by "translating" them into *drive* and *structure*. Freud initially suggests that a sharper distinction be drawn between *function* and *tendency*. In our terms, a tendency is a directional process, and hence, we can say, a *drive* process, whereas, in our model, we ascribe a *function* to both drive and structure: the drive has the function of "driving," while the function of structure is to "detain" the drives—that is, to combine, connect, and bind them, or, in other words, to regulate them homeostatically. Since we have already understood *tendency* as *drive*, we now "translate" *function* as *structure*. Freud is then saying the following. The pleasure principle (which is in fact a principle of regulation—i.e., a structure [*a*]) is a tendency (a drive [*b*]) in the service of a function (a structure [*c*]) whose aim is to keep the amount of excitation in the apparatus as low as possible—that is, to restore its equilibrium; and this function (structure [*c*]) is *involved* in the most universal *endeavor* (drive [*d*]), to return to the quiescence of the inorganic world—or, more precisely, in the death drive [*d*], which, in achieving this "quiescence of the inorganic world," at the same time establishes a state of absolute equilibrium (structure [e]), the state of absolute stability. This can be expressed as follows in terms of our two axioms:

$$\text{the structure } [a] = \text{a drive } [b] = \text{a structure } [c]$$
$$= \text{a drive } [d] = \text{a structure } [e]$$

This is by no means nonsense, but precisely the point at issue. For the movement represented by this sequence of ideas produces a *gestalt* that exemplifies the figure-and-ground illusion, in which *figure* and *ground* can constantly change places—provided that the observer undertakes a change of perspective, crosses a boundary, and considers one and the same system (our model) now from *within* and now from *beyond* this boundary. *Within* the boundary, a *drive* is a *directional* movement and a *structure* a stabilizing, *limiting* operation of switching to "zero" level; *beyond* it, however, *structure formation* can be seen as a *directional*— and hence "drive-like"—process that is constantly limited by the *drive excitations* because the drives have the effect of increasing systemic equilibrium by ever more extensive modification of the switch tension, whose end point is total unexcitability of the system as a whole. Let us consider this in more detail.

As we saw earlier (from the example of anxiety dreams in traumatic neurosis), the transformation of system tension into switch tension is a structure-forming measure in which the range of nonequilibrium is constantly reduced while that of equilibrium progressively expands. For this reason, *structural development* within the psychical apparatus, even when seen as a whole, *conforms to the pleasure principle*: what constituted excessive excitation and triggered unpleasure yesterday can today already be better regulated homeostatically, and may tomorrow no longer fall within the range of overexcitation of the relevant structural complex. However, this also implies that what excited the system (caused system tension) yesterday will have lost its exciting effect by tomorrow. The wider the tolerance of the switch tension becomes, the narrower will be the remaining range of possible system tension; once a theoretical end point has been reached, everything lies *within* the structurally fixed equilibrium range and nothing is any longer exciting. "The pleasure principle, then, is a tendency operating in the service of a function whose business it is to free the mental apparatus entirely from excitation." Moreover, what is here described as a tendency of the pleasure principle is also applied by Freud to the death drive, which is stated to be a tendency to conduct the organism (the psychical apparatus) into the inorganic state of total nonexcitability. Seen from *within* the boundary mentioned above, the *drives* are in the *service* of the *pleasure principle* (i.e., they are controlled by the principle of regulation, and used in a specific way to maintain homeostasis); but, considered from *beyond* the boundary, the opposite is the case: "the *pleasure principle* seems actually to serve the death *drives*" (p. 63, my emphasis).

Freud accurately described this as *a change of state of the system.* Having adduced the telling example of sexual excitation, which is extinguished when the maximum possible pleasure is attained (i.e., which, at the moment when pleasure [the pleasure principle] holds total sway, switches over into Nirvana [the Nirvana principle]), he continues:

> This raises the question of whether feelings of pleasure and unpleasure can be produced equally from bound and from unbound excitatory processes. And there seems to be no doubt whatever that the *unbound or primary processes give rise to far more intense feelings in both directions than the bound or secondary ones. Moreover, the primary processes are the earlier in time*; at the beginning of mental life there are no others, and we may infer that if the pleasure principle had not already been operative in *them* it would never have been established for the later ones. *We thus reach what is at bottom no very simple conclusion, namely that at the beginning of mental life the struggle for pleasure was far more intense than later* but not so unrestricted: it had to submit to frequent interruptions. *In later times the dominance of the pleasure principle is very much more secure, but in itself has no more escaped the process of taming than the other drives in general.* In any case, whatever it is that causes the appearance of feelings of pleasure and unpleasure in processes of excitation must be present

in the secondary process just as it is in the primary one. [ibid., my emphasis except for the word "them"]

In chronological terms, we *"reach what is at bottom no very simple conclusion."* At the beginning of structural development the unbound excitatory processes (primary processes) predominate; the switch tension has low tolerance values (a narrow bandwidth), and system tensions are correspondingly high, giving rise to extreme unpleasure, which is then followed in turn by great pleasure as they are reduced again. Hence the striving for pleasure is initially more intense because, first, greater unpleasure (system tension) has to be reduced and, second, the processes of structure formation meanwhile take a progressive course—and structure formation itself conforms to the pleasure principle. At the more mature stage when complex structures have formed, "the dominance of the pleasure principle is much more secure," the system as a whole is in much better equilibrium, and a high proportion of all possible system tension has been converted into switch tension. However, this securing *of the pleasure principle, or the attainment of its ends, at the same time amounts to its taming and limitation*: everything comes increasingly into balance, so that there is progressively less that is pleasurable and unpleasurable, and ultimately nothing at all that still excites. This, of course, is the essence of Nirvana: the extinction of all pleasure and all suffering—and indeed of all excitation and tension of any kind.

Let us consider this change of state again from a different perspective, that of an *attractor*. The denser the structural complexes become, the greater the attractive force emanating from them may be said to be. The structures so to speak *tend* to propagate outward (like the drives), and they develop expansively (like a drive process) in a single direction (the increasing direction), until, at the end of all possible growth (when all drive energy has been converted and all system tension conducted into switch tension), the flow of structural development congeals, and *movement* comes to a *halt*—that is, the *"drive element"* of this development has been transformed into *structure*. This aspect too—structure operating as an attractor—is described by Freud in *Beyond the Pleasure Principle*:

From the present case, then, we infer that a system which is itself highly cathected is capable of taking up an additional stream of fresh inflowing energy and of converting it into quiescent cathexis, that is of binding it psychically. *The higher the system's own quiescent cathexis, the greater seems to be its binding force.* [p. 30, my emphasis]

We found in the section on narcissism that the larger a structural complex becomes, the weaker is its effect as an attractor. Perhaps it would now be more accurate to say that the attraction exerted by an attractor initially increases with the growing accretion of structures around it, but then declines again as from a certain (maximum) value, with the "distance from what was originally repressed" (1915d, p. 149)—that is, with the distance from its core, or organizational center. Any such limitation of its capacity for absorption is neither asserted nor denied in the above quotation, which states that "a system which is itself highly cathected is capable of taking up an additional stream of fresh inflowing energy." However, the idea that this might be possible without limitation is inconsistent with the differentiation condition laid down for our formalized model: if an attractor's effect were unlimited and constantly increasing, we should ultimately have just a single structural complex, a big, undifferentiated "lump." *It is the limits of growth that permit differentiation.* Without this up-and-down alternation of growth and division, there would be no conscious (*Cs.*) and unconscious (*Ucs.*), no subject track and object track, and no id, ego, and superego in this model. We must therefore amend the above idea that the system congeals owing to a complete *binding* of all drive energy or, if you will, to a total conversion of all system tension into switch tension. The system as a whole congeals not because all energy has ultimately been consumed and absolutely all system tension reduced, but because the system has expanded to a point beyond which it cannot take up any more energies, because it can no longer bind them. This can be expressed by the image of a saturated system that has grown weary, expires, and dies.

In Chapter 7 of his *Beyond the Pleasure Principle*, Freud writes the *history* of his model; he describes the *evolution* and *decline* of the system he has constructed in terms of a *reversal of the functions of drive and structure* and a *reversal of its dynamic with time.* In the beginning, the pleasure principle holds sway—or, if you will, at the beginning of life the life drive is dominant and the tendency or striving assigned to it aims for pleasure. At the end, the Nirvana principle reigns—in other words, at the end of life the death drive predominates and the tendency or striving assigned to it aims for nothingness. In between, the reality principle is at the helm: "In this way we obtain a small but interesting set of connections. The *Nirvana* principle expresses the trend of the death drive; the *pleasure* principle represents the demands of the libido; and the modification of the latter principle, the *reality* principle, represents the influence of the external world" (1924c, p. 160).

We have always interpreted Freud's term "principle" (whether of constancy, pleasure, or unpleasure) in the sense of a homeostatic principle of regulation—that is, as a structure. Considered from *beyond* our boundary, however, the structure corresponds to a drive, so that the structural aspect of the system turns into the drive aspect. Hence we can now say that the pleasure and Nirvana *principles* (structures) can be understood as the (+) pleasure and (–) Nirvana *tendencies* (drives) of the system. It is then found that *the history of this living system corresponds, as regards its overall chronological course too, to the simple basic principles of its organization.* The proposition that applies to the elementary unity—that a *drive* triggers a *repression* on a *structure*—is now also true of the entire process: the (+) life-drive tendency (a striving for *pleasure*) undergoes combinatorial switching on a complex structure ("*reality*") and triggers the repressing (–) death-drive tendency (a *Nirvana* striving):

$$\text{pleasure} \rightarrow \text{reality} \rightarrow \text{Nirvana}$$
$$(+) \text{ life drive} \rightarrow \text{structure} \rightarrow (-) \text{ death drive}$$
$$\text{drive} \rightarrow \text{switch} \rightarrow \text{repression}$$

The macromovement of the system as a whole thus again corresponds to the micromovement from which it originated. From a higherlevel vantage point, the reversal of a unidirectional movement at the point of its maximum extension and the return from this point to its initial state have become visible.

It is this higher-order basic systemic idea that Freud is seeking to develop here and he does so in a number of variations, on the level of clinical psychology, biological theory, and cosmological speculation.

That brings us to the end of our reflections on *Beyond the Pleasure Principle*. We have understood why this work is so difficult and complex, why the concept of the death drive remains so obscure and enigmatic, and why a mixing or undifferentiation of the aspects of drive and structure is evident on numerous occasions in Freud's theoretical considerations. He did not invent the death drive because he was sick and sad; and he did not interweave the notions of drive and structure because he was unable to think clearly. It seems rather that, in his theoretical thought, Freud was suddenly able to bring about a change of gestalt and to discern something *beyond* the boundaries of his system. In my view, his theoretical genius had intuitively grasped this change of gestalt in his theory as a principle of development inherent in all living systems—that is to say, as a change of state, when the system goes into reverse at a certain point in its organization—and he had thus added a further level of complexity to his conception of the psychical apparatus. That explains why Freud always remained faithful to the theory advanced in *Beyond the Pleasure Principle*:

> To begin with it was only tentatively that I put forward the views I have developed here, but in the course of time they have gained such a hold upon me that I can no longer think in any other way. To my mind, they are far more serviceable from a theoretical standpoint than any other possible ones; they provide that simplification, without either ignoring or doing violence to the facts, for which we strive in scientific work. [1930a (1929), p. 119][11]

---

11 The concept of the death drive was controversial from the beginning. It was rejected, for example, by Penrose (1931), Fenichel (1935), Friedlander (1940), Brun (1953), and Graber (1953). Voices in favor include those of Alexander (1929), Bernfeld and Feitelberg (1930), Federn (1930), Bernfeld (1935), and Saul (1958). Westerman Holstijn (1930), Weiss (1935), and Lampl-De Groot (1956) adopted a wait-and-see attitude. The concept was accepted particularly readily, and further developed, by Melanie Klein (1933) and her successors, such as Rosenfeld (1952, 1971), Segal (1957), Bion (1957, 1959), and Joseph (1975, 1982). Kernberg (1969, 1980, 1983) has criticized the Kleinian conception of Freud's death drive, drawing attention to its "silent" aspects. (The Kleinian concepts are explained in Hinshelwood [1989],

THE DEFINITIVE VERSION OF THE STRUCTURE THEORY

In our attempt to establish a formalized consistent model of metapsychology, we have used the term *structure* from the beginning, although it does not occur in Freud until late on, and then only incidentally.[12] Whereas Freud (1923b) admittedly arrived at his new conceptualization of the psychical apparatus precisely from his "insight into the *structural conditions* of the mind" (p. 17, my emphasis), he as a rule refers, in this *second topography*—today usually known as the *structure theory*—to the *systems* or, as he now calls them, *agencies*, of the id, superego, and ego. The ideas he put forward in 1923 are "a further development of some trains of thought" on which he had embarked in *Beyond the Pleasure Principle*, in "an attempt... to arrive at new conclusions" (p. 12). These efforts, which he declares to be "in the nature of a synthesis," lead him not only to the conceptualization of the three agencies and their dynamic interaction, but also to matters that concern the model *as a whole*. As a result, the *shape* of the

---

while King and Steiner [1991] tackle the "Controversial Discussions" on the concept. Whereas the death-drive concept has virtually ceased to be an issue in the German and English-speaking countries, in France it is positively a focal point of metapsychological debate [Laplanche 1970, 1986, Donnet and Green 1973, Green 1983, 1986, Rosenberg 1991].)

12 Glover (1932) was one of the first to use the term "structure" systematically in metapsychology. Hartmann et al. (1946) attribute the formation of structure to the interaction of differentiation and integration. Gill (1963) introduces the term *macrostructure* for the agencies of the id, ego, and superego, and *microstructure* for ideas and memories, to indicate that the latter merely represent relatively stable organizations within the macrostructures and are subordinate to them. As we know, Rapaport (1960) based his examination of psychoanalytic theory on the notion of structure. For Guttman (1973), the question of structure is actually the key to any creative advance, whether in art or in science, and hence also in psychoanalysis. In this sense, the notion of structure is a topical issue in psychoanalysis (for an overview, see Arlow 1975, 1991, Schafer 1991, Shapiro 1991). The debate concerns, on the one hand, the *applications* of the notion of structure—for example, development theory (Tyson 1988, Greenspan 1991, Lichtenberg 1991), or structural changes within psychoanalyses (Wallerstein 1983, 1991, Goldberg 1991, Modell 1991, Weinshel 1991)—and, on the other, the *clarification* of the term in psychoanalysis (Pulver, 1991), as well as its use in the *structure-function* relationship borrowed from the biological sciences. Since this book attempts to conceive metapsychology as a *theory on the boundary between psychic and somatic processes*, the present *conception of structure as a switch* or, if you will, as a series of switches organized in a hierarchy and operating on an integrated basis *within a dynamically stable system*, has deliberately been made as parsimonious as possible.

psychical apparatus as developed by Freud becomes visible in its entirety. He so to speak takes a step back, synoptically assembling the major functional unities on which he had undertaken such minute and detailed labors of construction in earlier years (1895, 1900, 1910–1915, and 1920) into a coherent system, of which only a few aspects remain to be "supplemented, built on to, and so set right" (1940a [1938], p. 205). This new vision of the whole is found to be predicated on his *Beyond the Pleasure Principle*, in which he had succeeded in taking this step outside the boundaries of his model; now, as it were from this external vantage point, he is able to reflect again on the entire edifice from a new perspective.

However, there is a further reason why a crossing of boundaries— in effect changing from an internal to an external view of the psyche— is necessary in this final revision of metapsychology. What in Freud's view characterizes the individual configurations assumed by these three major agencies are, of course, the *identifications* with the main persons in a child's life in the most important years of its development. Because Freud's model is thus an *open system*, it is incumbent upon us to explain how the external world acts on the internal world in such a way as to form structure—that is, to arrive at a conceptualization of this *relationship between inside and outside*.

The Superego and Identification

Let us begin with a general caveat. Just as, in a formalized model, there are no such things as the psychic and the somatic *per se*, or conscious or unconscious *as concrete phenomena*—let alone *in the form of specific contents*—so too, for a "psychical apparatus," there is no such thing as an "external object" in the sense of a living human being of flesh and blood who loves or hates, and who is present or absent. However, to describe his *metapsychological* view of the relationship between inside and outside, Freud usually resorted to examples in which a child (a baby, a little son, or a daughter) is involved in an interaction specific to its stage of development with the mother and father. If, for the sake of our formalized perspective, we now abandon this more graphic form of presentation, the first and most fundamental question must be: How can a psychical apparatus of this kind communicate at all with its environment? In simple terms, what enters it from the outside, and, conversely, what passes from inside to outside? Freud's answer is that it is *wishes* that are directed from the inside outward, whereas the reactions to these wishes, as well as, of course, wishes of external origin, are what penetrate inside. A wish, in our model, is a process that involves all three systems (D, P, and M)—that is, a complex unity composed of various components. At an even more basic level, simple logic yields the following proposition: the psychical apparatus, in the version developed here, operating as it does with nothing but drives (variables) and structures (switches), cannot "transmit" or "receive" anything other than drive excitations (the drive aspect) in the specific form of their combinations (the structural aspect). A combination, or combinatorial switching operation, turns a (psychic) process into a drive-repression unity—so that what passes to the outside is a drive-repression combination, or the result of a whole series of such combinations, performed in accordance with different modalities via all three systems (D, P, and M), yielding a pattern formation determined by this process. What is perceived by the psychical apparatus is then this specific, highly complex *pattern*.

Let us consider first the relationship between inside and outside (in concrete terms, between subject and object) as an *extension* of our system (for in principle there is also no such thing as an inside or an outside for such a system), and, for the sake of clarity, begin with a simplified model—on a level particularly suited to the formulation of hypotheses on the early processes of structure formation in subject– object interaction. Take the example of need and its satisfaction. A small child's psychical apparatus C emits an elementary drive wish. It is the function of a parent P to satisfy this wish—that is, in formal terms, the psychical apparatus P of the object acts as a switch, or (auxiliary) structure,[13] that limits the drive excitation of C, combining the drive with a repression. The object thus corresponds to an *external regulator* having the function of contributing (decisively) to the dynamic stability of the system C—particularly if we assume that the primordial structures of this psychical apparatus are not yet capable of automatically establishing and permanently maintaining its homeostasis. If we regard the object as an external structure, it follows, from the internal perspective of the psychical apparatus, that a *libidinal* (drive) excitation emanating from C activates in P, by combinatorial

---

13 Spitz (1951) describes the baby–mother relationship in the child's first year of life as a "closed system," in which the mother is assigned the function of a "*substitute ego*": "During the whole period of which we are speaking, i.e., the first year of life, this ego remains rudimentary. It would be completely inadequate for self-preservation were it not *complemented* by an external helper, a *substitute ego* as it were, to whom the major part of the executive, defensive, and perceptive functions are delegated. This delegate, who complements the infant's ego, is its mother or her substitute. We can speak of her as the infant's ego; like the adult's internal ego, the infant's external ego controls the pathways leading to motility during the first year of infancy" (p. 255f., my emphasis). Beres and Joseph (1970) see the parents as "*regulating agents*"; in these authors' view, one of the main tasks of psychic development is the internalization of the regulative function, which they regard as the foundation of *superego* development. Instead of Spitz's term *substitute ego* or the *regulating agents* postulated by Beres and Joseph as precursors of the superego, I shall use the more neutral formulation *auxiliary structure* or *external structure*, deliberately leaving open the question of which of the three macrostructures is later to be deemed the site of the precipitate of these external structures. Loewald (1980) stresses that the principal task of the psyche is not to get rid of stimuli but to generate representations of them—that is, to generate drive activities—*the drives being organized by interaction within a psychic field* originally consisting of the *mother–child unity* (p. 119). I consider that Bowlby's (1958, 1960, 1969) theory of *attachment* also belongs in this context. In his view, bonding is facilitated by a series of "instinctual response systems," which are primarily and partially independent of each other—namely, sucking, clinging, following, screaming, and smiling (the theory of component instinct reactions). For Bowlby, these primary instinctual reactions become integrated, during the first year of life, into bonding behavior, a complex behavioral pattern integrated by the relationship with the mother through her individual reactions (the theory of the control of bonding behavior). In the view developed here, behavioral systems are already complex pattern formations (and hence structures), whose genesis is based on drive-structure processes; to that extent, the drive theory that Bowlby rejects is as it were fused in with his bonding theory. At any rate, Bowlby's term "bonding" expresses precisely what is meant in our formalized conception when we describe the object, or structure, as the regulator of the drive, and postulate that *bonding* with an external structure (the mother) corresponds to the regulation of the drive by this structure. In the same way, Sandler's (1960a) thesis of the "background of safety," which he sees as a *non-drive-based* need of the infant, ought in my opinion to be conceptualized as also involving regulation by an external structure.

switching, a *lethic* (repression) excitation, and that a *lethic* (drive) excitation emanating from *C* triggers a *libidinal* (repression) excitation in *P*. In other words, a libidinal or lethic cathexis of *P* leads respectively to a lethic or libidinal cathexis of *C*; the equilibrium of the two structures *C* and *P* of the extended system *CP* is restored after this "exchange."

However, even this conceptualization accounts for only one half of the situation, because it has so far ascribed the switching function solely to the external structure *P*, but this is of course impossible because, in systemic terms, at least two structures are always needed to form a complete loop. We must assume that libidinal or lethic cathexes emanating from *P* are also undertaken on *C*, and are perceived, responded to, and stored by *C* lethically or libidinally respectively.[14] Again, what is excited in *C* is not only a drive, but at the same time (even if at first insufficiently) its repression; that is to say, both antagonistic drives are always involved in a process. Hence the repression of *C* will also be combined with the repression of *P*—or, more precisely, a particular drive-repression combination of *C* will combine with a drive-repression combination of *P*. For this reason, what is recorded in C is not an identical copy of *P* but a mixed copy *CP* (which undergoes constant modification during structure development), and this mixed copy becomes the basis of an *individual pattern formation* in *C*.[15] How, then, might the development of structure in the oral, anal, and phallic-oedipal stages of libido organization be describable in the light of these general considerations?

> At the very beginning, in the individual's primitive oral phase, object-cathexis and identification are no doubt indistinguishable from each other. [1923b, p. 29]

---

14 Cf. Laplanche's "enigmatic messages" (1986).

15 According to Kernberg's (1993b) conception of the internalization of object relations, "What the child internalizes is not the image or representation of the other, but the relationship between self and other—in the form of an interaction between self-representation and object imago or object representation" (p. 97, translated for this edition).

[T]he effects of the first identifications made in earliest childhood will be general and lasting. This leads us back to the origin of the ego ideal; for behind it there lies hidden an individual's first and most important identification, his identification with the father in his own personal prehistory. This is apparently not in the first instance the consequence or outcome of an object-cathexis; it is a direct and immediate identification and takes place earlier than any object-cathexis. [p. 31]

This may be translated into our terminology as follows. Before the formation of the subject and object tracks, object cathexis and identification are indistinguishable. Rather, the drive tendencies emitted by C will, together with the repression responses received from P, contribute to the formation of structures in C, these structures being molded to some extent both by the switching law of the father F and by that of the mother M; more precisely, they form in C one structural complex with the switching law of a mixed copy CF and another with the switching law CM.[16] The representations formed in this early phase have lasting significance—because, according to Freud, they are fundamental building blocks of the ego ideal, and will influence the subsequent differentiation of the two tracks of drive organization. As Freud explains: "The two [identification and object cathexis] subsist side by side for a time without any mutual influence or interference. *In consequence of the irresistible advance towards a unification of mental life, they come together at last*; and the normal Oedipus complex originates from their *confluence*" (1921c, p. 105, my emphasis). On the basis of our assumption that the activity of each structure results in an excitation that is perceived by another structure as a drive, we can see this "confluence" as *drive activity*, as follows: the CM and CF currents "come together at last"—that is to say, they are combined in a new structure on a higher hierarchical level, C_{MF}. This combination could be regarded as the outcome and conclusion of the first oral phase of libidinal

---

16 The CM and CF complexes could be seen as the formal counterpart of Kohut's "selfobjects," or as the "bipolar self" deemed by Ornstein (1989) to be "an intrapsychic concept that describes how the self can achieve its own developmental aims through the functions of the other" (p. 38, translated for this edition).

organization, establishing a *first stage in the ego ideal*, which we may—for simplicity—call the C_{MF1} structure, containing an *initial complete triangular configuration of the ideal self and the two primitive idealized (self)objects.*

Freud established that the crucial feature of the anal phase that now ensues is the *obstinacy* of the child that wishes to *do everything itself*: this corresponds to an attempt at *self-regulation*—at (partial, structurerelated) detachment of the system *C* from the external structure *P*. Further important achievements of the anal phase are considered to be the development of the concepts of *I* and *you* and the crystallization of the polarities of *active* and *passive*. The *active/passive* antithesis has effects in two dimensions. With regard to the function of the *structures*, it corresponds to the antithesis of *efferent* and *afferent*: "active/efferent" means that something emanates from a structure ("doing it oneself"), while "passive/afferent" indicates that something is acting on a structure. Each structure thus has an *effector side* and a *receptor side*. The second dimension of this opposition of *active* and *passive* accrues from our characterization of the two *drives*, if we connect "active" with *libidinal* and "passive" with *lethic*. The predominantly libidinally controlled structural complexes can now be said to become differentiated from those in which lethic control predominates; the lethic trends are directed inward and hence mainly toward the *self*, while the libidinal ones are directed outward toward the *object*. The anal phase of drive organization thus lays the foundations for the emergence and differentiation of the object track—the end of this phase being marked by the important achievement that the "extraneous object [is] already observable" (1905d, p. 198f.). We may therefore deem the principal factors in *anal-phase structure formation* to be the following: (*1*) *the differentiation between the lethically and libidinally controlled groups of representations, and hence between the subject and object tracks of drive organization; and* (*2*) *the differentiation between the afferent and efferent regulatory functions of the structures.*

In accordance with our conception, the modified intervention— aligned as it now is with the anal (behavioral) pattern—of the two parents in their external regulatory function will, of course, produce a structural precipitate in this phase too, in the form of the generation of phase-specific *CF* and *CM* complexes, both of which are ultimately integrated into a structural complex C_{FM2}.[17] *At the end of the anal phase*, we thus have a *second structural complex*, C_{FM2}, which may be described *as the second stage in the ego ideal*. Now we saw in our discussion of its genesis (Figure 2–7) that the ego ideal arises from the integration of two prior structural complexes; we called the side cathected predominantly with libido *narcissism*, and gave the provisional name *egoism* to that in which lethic cathexis is dominant. We are now able to refine this concept, as follows. The complete ego ideal arises as the integration product of the oral, primary-narcissistic C_{MF1} complex (*narcissism*) and the anal C_{FM2} complex (*egoism*). Hence *the ego ideal*, which will have come into being by the time of entry into the oedipal crisis, is already *a structural complex formed from a number of stages of differentiation and integration—a complex in which, now, the two triangular subunities C_{MF1} and C_{FM2} are amalgamated into another triangular organizational unity, the structural complex C_{FM3}*[18] (see Figure III–1).

The onset of the third phase of development, the oedipal crisis, thus proceeds from a stage of formation of the psychical apparatus in which an initial structurally based differentiation between libidinal and lethic tendencies, subject and object, and afferent and efferent processes has been achieved. The representations of an *efficient* and a *receptive self*, and of an *efficient* and a *receptive object*, now exist. However, in the anal phase, the opposition of *male* and *female* does not yet arise in the sense of a *sex-specific dominant identification* with a self-representation (or group of self-representations) on the subject track, or of a corresponding differentiation on the object track (although this does not mean in practice that the phenomenal differences between the sexes are not yet *known* at this time). The definitive formation of this sexual distinction is the

---

17 There is insufficient space in the shortened version of this book to show on the basis of Freud's texts why I sometimes use the notation C_{MF} and sometimes C_{FM}; however, since these are in any case intended only as simplifications to facilitate understanding, and since we are quite prepared to accept that now the maternal and now the paternal influence predominates, I shall not dwell on this variation here.

18 Chasseguet-Smirgel (1976, 1984) has given an especially precise account of the primary narcissistic and, in particular, anal aspects of the ego ideal.

task of the oedipal phase. "The whole subject, however, is so complicated that it will be necessary to go into it in greater detail. *The intricacy of the problem is due to two factors: the triangular character of the Oedipus situation and the constitutional bisexuality of each individual*" (1923b, p. 31, my emphasis).

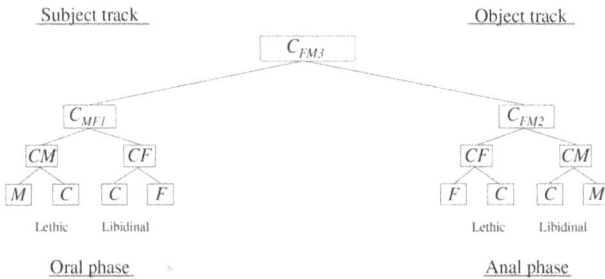

FIGURE III–I illustrates the stages of structure formation (from bottom to top). The bottom row treats the child and the parents as separate structures, which are combined as functional unities in the CM and CF complexes in the next row up (in accordance with our view of the parents as external structures, or external regulators, of the psychical apparatus). The CF and CM complexes are then consolidated in the third row into the two stages of the ego ideal distinguished here, the C_{MF1} complex and the C_{FM2} complex, which mark the emergence of the two differentiated tracks of drive organization. The C_{FM3} complex above subsumes both, on a higher hierarchical level, into the ego ideal, thus ensuring the functional integration of the two subordinate structural complexes and the drive processes emanating from them.

In Freud's conception there are always *three structural unities* within which the entire dynamics of the psychic processes unfold (in our terms the three structural complexes C_{MF1-3}), as well as *two drives*, which we have called the (+) sexual drive and the (–) preservative drive. We must therefore locate "constitutional bisexuality" within the (+) sexual drive—which thus involves a further stage of differentiation within the (+) drive tendency. As we know, Freud quite often links activity with masculinity and passivity with femininity, seeing these connections as a "biological fact" (1915c, p. 134), although he does always point out that this passivity on the phenomenal level corresponds to a libidinal drive *activity*.

We have called the drive force of sexual life "the libido." Sexual life is dominated by the polarity of masculine-feminine; thus the notion suggests itself of considering the relation of the libido to this antithesis. *There is only one libido, which serves both the masculine and the feminine sexual functions. . . .* Furthermore, it is our impression that *more constraint has been applied to the libido when it is pressed into the service of the feminine function.* [1933a [1932], p. 131, my emphasis]

Freud's thesis is thus that, in female development, the libido is *pressed* by force (*constraint*) in a particular *direction* (the feminine function); "constraint" and "pressing (into)" appear to indicate a repression, or, in more neutral language, a combinatorial switching operation. Moreover, each such combination takes place in accordance with a specific mode, which we can here determine from its *direction*, toward the "feminine sexual *function*," and comprehend as a *turning inward*. "Turning against one's own person" is a combinatorial switching operation involving feedback whereby a (+) tendency is preserved— that is, it remains a predominantly libidinal trend. This means that the (phenomenally) passive feminine trends are active libidinal trends directed inward. In other words, libido remains libido, and it remains the dominant influence in the sexual function. What differs as between the two sexes is its *drive vicissitude*[19]—that is, the particular modality of the relevant drive-repression combinations that leads to the specific pattern formations in which the psychic sexual function ultimately becomes constituted. It follows logically from this conception that, owing to the identification with both parents, both "feminine" and "masculine" drive vicissitudes are learned and activated. These are not only correlated with the constitutional bisexuality of human beings but also pave the way for the "complete Oedipus complex":

---

19 I first attempted, more comprehensively than here, to demonstrate the *specificity of female development as a consequence of certain drive vicissitudes* (driverepression combinations in accordance with different modalities) in a study of Freud's metapsychological conception of female development (Schmidt-Hellerau 1988).

Closer study usually discloses the *more complete* Oedipus complex, which is twofold, positive and negative, and is due to the bisexuality originally present in children: that is to say, a boy has not merely an ambivalent attitude towards his father and an affectionate object-choice towards his mother, but at the same time he also behaves like a girl and displays an affectionate feminine attitude to his father and a corresponding jealousy and hostility towards his mother. It is this complicating element introduced by bisexuality that makes it so difficult to obtain a clear view of the facts in connection with the earliest object-choices and identifications, and still more difficult to describe them intelligibly. [1923b, p. 33]

What is special about the concept of the complete Oedipus complex is that it describes *two* further differentiations within the subject-object track. The first (resulting from bisexuality) concerns the organization of the sexual drive: a distinction between *male* and *female* is now to be introduced on both the subject track and the object track. However, the introduction of the sexual dimension, according to the conception consistently maintained here, now gives rise to a second differentiation: a predominantly lethically controlled branch and a predominantly libidinally controlled branch must additionally be formed on each track of the drive organization. This can be put as follows: a distinction must now be made between a *biogenic* and an *erotogenic self*, and between a *biogenic* and an *erotogenic object*—and the erotogenic self and objects must in addition be identified as *male* or *female*. This at the same time implies the formation of a *female oedipal mother*, assigned the structural complexes of the anal and the oral mother, and of a *male oedipal father* who is at the same time also the anal and oral father. The division of the structures by sex-specific combinatorial switching modalities for the predominantly libidinal trends (in the sense of a coordination of pattern formations) thus necessitates a further reorganization of all representations hitherto formed. This new, third order does not supersede its two predecessors, but—being at a higher hierarchical level—when activated determines future access to the earlier stages of structure formation.

At the dissolution of the Oedipus complex the four trends of which it consists will group themselves in such a way as to produce a father-identification and a mother-identification. The father-identification will preserve the object-relation to the mother which belonged to the positive complex and will at the same time replace the object-relation to the father which belonged to the inverted complex: and the same will be true, mutatis mutandis, of the mother-identification. [1923b, p. 34, my emphasis]

What are these four trends? We have:

1.   The positive Oedipus complex:
     the boy, identified   *loves*   and fights
     with the father,   the mother ($_cFM$)[20]   against the father
2.   The negative Oedipus complex:
     the boy, identified   *loves*   and fights
     with the mother,   the father ($_cMF$)   against the mother.

However, two trends are lacking here. Now the fights against the father and the mother respectively could be seen as separate trends, especially if aggression is regarded as a drive in its own right, and in this case the first two (classical) trends would be doubled to yield *four*. But how do these aggressive trends then combine? Moreover, are these not *libidinal* trends—in which the fight against the third party is only a secondary consequence? Since I have not conceived aggression, on the formalized level of metapsychology, as a drive in its own right, or as the drive antagonist to the sexual drive, an explanation is called for. Some progress will be made if we consider the intended—and

---

20   Strictly speaking, this notation is no longer appropriate for representing the situation at this level of complexity. I use it nevertheless because it will ultimately illustrate a very important train of ideas. In this consideration, I am omitting the developmental stages so far attained (as far as C_{FM3} and again treating the oedipal phase separately; the change in character size from C_{MF} to $_cFM$ is intended to indicate that the boy endows himself with the paternal potency and attractiveness, thereby as it were enhancing his own value and enlarging himself into a suitable partner for the other parent. [Translator's note: To avoid possible confusion due to excessive numbers of symbols, the letter "c" (child) is retained even where only boys are meant.]

possible—meanings of *active* and *passive*. After all, trends 1 and 2 above are only one side of the coin, referring as they do solely to the *"active"/efferent* side of the representations, the *efficient self*: the boy *loves* the mother or *loves* the father. Precisely in the latter case, however, phenomenal passivity and drive activity are mixed: if both female and male sexuality are controlled by way of the (+) sexual drive and appear as "active" or "passive" only according to how they are switched (i.e., whether they are directed inward or outward), then the seemingly passive *female wanting-to-be-loved* is initially a *drive activity*—a specifically female form of *actively loving*. At the same time, however—and this is the crucial point—there is another form of wanting-to-be-loved, which emanates from the *"passive"/afferent* side of the representations, from the *receptive self*, and this form, as such, is no longer specifically female: men too want to be loved, loved back, have their love returned, by the beloved woman. That is ultimately a question of homeostasis—of libidinal economy, as Freud calls it—and, in addition, of object relations (which are, of course, also represented endosystemically). This distinction between feminine libidinal *activity* on the *efferent* side of the representation and *passivity* on its *afferent* side has fallen by the wayside in Freud's treatment of female sexuality (hence his difficulties in its conceptualization). But it is precisely here, on this reverse side, the afferent side of the representations, that the outstanding two of the four trends belong. The complete picture is therefore as follows:

In the positive Oedipus complex:

1a →)	The boy, identified	*loves*		and fights
	with the father,	the mother ($_cF \to M$)	against the father[21]
1b ←)	The boy, identified	*would like to be loved*		and fears
	with the father,	by the mother ($_cF \leftarrow M$)	the father

---

21 The arrows now indicate the efferent (→) and afferent (←) trends (sides of the erotogenic representation). For further elaboration of the Oedipus complex regarding these considerations see Schmidt-Hellerau 2005b, 2008, 2010 .

In the negative Oedipus complex:

2a →)	The boy, identified with the mother,	*loves* the father ($_cM \rightarrow F$)	and fights against the mother
2b ←)	The boy, identified with the mother,	*would like to be loved* by the father ($_cM \leftarrow F$)	and fears the mother

The side of the erotogenic self-representation on which the positive and negative Oedipus complexes leave their structural precipitate now assumes decisive importance. If the positive Oedipus complex molds the efferent side of the self-representation and the negative Oedipus complex the afferent side, the four trends combine in such a way that 2b is retained, so that 1b is replaced (A), and that 1a is retained and consequently 2a is replaced (B):

(A) From the *mother identification*, the "passive"/afferent object cathexis: the boy wants to be loved by the father ($_cM \leftarrow F$).

(B) From the *father identification*, the "active"/efferent object cathexis: the boy loves the mother ($_cF \rightarrow M$).

Combining the two trends (A) and (B) in a single proposition, we then have: *The boy wants to be loved by the father—in order to love the mother (like the father).* We are then inclined to agree with Freud that the boy "borrowed strength to do this, so to speak, from the father, and this loan was an extraordinarily momentous act" (ibid., p. 34). Freud is here already referring to the elements that mold the superego, but one important combinatorial stage is still lacking. Consider the following point, on which Freud lays particular emphasis:

> *The broad general outcome of the sexual phase dominated by the Oedipus complex, may, therefore, be taken to be the forming of a precipitate in the ego, consisting of these two identifications in some way united with each other. This modification*

of the ego retains its special position; it confronts the other contents of the ego as
an ego ideal or super-ego. [ibid.]

These two *identifications* (A) and (B) must therefore *somehow* come to be
united (illustrated graphically in Figure III-2).

Might a less complicated account not be possible? In the case of the boy
in the above model, for example, could the efferent and afferent sides of the
positive Oedipus complex not simply be intensified and everything else be
rejected? In my view, the afferent part of the positive Oedipus complex—"the
boy wants to be loved by the mother"—still corresponds, at this first stage (of
combinatorial switching), to the self-related narcissistic trend derived from
the ego ideal. Conversely, the fully assimilated mature Oedipus complex is
the result of a much more complex process (of combinatorial switching); in
psychological terms, it develops via a primary identification with a mother
who wants to be loved by the father (first stage: the negative Oedipus
complex), into the subsequent wish (the positive Oedipus complex) to be
loved (later) oneself as a man (father identification) by (a woman like) the
mother. On the basis of Freud's suggested unification of father and mother
Identifications (as comprehensively formulated in the above tabulation), this
process—together with the integration of passivehomosexual wishes—yields
the proposition "the father loves the mother" for the efferent side and "the
mother wants to be loved by the father" for the afferent side. We see that, in
this combination, the afferent side now actually supports the efferent side, for
the two wishes combine to give the following: "The father loves the mother,
and the mother wants that too—that is, to be loved by the father." This is the
basis of the crucial intensification of the male position; in formalized terms,
the mother identification on the afferent side intensifies and stabilizes the
father identification on the efferent side of the erotogenic self.

Positive Oedipus complex		Father identification	Subject track	Object track	
"Active"/ efferent	$_cF{\to}M$		$F{\to}M$ $\underline{M{\leftarrow}F}$	$M{\to}F$ $M{\leftarrow}F$	$F{\to}M$ $\underline{F{\leftarrow}M}$
		$_cF{\to}M$			
"Passive"/ afferent	$_cF{\leftarrow}M$		$F{\to}M{\leftarrow}F$	$M\Leftrightarrow F$	$F\Leftarrow M$
Negative Oedipus complex		Mother identification			
"Active"/ efferent	$_cM{\to}F$		$C_{F{\to}M{\leftarrow}F}$	$_c{\leftrightarrow}M\Leftrightarrow F$	$_c{\leftrightarrow}F\Leftrightarrow M$
		$_cM{\leftarrow}F$			
"Passive"/ afferent	$_cM{\leftarrow}F$		Masculine self-representation	Mother represent-ation	Father represent-ation

FIGURE III–2 shows, the association of the efferent father identification from the positive Oedipus complex with the afferent mother identification from the negative Oedipus complex constitutes a self-representation on the subject track in which the *mother object cathexis and the mother identification are superimposed* and reinforce each other. In consequence, the positive efferent father identification and the negative afferent father object cathexis become centered around the mother trend: the resulting erotogenic self-representation is predominantly male (paternal), and thus efferently and afferently directed in the female (maternal) direction. Finally, the transfer of representations from the positive Oedipus complex (the father representation) and the negative Oedipus complex (the mother representation) on to the object track is indicated; this intensifies the representation of the mother–father relationship. The simple double arrow (↔) between C and the mother and father representations shows that the relationship between C and both parents is "cut in half" for C by the fact that, with regard to the father and mother identifications (second column), one side in each case has been transferred on to the object track in "repressed" form—that is, actually, in a "crossover." This means that the afferent trend from the positive Oedipus complex and the efferent trend from the negative Oedipus complex have not disappeared or been lost, but have been used to form the object representations, where they stabilize the representation of the father's and mother's belonging together and being in relation to each other.

That would appear to conclude our reflections on the formation of sexual identification—but we have not yet finished with the Oedipus complex, because, at this juncture, the boy would be expected to unleash his freshly concentrated masculinity on the mother, and this must now be stopped. An important step is thus still lacking, namely the formation of the *superego*. Freud explains:

> Along with the demolition of the Oedipus complex, the boy's objectcathexis of his mother must be given up. Its place may be filled by one of two things: either an identification with his mother or an intensification of his identification with his father. We are accustomed to regard the latter outcome as the more normal; it permits the affectionate relation to the mother to be in a measure retained. [ibid., p. 32]

What is meant by "the *affectionate* relation to the mother"? Is an "affectionate" relation a *libidinal* one that has been reduced (sublimated)—or is it perhaps a way of loving the mother in which love means *concern* and *caring*? At any rate, what is at issue is the *preservation* of the relationship with the mother. Now Freud refers to a "*demolition* of the Oedipus complex," characterizing this process, therefore, as a rabid, *destructive* act—as we know mainly from the side of the *father*, who chases the little boy back into the nursery with his powerful *threat of castration*. In this way the father *represses* the son—or, if you will, he represses the son's mother-directed object-libidinal aspirations—and is thereby, so to speak, reacting totally *egoistically*, wanting to have the mother all to himself. *Egoism*, in our classification, belongs on the side of the *self-preservative drives*, and the threat of castration must in any case mobilize the *self-preservative drives* in the boy—to preserve the valued organ, and to save his own life. Suddenly, then, we are talking about processes that we associate with the self-preservative drive, which has not been mentioned for so long. Here, in the development of the superego, it emerges from the shadows into which oedipal love had banished it; here it again gives a sign of its presence. It must in fact have been active all the time; it is just that we have not thought any more about it since our initial reflection that, in addition to the libidinally controlled branch, a predominantly lethically controlled branch—the precipitate of whose structures would lie in the biogenic self and the biogenic objects—must now also come into being on both the subject and object tracks. Since Freud does not pursue these lethic processes of structure formation during the phallic phase, let us try, using our own resources first, to throw some light on this other side of the oedipal phase.

For this purpose we may take as our starting point the antagonistic configuration of the drives—that is, our basic postulate that whichever drive we are considering represses the other. It follows that excitations of the sexual drive must elicit the self-preservative drive in one form or other. In the case of the positive Oedipus complex, we had established, for the efferent side, that "the boy wants to love the mother": the aim is the institution of a "two-person" relationship, and the presence of the third party is to be repressed. Although the third party reappears in the secondary action—"and fights against the father"—it does so in the context of its *elimination*, which is not reconcilable with the "triangular character" of the Oedipus complex as described by Freud. The question is, therefore, whether this third party is not also represented in a position other than this one that is so violently fought against—that is, whether the third party might not in effect be represented lethically on the *reverse side* of the Oedipus complex, thus performing a stabilizing function as a structure (in the process of formation). Proceeding in the same order as before, let us review all the possibilities for the positive and negative Oedipus complex on the efferent and afferent sides. The first line in each case applies to the predominantly libidinal (+) drive trend, and the second line to the *directionally opposed* lethic (−) drive trend (see p. 226).

Let us consider the first situation—1a (+/−)—in more detail. The libidinal wish is *to love the mother*, which would exclude the third party (the father). The lethic repression of this wish consequently mobilizes precisely this third party: *to preserve the father*. This lethic counter-wish mitigates the appended clause (the secondary action): fight against the father. In relation to the father, the conflict is therefore of *fighting versus preserving*. However, since *preserving the father* is at the same time a lethic wish that competes with the mother's actions, the *fight* against the mother, conversely, mitigates the *love* for the mother. The same applies to the "active"/efferent side of the negative Oedipus complex—2a (+/−)—the conflict here being between *loving the father* and nevertheless *preserving the mother*. The same applies again in the "passive"/ afferent versions, the wishes this time being directed to the subject's own person. For example, in the negative Oedipus complex—2b (+/−)—the afferent libidinal wish is *to be loved by the father*. This excludes the third party (the mother), who must first be brought back by the lethic countercurrent, namely, *to be preserved by the mother*. The lethic counterwish mitigates the appended clause of the libidinal current: the wish to be preserved by the mother is offset by the fear of the mother. Similarly, the fear of the father, stemming from the afferent lethic trend, moderates the passive homosexual wish *to be loved by the father*. The same is again true in case 1b (+/−): *wanting to be loved by the mother* and nevertheless *to be preserved by the father*. Clearly, then, in all four variations of the Oedipus complex *the lethic trend counterbalances the libidinal trend*. It is not only *fear* of the father/mother that holds the son back, but also *concern* for the father/mother, the wish to *preserve* him/her; and it is not only *fear* of the mother/father that puts an end to the passive/libidinal wishes, but also the simultaneous wish to be *preserved* and *supported* by the father/mother. In other words, the lethic and libidinal trends are simultaneously apportioned, in all four variants, to both parents: in effect, if the son loves the mother in the "foreground," his object-preserving trends are then directed to the father in the "background"—and vice versa. It seems to me that *this is the classical conflict between the two drive trends in the triangular Oedipus situation: loving one parent and nevertheless preserving the other.*

1a (+) →)	The boy wants	to love the mother	like the father	and fights against the father
1a (–) →)	The boy wants	to preserve the father	like the mother	and fights against the mother
1b (+) ←)	The boy wants	to be loved by the mother	like the father	and fears the father
1b (–) ←)	The boy wants	to be preserved by the father	like the mother	and fears the mother
2a (+) →)	The boy wants	to love the father	like the mother	and fights against the mother
2a (–) →)	The boy wants	to preserve the mother	like the father	and fights against the father
2b (+) ←)	The boy wants	to be loved by the father	like the mother	and fears the mother
2b (–) ←)	The boy wants	to be preserved by the mother	like the father	and fears the father

The complexity with which the representations of the erotogenic self and objects have come into being for the libidinal trends is paralleled (as it were, in the shadow of that drama) by that of the genesis of the representations of the biogenic self and objects based on the lethic drive trends in the functions of self-preservation and preservation of the object. This is the theoretical justification for what we had provisionally, and solely for the sake of symmetry, assigned at the end of our consideration on narcissism (Figure II–7) to the notion "*object preservation*" on the object track. As Freud too notes: "What guarantees the safety of the ego is the *fact that the object has been preserved* "[22] (ibid., p. 53, my emphasis). This means that we now have two main currents on each of the two tracks: *self-preservation* and *self-love* on the subject track, and *object love*

---

22 [Translator's note: Strachey renders Freud's *Erhaltung* as "retained," but, since the same German word is used for "preservation"—e.g., in the term "selfpreservation"—"preserved" is preferred here.]

and *object preservation* on the object track. Following this *differentiation*, we may expect the next step to be another *integration*, and postulate, for the fully developed (mature) structural level of the psychical apparatus, a combination of the erotogenic and biogenic self and of the erotogenic and biogenic object: the integrated self then contains an erotogenic and a biogenic component, while the integrated object is also not only *either* a sexual or a feeding object, but both together—that is, an object that performs both an erotogenic and a biogenic function (see Figure III–3, p. 236).

Purely theoretical as these considerations are, they can nevertheless clarify for us certain aspects of lethic structural development during the oedipal phase. In the foreground now are not *aggression* and *fear*, but *concern*[23] for and *care* of the object, *both of which must first be learned* as an important, and indeed life-preserving, component of the psychical apparatus's "moral agency" that is to be formed. Now that we have established the conceptual foundations of these aspects of the superego, it seems to me that they emphasize the need *to preserve* the self-preservative drive as the antagonist of the sexual drive in drive theory: these functions could not have been established with aggression as the opponent of libido. Thus prepared, we can now turn to Freud's account of the *superego*, with which the lethic trends emphasized above can readily be reconciled.

> The super-ego is, however, not simply a residue of the earliest object-choices of the id; it also represents an energetic reaction-formation against those choices. Its relation to the ego is not exhausted by the precept: "You *ought to be* like this (like your father)." It also comprises the prohibition: "You *may not be* like this (like your father)—that is, you may not do all that he does; some things are his prerogative." This double aspect of the ego ideal derives from the fact that the ego ideal had the task of repressing the Oedipus complex; indeed, it is to that revolutionary event that it owes its existence. Clearly the repression of the Oedipus complex was no easy task. The child's parents, and especially

---

23 Winnicott (1963, p. 167) stressed the capacity for concern so as "to cover in a positive way a phenomenon that is covered in a negative way by the word 'guilt.'"

his father, were perceived as the obstacle to a realization of his Oedipus wishes; so his infantile ego fortified itself for the carrying out of the repression by erecting this same obstacle within itself. It borrowed strength to do this, so to speak, from the father, and this loan was an extraordinarily momentous act. The super-ego retains the character of the father, while the more powerful the Oedipus complex was and the more rapidly it succumbed to repression (under the influence of authority, religious teaching, schooling and reading), the stricter will be the domination of the super-ego over the ego later on—in the form of *conscience* [my emphasis] or perhaps of an unconscious sense of guilt. [ibid., p. 34f.]

As we know, Freud failed to differentiate clearly between the *ego ideal* and the *superego*—in my view, owing perhaps to the "double aspect" of this agency. If we take it that the ego ideal is to be controlled *predominantly libidinally*, so that it constitutes the libidinal side of this double aspect, then Freud's description of *conscience* might prove to correspond to the other, lethically cathected, side. At any rate, I contend that *the libidinal ego ideal and the lethic conscience undergo combinatorial switching in the higher-level macrostructure of the superego, thus forming a single functional organizational unity, which is also conceived as triangular.* This conception is borne out by a number of indications in the passage quoted above:

1.   The superego is described *not only* as a "residue of the earliest object-choices," *but also* as constituting an "energetic *reactionformation*" against them. Now a reaction presupposes an action: the libidinal object choice (the action) leads (by combinatorial switching in a structure) to the activation of the drive antagonist (the reaction)—that is to say, the libidinal trend is repressed lethically. The structure *formations* of both drives—the libidinal object cathexes and the lethic reactive (anti)cathexes—meet or combine in the superego.

2.   The superego contains not only the *precept* of the *ego ideal*—"You *ought* to be like this (like your father)"—but also the *prohibition* dictated by *conscience*: "You *may not be* like this (like your father)—

that is, *you may not* do all that he does." In formal terms, this is a matter of *yes* and *no* or, if you will, of a (+) drive impulse, the *precept* with its function of *orientation*, and a (–) drive impulse, the *prohibition* with its function of *limitation*.

3. The *double aspect* of the *superego* owes its existence to the *revolutionary event* that took place in the *repression* of the Oedipus complex, namely, to the changeover (involving combinatorial switching) from the predominantly *libidinal ego-ideal trends* to the predominantly *lethic trends of conscience*. In other words, the superego arises, in structural terms, from the "conjoining" of the ego ideal and conscience, or, in drive-process terms, from the coalescence of trends of the ego ideal and of conscience.

4. According to Freud, *superego formation* is based solely on the *repression* of the *Oedipus* complex. If the engine of the Oedipus complex is *libidinal*, this *repression* (this taming and restraining of the libidinal aspirations) can only be effected *lethically*. Here the *conscience* is supposed to be an inner *obstacle* to the powerful Oedipus wishes: the "infantile ego" *fortifies itself* for the carrying out of this repression by *identification* with the parents, who, after all, have *prevented* the "realization of the Oedipus wishes"—that is, it does so "by erecting this same obstacle within itself." Hence the lethic branches of both the subject track and the object track also see the precipitation of various identifications and object cathexes, the decisive character (both efferent and afferent) of which must first be elaborated by way of multiple combinatorial switching. Just as the ego ideal lives from the libidinal perfection of the parental love object, so, too, *conscience* is (partly) molded by the parents' lethic repression responses. According to Freud, it is the father's influence that is particularly relevant here, but, in my opinion, if the ego ideal is supposed to be predominantly libidinal in character and molded by the father, it is only logical to conceive the conscience as being predominantly lethic in character and molded by the maternal influence. The superego

too—as well as its two substructures—would then show the same triangular composition. *The (libidinally characterized) ego ideal molded by the father and the (lethically characterized) conscience molded by the mother together form the superego (macrostructure), in which the precepts and prohibitions of both parents—the (postoedipally) united parental couple—are conjoined, both moderating and supporting each other*; and the superego, when it later comes to represent the "influence of authority, religious teaching, schooling and reading," will stand for everything regarded by the mature adult as constituting value and *morality*.

The fact that Freud retained two names for these agencies, the ego ideal and superego, might indicate that he wanted to distinguish *two functions*—because the striving for an ideal indicates a libidinal movement diametrically opposed in direction to the lethic trend of an oppressive conscience. Having, in accordance with the results of his final drive theory, substantially neglected to investigate the tendencies of the self-preservative drive in the oedipal phase in favor of the "destructive component" (ibid., p. 53) of the death drive, he lacked a position antithetical to the ego ideal that would have enabled him to arrive at an autonomous, self-contained triangular conceptualization of the superego. What is missing are the (–) drives—that is, the death or self-preservative drives—and their structural precipitate in the psychical apparatus. A gap remains to be filled here. In my view, there is in the phallic phase, alongside the clamor of oedipal love, also a more silent, if not indeed "mute," form of drive activity: a lethic trend that learns *concern* and *care* and *preservation* (something *not* identical with the specificity of female sexuality)—a trend that contributes just as much to the formation of structure and identity as do the libidinal identifications and object cathexes with which we are familiar in this role. I contend that, in this process, lethic positions are marked on both the subject and object tracks, and indeed that lethic development always accompanies and counterbalances libidinal development, even if—or precisely because—it forms a branch of its own on the subject–object track.

Finally, then, we are left with the question of where to place the superego, with its substructures of the ego ideal and conscience, within our model of the subject–object track. In our discussion of "On Narcissism: An Introduction" (1914c), we assigned the ego ideal a place at the foot of the subject track on the grounds that, with its libidinal orientation, it had the function of, so to speak, offsetting the lethic trends directed toward the self; in this way we had established an antagonistic tension between the self and the ego ideal. Our view now is more differentiated. We have found that, in addition to the first stage in the ego ideal at the foot of the subject track in the anal phase of libidinal organization, a second ego-ideal stage is formed at the foot of the object track, and that both are ultimately combined in the C_{FM3} complex, the ego ideal at the beginning of the phallic-oedipal phase. Now, however, we have postulated an additional parallel process under predominantly lethic control, which also forms structural complexes that become established at the foot of the subject–object track; this substructure of the superego, the "conscience," likewise originates from a first, oral, preliminary stage and a second one that is anal, which leave offshoots on the subject–object track. The superego thus combines not only the subject and object tracks but also the libidinal and lethic branches of drive organization that have become differentiated on both tracks. The tendencies of *self-love* and *self-preservation* have their counterpole in the first stage of the conscience and ego ideal, while the trends of *object love* and *object preservation* are limited by the second stage of the conscience and ego ideal. At the same time we may postulate an antagonistic tension between the trends directed toward the *biogenic self* on the one hand and *ego ideal I* on the other, as well as between the *erotogenic self* and *conscience I*, and an analogous one on the object track between the *erotogenic object* and *conscience II*, as well as between the *biogenic object* and *ego ideal II*. When these are combined in the superego, therefore, the computation again involves *four different trends*, so that both the formation and the activities of the superego are seen to be highly complex processes. This is illustrated graphically in Figure III–3.

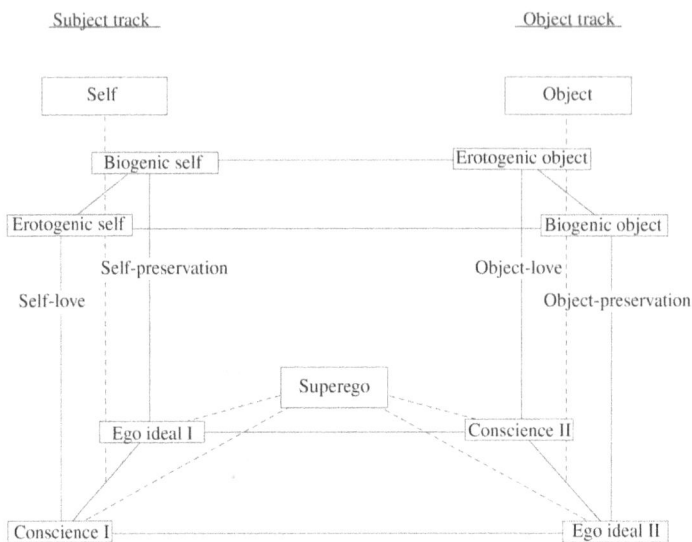

FIGURE III–3. The diagram shows that the superego is not confined to a combination of the tendencies on the subject and object tracks, but integrates four different tendencies: the resultants of the two predominantly libidinal and the two predominantly lethic structural complexes of ego ideals I and II and consciences I and II. The arrangement of the structures is determined by their opposing orientations—for example, erotogenic self vs lethic conscience I, biogenic object vs libidinal ego ideal II, and so on.

The following have therefore been accomplished at the end of the oedipal phase:

1. On the libidinally controlled branch of the subject track, the male and female identifications have become integrated into a single dominant *sexual identity*; the representations organized in this way by a specific switching modality of the libidinal currents form the *male* or *female erotogenic self*.

2. On the libidinally controlled branch of the object track, the representations of the various objects have also become grouped sex-specifically according to the "father" and "mother" models;

these representational configurations may be referred to as the *male* and *female erotogenic objects.*

3. In parallel with the above, the same has occurred on the two lethically controlled branches of the subject and object tracks; we therefore now also have the structures of the *biogenic self* and of the *biogenic objects.*

4. Extrapolating, we may assume that this *differentiation* will be followed by another *integration* at a higher level of organization, that the erotogenic and biogenic selves will be combined to form the more comprehensive entity of the self, and that the erotogenic and biogenic objects will also have to come together if the object is to be represented in its totality.

5. We further stated that the early structural formations on the subject–object track constituted the *ego ideal* with its two preliminary stages; it initiates the Oedipus complex and continues its development from then on with the idealization of one sex, either male or female. In its shadow, the *conscience* with its two preliminary stages and the associated functions of self-preservation and object preservation has formed on the lethic branch of the subject and object tracks by parallel processes of identification and object cathexis. As a crude simplification, the ego ideal may be said to be the *residence of the life drives*, and *conscience* a *"gathering-place for the death drives"* (ibid., p. 54); the ego ideal is fueled by the (+) drives, contains the *precepts*, and performs *functions of orientation*, whereas conscience energizes the (–) drives, contains the prohibitions, and performs *limiting functions*.[24] In

---

24 In an earlier contribution based on a bipolar conception (Schmidt-Hellerau 1990), I assigned the function of orientation to the ego ideal and that of limitation to the superego; however, in accordance with the triangular conception developed here, these ascriptions call for revision. The literature on the superego and the ego ideal distinguishes, for example, "superego nuclei" (Glover 1956) or "superego components" (Spitz 1958); the two entities are treated sometimes separately with differentiated functions, and sometimes as integrated (on the development of the superego, see also Sandler 1960b, 1962, Danneberg 1968, Cambor 1970).

the repression of the Oedipus complex, the two substructures, the *ego ideal* and *conscience*, with their respective oral and anal precursors on the subject–object track, are combined in the higher-level macrostructure of the *superego*, and a resultant is computed from the four different trends, which are thus integrated into an ultimately predominant trend; in psychological terms, this combination restrains the carelessness and extravagances of the ego ideal, and mitigates the severity and pitilessness of the conscience. Freud described these two functions of the superego as follows: the ego is concerned to be "*loved* by the super-ego" (in our terms, this is its libidinal task), while the superego at the same time has to fulfill a "function of *protection* and *saving*" (its lethic task) (p. 58, my emphasis). The superego is thus a synthesis of the ego ideal and of conscience, or, as we might say, it proves its worth in the performance of this synthesizing function.

The Ego and Perception

In the above considerations on the structure-forming processes of identification and object cathexis, we attempted to give a formal description of the relationship between inside and outside, subject and object, using the model of the *subject–object track* as a guide. We now need to be able to

---

In an early paper [translator's note: this apparently exists in German only], Grunberger (1974) postulated a maternal "Ober-Ich" ["superego" or "over-ego"] originating in the passive-anal phase and characterized by unbridled aggression, whereas the ensuing active-anal phase witnessed an identification with the father and an introjection of the paternal phallus, which conferred a phallic-narcissistic character on the early superego (it is interesting in the present context that Grunberger considers the early superego to have two orientations, *inward* and *outward* respectively). Chasseguet-Smirgel (1976) devoted a comprehensive essay to the ego ideal, casting light in particular on the implications of anal fixations for the development of perversion on the one hand and creativity on the other; she distinguishes between the ego ideal as the heir to primary narcissism, and the superego as the heir to the Oedipus complex—the ego ideal again being seen as the first stage of ego development and the superego the last.

show more precisely how this differentiated *process of perception* is conceived within our model. Perception had a place in Freud's model from the beginning (first in the φ system and then in the system *Pcpt.*), and so the basis of our investigation now will be the *D-P-M systems* configuration. This at the same time involves the *ego*, which, after all, has particularly "*intimate connections with the perceptual system*—connections *which, as we know, constitute its essence and provide the basis of its differentiation from the id*" (1926d [1925], p. 92, my emphasis)—especially, of course, where conscious perception (that is, the conscious mind) is concerned. Let us now try to find a way into this complex subject-matter of *perception* and *consciousness*, and thereby into the construction of the *macrostructure of the ego*, starting, like Freud, from the system *borderline*:

> What consciousness yields consists essentially of perceptions of excitations coming from the external world and of feelings of pleasure and unpleasure which can only arise from within the mental apparatus; it is therefore possible to assign to the system *Pcpt.-Cs.* a position in space. It must lie on the borderline between outside and inside; it must be turned towards the external world and must envelop the other psychical systems. [1920g, p. 24]

External and internal stimuli meet in the subject "on the borderline between outside and inside," and this borderline is also stated to be the location of the system *Pcpt.-Cs.* In an interesting speculation (ibid., p. 26 ff.), Freud likens the "living organism" to an initially "undifferentiated vesicle of a substance that is susceptible to stimulation," whose surface is permanently modified to a certain depth by the "ceaseless impact of external stimuli"—it is "baked through" and then becomes incapable of any further modification. This surface acts like a membrane against stimuli, which reduces energies of external origin to fractions of their original magnitude (the protective shield against stimuli), and conducts only a tiny proportion of them to the inside via the sense organs (reception of stimuli), where the stimuli leave "permanent traces... which form the foundation of memory" (p. 25). Since memory consists in specific *modifications* of structures, but both external and internal stimuli must always meet with the *same* conditions of reception if they are to provide us with a reliable perception of ourselves and the external world, perception and memory are accommodated in different places within the psychical apparatus (outside and inside). Moreover, what applies to perception in general is also true of a specific perceptual organ, namely consciousness: in the system *Cs.*, too, the recording of permanent memory traces would "very soon set limits to the system's aptitude for receiving fresh excitations" (p. 25). Freud concludes that "the excitatory process becomes conscious in the system *Cs.* but leaves no permanent trace behind there; but that the excitation is transmitted to the systems lying next within and that it is in *them* that its traces are left" (ibid.). Perception and consciousness are thus conceived as separate from the memory traces; they are functions that Freud connects by the hyphen in his term "system *Pcpt.Cs.*," but also distinguishes from each other. The difference is that perception (both internal and external) is more all-embracing than its consciousness: consciousness registers only a very limited segment of the sum of all internal and external perceptions excited at any given time.

Freud situates the *protective shield against stimuli* in the "baked-through" outer crust of his hypothetical vesicle. However, the conversion (breaking down) of external (physicochemical) stimuli (large quantities) into appropriate (quantitatively smaller) internal excitations that takes place there constitutes only an initial stage of protection against stimuli. Our previous reflections now afford a deeper insight into this important psychic function of the protective shield against stimuli. We postulated that external objects, through their function as external regulators, protect the developing psychical apparatus from overexcitation by effecting (preliminary) combinatorial switching of stimuli of both internal and external origin, thereby safeguarding the homeostasis of the psychical apparatus *C*. The identification and object cathexis that lead to the formation of self and object representations then simply constitute the *internalization of these switching functions*. This shows that the actual "borderline between outside and inside" is established not in the organs of perception but in the mnemic systems that lie behind them. Since protection against stimuli can, within our formalized model, be nothing but the combinatorial switching of different excitatory values with a view to making the system dynamically stable, we can say that *the activation of memory traces (of self and object representations) constitutes the system's protective shield against both internal and external stimuli.*[25]

Having placed the protective shield against stimuli in the deeper layers of the psychical apparatus (*P2*), Freud can now achieve a more differentiated view of perception, which he presents not only concisely but also with great precision at the end of "A Note upon the 'Mystic Writing-Pad'" (1925a [1924]). After comparing the "perceptual apparatus of our mind" with the two principal components of the Mystic Pad, "the celluloid and waxed paper cover with the system *Pcpt.-Cs.* and its protective shield, the wax slab with the unconscious behind them" (p. 230f.)—the writing being legible only when the cover is in contact with the wax slab, and disappearing when they are separated— he goes on:

> This agrees with a notion which I have long had about the method by which the perceptual apparatus of our mind functions, but which I have hitherto kept to myself. My theory was that cathectic innervations are sent out and withdrawn in rapid periodic impulses from within into the completely pervious system *Pcpt.-Cs.* So long as that system is cathected in this manner, it receives perceptions (which are accompanied by consciousness) and passes the excitation on to the unconscious mnemic systems; but as soon as the cathexis is withdrawn, consciousness is extinguished and the functioning of the system comes to a standstill. It is as though the unconscious stretches out feelers, through the medium of the system *Pcpt.-Cs.*, towards theexternal world and hastily withdraws them as soon as they have sampled the excitations coming from it. Thus the interruptions, which in the case of the Mystic Pad have an external origin, were attributed by my hypothesis to the discontinuity

---

25 Hartmann (1952) tends to regard the protective shield against stimuli too as an inborn, autonomous factor in ego development. The above considerations show that—irrespective of the relative quantitative roles of constitution and experience in the development of the protective shield against stimuli (both factors are always involved in all drive and structure processes)—the epithet "inborn" in no way facilitates our understanding, but if anything constricts our vision of this concept.

in the current of innervation; and the actual breaking of contact which occurs in the Mystic Pad was replaced in my theory by the periodic non-excitability of the perceptual system. I further had a suspicion that this discontinuous method of functioning of the system *Pcpt.-Cs.* lies at the bottom of the origin of the concept of time. [p. 231]

Transposing these ideas to our *D-P-M* system, we find first of all that sensory perception belongs on the lowest level of the *P* system (*P*1)—the place where we had located the *biogenic* and *erotogenic zones*, and, among them, also the *sense organs*. Perception being a receptive process, we are here concerned with an afferent side of *P*1. Now *P*1 is primarily cathected, within our model, from the *D* system; according to Freud, this cathexis comes "from within"—"as though the *unconscious* [my emphasis] stretches out feelers, through the medium of the system *Pcpt.-Cs.*, towards the external world." Hence this "attention cathexis" consists in the unconscious cathexis of specific patterns on the afferent side of these organs of perception from the inside of the psychical apparatus. The perceptual system, cathected (or hypercathected) in this way, receives the stimuli impinging on its sense organs and passes them on from its efferent side "to the unconscious mnemic systems"—that is, to *P*2. As soon as the cathexis is displaced from *P*1 to *P*2, the perception in *P*1 comes to a standstill and the perceptual system is briefly incapable of being excited. In the unconscious mnemic systems, the stimuli are "sampled"—that is, they undergo combinatorial switching—and the result of this combination is fed on from *P*2 to *P*1, constituting a subsequent specific cathexis of certain patterns of afference in *P*1, leading to the next perceptions, which in turn undergo combinatorial switching in *P*2, and so on. The process of perception here is subject to a rhythm corresponding to the constant alternation of extroversive and introversive—(+) drive and (–) drive—excitations; and the *P*1 and *P*2 systems are, once again, simply the structures that perform combinatorial switching of the incoming drive stimulus and trigger "its repression"—which in turn gives rise, in the next cathexis of a structure, to an antagonistic drive excitation for the purpose of homeostasis.

This has the following implication for the relationship between perception and the protective shield against stimuli. The first stage of protection against stimuli lies in the combinatorial switching in the sense organs in $P1$ (corresponding to the celluloid that protects the waxed paper from scoring). The second stage of protection against stimuli is provided by the mnemic systems of $P2$, where the "samples" from $P1$ are combined and passed on in such a way that, upon the subsequent recathexis of $P1$, perceptions that would lead to overexcitation (i.e., which had already resulted in an "overexcitation" in the first "sample") are either avoided (by withdrawal of cathexis and/or flight from the stimulus), or made more amenable to homeostatic regulation (so to speak, brought into balance) by a correspondingly increased "anticathexis" of the relevant afferent locations. The idea of such a regulation implies a circulation of excitations between $P1$ and $P2$, in which the D system is constantly involved (via feedback from $P1$ and $P2$). At any rate, Freud's conception of the sending out and withdrawal of cathexes from the unconscious (the $P2/D$ system) allows subtle adjustment (and adaptation) of the system to the instantaneous requirements of the process of perception. It is further assumed that this process is not confined to the systems $P1$ and $P2$, but is also passed on to tier $P3$— thereby providing this complicated sequence of miscellaneous combinatorial switching operations in all three P systems with ample scope for deploying the entire spectrum of familiar defense mechanisms (drive vicissitudes) that together ultimately make up the protective shield against stimuli. This conception simply means that we perceive not only with the sense organs ($P1$) but also with the mnemic systems ($P2$), or, as we say, that we see not only with our eyes, but also (perhaps even mainly) with our minds. Moreover, this is how the unconscious interferes with perception. Hence the outline of the "method by which the perceptual apparatus of our mind functions" given in the "Mystic Writing-Pad" contains the entire conception of perception, whether normal (structured), selective, or neurotically distorted (as, for example, in the transference).

So far, then, we have seen that all external and internal stimuli are perceived (i.e., undergo initial combinatorial switching) in $P1$, experience further combination in the mnemic systems $P2$, and then again in $P1$, and so on. This means that $P1$ is oriented not only afferently toward the sensory stimuli, but also efferently to the self and object representations in $P2$—suggesting that consciousness, as a special perceptual process, should not only be associated with the activation of $P1$, but is also conditional upon the involvement of $P2$. Freud reflects:

> The question, "How does a thing become conscious?" would thus be more advantageously stated: "How does a thing become preconscious?" And the answer would be: "Through becoming connected with the word-presentations corresponding to it."
>
> These word-presentations are residues of memories; they were at one time perceptions, and like all mnemic residues they can become conscious again. Before we concern ourselves further with their nature, it dawns upon us like a new discovery that only something which has once been a Cs. perception can become conscious, and that anything arising from within (apart from feelings) that seeks to become conscious must try to transform itself into external perceptions: this becomes possible by means of memory-traces. [1923b, p. 20]

So far we have examined the process of perception solely on the basis of process cycles within the D and P systems, but Freud now also involves the M system. It is the fact of "*becoming connected with... word-presentations*" ($M3$) that brings a thought process to consciousness. The word presentations stem from memory traces ($P2$) that arose from processes of perception ($P1$). Hence only a complete psychic process cycle, of which, according to our conception, all three D-P-M systems always partake, can become conscious.

Freud had shown in *On Aphasia* (1891b—see Figure III–4) that words (word representations) proceed from the integration of various pattern formations that are themselves already complex (sound and kinesthetic images, and visual images for print and script), which are associated with the object representation, whose structure is even more complex. The full differentiation of the individual components of the word representation that takes place in the object representation indicates that what we understand as a word results from an infinitely complex computational process ultimately made up of nothing but yes/ no, on/off, or plus/minus steps—that is, of (+) drive and (−) drive processes. In terms of the conceptualization of the relationship between inside and outside, this means that what we "send out" is the pattern formation, deposited in the M system, resulting from such (+/−) computational processes; and that what we "receive" are also pattern formations of this kind, which we register and subject to further processing in the P system (as proprioceptions or exteroceptions). The psychical apparatus thus appears as a system that not only instantaneously integrates and synthesizes (by combinatorial computation) highly complex individual process cycles, thereby generating specific patterns, but also, conversely, instantaneously analyzes and classifies the perception of such process cycles and patterns.

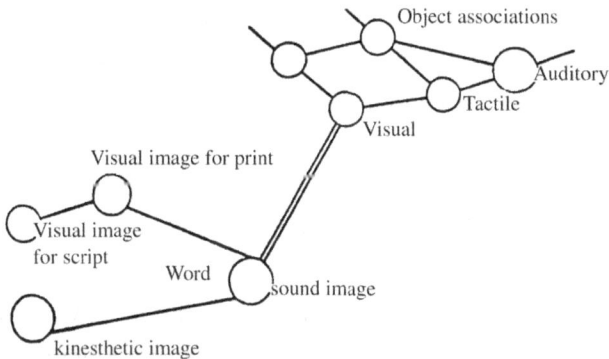

FIGURE III–4. Freud explains his diagram as follows: "The word concept[26] appears as a closed complex of images, the object concept as an open one. The word concept is linked to the concept of the object via the sound image only. Among the object associations, the visual ones play a part similar to that played by the sound image among the word associations. The connections of the word sound image with object associations other than the visual are not presented in this schema" (1891b, p. 77).

---

26 [Translator's note: i.e., word presentation.]

Now what microstructure within the psychical apparatus might perform such a complex operation? The overall answer can only be that the *entire system* is involved in these computational processes—but the ego clearly plays a particular part in them:

> We have formed the idea that in each individual there is a coherent organization of mental processes; and we call this his ego. It is to this ego that consciousness is attached; the ego controls the approaches to motility—that is, to the discharge of excitations into the external world; it is the mental agency which supervises all its own constituent processes, and which goes to sleep at night, though even then it exercises the censorship on dreams. From this ego proceed the repressions, too, by means of which it is sought to exclude certain trends in the mind not merely from consciousness but also from other forms of effectiveness and activity. [1923b, p. 17]

The ego is a hierarchically supraordinate *organizational and integrative center* having the functions of *control, selection* (the exclusion of certain trends), and *coordination* (e.g., in relation to constituent processes): "*But what distinguishes the ego from the id quite especially is a tendency to synthesis in its content*, to a combination and unification in its mental processes which are totally lacking in the id" (1933a [1932], p. 76, my emphasis). If it is to be able to perform these comprehensive synthesizing tasks, the ego must not only have access to all components of the *D-P-M* system, but also communicate with the other two agencies, the id and the superego. This is illustrated by Figure III–5, Freud's diagram (p. 78):

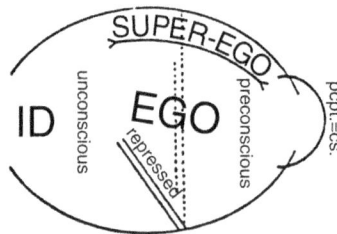

FIGURE III–5.

This drawing is Freud's attempt to integrate his first topography with his new conception of the agencies. The absence of sharp lines of demarcation shows that, whereas the id is entirely confined to the domain of (preunconscious and) unconscious processes, the processes in the ego and superego extend over the entire spectrum of possible functional states—from the unconscious via the preconscious to the conscious sphere. The ego is "a portion of the *id*"; it is what the *sensory perceptions* of the external world have made of it, with the traces these have left inside it, as well as what the *superego* demands of it; it obeys its "three tyrannical masters"—the external world, the superego, and the id (p. 77), and in so doing struggles to perform its *economic* (!) task of integrating the various influences. The ego is thus an organization of psychic process cycles *between* the id, the superego, and the system *Pcpt.-Cs.*, which, in the performance of its functions, is dependent on these various forces and influences "working *in it* [the ego] and *upon it*," and which is therefore also exposed to a huge diversity of influences and disturbances from these three sides. It is in fact only out of these incoming elements that the ego is *generated* in the first place, through the *process* of this organization (of the various elements) itself becoming *structure* (a kind of frozen action). That is to say, the functional level of the ego's process cycles at any given time leaves behind a structural precipitate that gradually develops into a functionally autonomous structural complex. It is precisely this line of descent from the id, superego, and perception that makes the ego the appropriate—or, indeed, specifically calibrated— "sense-organ of the entire apparatus" (p. 75). Let us pursue this aspect a little further:

> It starts out, as we see, *from the system Pcpt., which is its nucleus*, and begins by embracing the *Pcs.*, which is adjacent to the mnemic residues. [1923b, p. 23, my emphasis]
>
> It is easy to see that the ego is that part of the id which has been modified by the direct influence of the external world through the medium

of the *Pcpt.-Cs.*; in a sense it is an extension of the surfacedifferentiation. Moreover, the ego *seeks to bring the influence of the external world to bear upon the id and its tendencies*, and endeavours to substitute the reality principle for the pleasure principle which reigns unrestrictedly in the id. *For the ego, perception plays the part which in the id falls to the drive.* [p. 25, my emphasis]

Another factor, besides the influence of the system *Pcpt.*, seems to have played a part in bringing about the formation of the ego and its differentiation from the id. A person's own *body*, and above all its *surface*, is a place from which *both external and internal perceptions* may spring. It is seen like any other object, but to the *touch* it yields two kinds of sensations, one of which may be equivalent to an internal perception. The ego is first and foremost a bodily ego; it is not merely a surface entity, but is itself the projection of a surface. If we wish to find an anatomical analogy for it we can best identify it with the *"cortical homunculus"* of the anatomists, which stands on its head in the cortex, sticks up its heels, faces backwards and, as we know, has its speech-area on the left-hand side. [p. 25f., my emphasis except for the words "seen" and "touch"]

The ego, then, starts out from the "system *Pcpt.*, which is its nucleus"— the *P*1 system with its drive sources (the erotogenic and biogenic zones with their various sense organs), and also encompasses the "mnemic residues"—the self and object representations in *P*2. Every excitation of an erotogenic or biogenic zone, and indeed any *sensory excitation*, operates within our formalized model as a *component drive*, and for this reason Freud rightly states that, for "the ego, perception plays the part which in the id falls to the drive." Even a person's "own body, and above all its surface," in the conception developed here, is not "[a]nother factor, besides the influence of the system *Pcpt.*," but also a location within *P*1 at which "both external and internal perceptions" are excited[27]—for *P*1 can be subdivided into a number of different (exteroceptive and interoceptive) cathectic sites. In every respect, therefore, the ego, which

---

27 On this point, cf. in particular Anzieu's (1985) concept of the "skin ego."

starts out from the system *Pcpt.*, is exposed both to the "direct influence of the external world" and to the action of the internal world (and hence of the id and the superego)—or, if you will, it acts as a switching center for excitations originating there. *The ego is the central integrating and mediating station within the psychical apparatus for all kinds of conscious, preconscious, and unconscious internal and external perceptions.*[28]

---

28 Hartmann (1950) sees the ego as a "substructure of personality" determined by its *inhibiting* functions (p. 75). In his view, ego development results from three sets of factors: outer reality, the drives, and "inherited ego characteristics. Some aspects of early ego development appear in a different light if we familiarize ourselves with the thought that the ego may be *more*—and very likely is more—than a developmental *by-product of the influence of reality on instinctual drives*: that it has a partly *independent origin*—apart from these formative influences. Of course, this is not to say that the ego as a definite psychic system is inborn; it rather stresses the point that the development of this system is traceable not only to the impact of reality and of the instinctual drives, but also to a set of *factors* that can*not* be *identified* with either one of them" (p. 78f., my emphasis). According to Hartmann (1939), these factors are the so-called inborn ego apparatuses, motoricity, perception, memory, and the protective shield against stimuli, which he subsumes in the concept of the "conflict-free ego sphere": "Not every adaptation to the environment, or every learning and maturation process, is a conflict. I refer to the development *outside of conflict* of perception, intention, object comprehension, thinking, language, recall-phenomena, productivity, to the well-known phases of motor development, grasping, calling, walking, and to the maturation and learning processes implicit in all these and many others" (p. 8). "I propose that we adopt the provisional term *conflict-free ego sphere* for that ensemble of functions which at any given time exert their effects outside the region of mental conflicts" (p. 8f.). Against the background of the formalized conception of psychoanalytic theory developed in this book, it is clear that Hartmann is using the terms "conflict" and "ego" in a *phenomenological* and not a *metapsychological* sense; however, the clinical practice of psychoanalysis shows that what he calls the "conflictfree ego sphere"—perception, intention, language, thought, memory, and motoricity—may be disturbed in a variety of ways by neurotic conflicts. According to our present conception, there can be no conflict-free sphere within the psychical apparatus, because conflict, in formal terms, is nothing other than a drive-repression process, and is therefore constitutive of every psychic process. Because they are often *phenomenologically* conflict-free (i.e., because they are so experienced), Hartmann detaches various functions from drive theory; for example, he sees learning (and learning to think) as "independent biological functions which exist alongside, and in part *independent of, instinctual drives and defenses*" (p. 14, my emphasis). The main conceptual problem resulting from this view, and my central criticism of Hartmann's ego psychology, is that it assumes *separate* apparatuses, working independently of the drives, *inside* or *outside* the psychical apparatus. Such a postulate would call for a clear theorization of the way these various apparatuses are deemed to interact within a logically consistent model that would have to link "drive-related" with "non-drive-related" elements, and "conflict-free" elements with drive-defense processes; however, this has not hitherto been done—nor, in my view, is it feasible, for methodological reasons.

Now, however, Freud uses a particular image. He says that the ego "is not merely a surface entity" (which combines internal and external stimuli), "but is itself the *projection of a surface*"—and, moreover, it is a projection that is in every respect *mirror-reversed*, being equivalent to the "'cortical homunculus'... which stands on its head in the cortex, sticks up its heels, faces backwards and... has its speech-area on the left-hand side." This idea, which directly corresponds to the somatotopic projection in the homunculus, conveys some essential information about Freud's theoretical conception of the ego—for if we see the ego not only as the *perceptual surface* of the psychical apparatus, but also as the *mirror-reversed projection* of this surface (that is, if, within it, we exchange outside for inside, top for bottom, front for back, and right for left), a new perspective on the functioning of the ego is obtained.

Returning to our considerations on *Beyond the Pleasure Principle*, we can regard the projection that gives rise to the mirror reversal in the ego as a step across the boundary. Considered thus from outside, the psychical apparatus is then "seen like any other object," in the same way as the body. It could then be postulated that a part of the ego operates from a position *beyond the boundary*, and that a change of perspective—a mirror reversal of "figure and ground" (i.e., of drive and structure)—takes place here, with the result that the ego's

---

Following Hartmann, Rapaport (1967) suggests distinguishing between the *motivation* and the *cause* of behavior, and, within motivation, between drive motivations, derived drive motivations, and autonomous motivations, whose origin may also be non-drive-related. Motivations, for Rapaport, are always a cause of behavior, but not all causes are at the same time motivations—for example, curiosity, exploration, or activity are not (drive) motivations, but causes of behavior, which call for explanation by a psychoanalytic theory of consciousness and of attention cathexis that is a causal and not a motivational theory. Rapaport considers that, if the drives are seen as the sole cause of behavior, other intrapsychic factors are being overlooked as determinants or codeterminants—for example, the ego and defense. In his view, *repression* plays a *causal* and not a motivational role in the determination of behavior: "Here we encounter for the first time a mental (psychological) factor which is a cause but not a motivation of behavior. This opens up the possibility that other mental structures (e.g., ideas, associative relations, and so forth) too may likewise play a causal but nonmotivational role in determining behavior" (p. 890). Rapaport therefore advocates acknowledging the ego as a determinant of behavior *as opposed to the drives*. From this point of view, my critique of his attempt to establish a non-drive domain within metapsychology is of course the same as in the case of Hartmann: since I regard repression as a drive, the mental non-drive factor cited above can also not constitute a cause.

structural activities within the boundary (the *processes of pattern generation*) are the *moving, driving* factor for the ego beyond the boundary, whereas the originators of *movement* within the boundary (the *drives*) *limit, halt*, or *structure* the processes of pattern formation beyond the boundary. This hypothesis would imply a changeover of system functioning at a particular level or degree of complexity, of its organization. Moreover, since every changeover of system functions to a higher organizational level is accompanied by an increase in complexity and a loss, or economization, of detailed perception, and since we deem the conscious mind to perceive only a small segment of all ego processes, I contend that *this part of the ego beyond the boundary constitutes the conscious mind, or system Cs.* The system *Cs.* would then differ from the rest of the ego in that, by virtue of its type of perception from *beyond the boundary*—a type specific to it, based on the sequence of pattern formations—it registers only a limited and highly complex segment of all ego perceptions on the "within" side of the boundary; that it is separate from the mnemic systems (which would thus be situated in the part of the ego within the boundary, as in the id and superego); and that the excitatory process in it "expire[s], as it were, in the phenomenon of becoming conscious" (1920g, p. 25). Two indications tend to bear out this view.

The first concerns the assumption of a so-called *neutralized energy*. Freud (1923b) postulates that there exists "in the mind—whether in the ego or in the id—a displaceable energy, which, neutral in itself, can be added to a qualitatively differentiated erotic or destructive impulse, and augment its total cathexis" (p. 44). Throughout our examination of Freud's metapsychological concepts, we have maintained that there are to be only two basic drives, for whose energy we have used the notation (+) libido and (−) lethe. On this basis, the postulated neutralized energy could be seen as an energy wholly in balance, which would then assume the value 0; in purely arithmetical terms, however, a total cathexis could not be augmented with such a "0" value. Another way of conceiving a neutralized energy of this kind, which is to be neither libidinal nor lethic, but nevertheless capable of augmenting the cathectic amounts present, would be to assign this "neutralized energy" (this ego energy) to the domain of the ego *beyond the boundary*—to its system *Cs*. It would then, drive and structure having been interchanged, be *the expression of the structural activities of the psychical apparatus* (and every structure, after all, is subject to the principle that the switching law established in it can be denoted by the imaginary equilibrium value, or "neutrality value," of *zero*). This "neutralized energy" could then be understood as an easily displaceable "energy of consciousness," capable of cathecting id and superego processes, but also mainly ego processes, and thereby of "augmenting" their total cathexis to a level above the threshold of consciousness.

The second indication in favor of this conception of the conscious part of the ego as "beyond the boundary" is to be found in *Inhibitions, Symptoms and Anxiety* (1926d [1925]). Freud here declares the ego to be the sole locus of anxiety, and abandons his earlier view of anxiety as a direct product of the conversion of undischarged libido. His justification for this revision is the idea of a neutralized energy in the ego, which makes the theory of anxiety as a signal possible:

> Thinking is an experimental action carried out with small amounts of energy. Thus the ego *anticipates* the satisfaction of the questionable drive impulse and permits it to bring about the *reproduction* of the unpleasurable feelings at the beginning of the feared situation of danger. With this the automatism of the pleasure–unpleasure principle is brought into operation and now carries out the repression of the dangerous drive impulse. [1933a (1932), p. 89, my emphasis]

The economic advantage of this new conception of anxiety is that the psychical apparatus can now restrict "the generation of anxiety... to a mere *signal*" (ibid., p. 90, my emphasis). This becomes possible by the *anticipation* of a sequence *reproduced* in accordance with the *pattern* of an earlier situation (of helplessness). Now the reproduction of patterns consists in the cathexis of existing memory traces (patterns) and of others added by association in the cathectic process, and anticipation is possible only within these traces; in other words, this new theory of anxiety is concerned not directly with drive energies—"the question of what the material is out of which anxiety is made loses interest" (p. 85)—but with perception of the processes of pattern formation stored in the mnemic systems. Our thesis is, then, that these processes of pattern formation—these structuring activities—are the driving factor, the drive, in the domain of the conscious ego beyond the boundary. However, even if we thus follow Freud in declaring the basis of anxiety—as well as, perhaps, of all conscious perception—to be no longer the drive but the pattern formation embodied in the structures, the signal theory does not invalidate the drive theory within our formalized model. After all, if the *signal* is based on the activation of pattern formations or—however rudimentarily—corresponds to them, the configuration of such pattern formations depends on prior drive process cycles, which are therefore genuinely contained in the signals. In other words, Freud's first theory of anxiety is based on the notion of the drive "within" the boundary and his last theory of anxiety on that "beyond" the boundary. These ideas are expressed graphically in Figure III–6.

Having thus established a relationship between the ego and the three *D-P-M* systems, we can now use Freud's illustration of the psychical apparatus (Figure III–5) as the basis for a mental addition to Figure III–6, inserting the id at the bottom and the superego at the side.

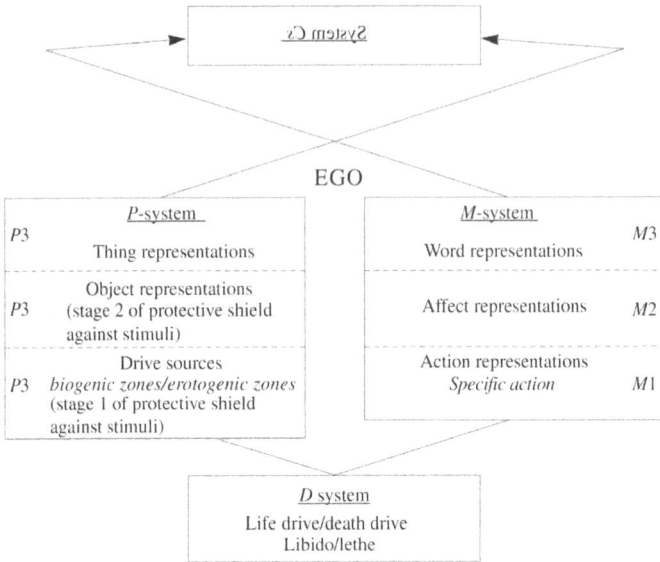

FIGURE III–6 is an isolated representation of the ego macrostructure with its possible ways of accessing the three D-P-M systems. The crossover to the system Cs. is indicated by the mirror-reversed typeface. This also shows that cathexis of the **M** system is essential to the complete crossing over of the psychic process into the system Cs. (without the **M** system, only a "half" consciousness would so to speak arise). This corresponds to Freud's requirement of linking with a word representation as a necessary condition for a psychic process to become conscious—that is, properly speaking, for a process to become **preconscious** (i.e., capable of consciousness).

Our ideas about the ego are beginning to clear, and its various relationships are gaining distinctness. We now see the ego in its strength and its weaknesses. It is entrusted with important functions. By virtue of its relation to the *perceptual system* it gives mental processes an *order in time* and submits them to *"reality-testing."* By interposing the *processes of thinking*, it secures a postponement of motor discharges and controls the *access to motility*. This last power is, to be sure, a question more of form than of fact; in the matter of action the ego's position is like that of a constitutional monarch, without whose sanction no law can be passed but who hesitates long before imposing his veto on any measure put forward by Parliament. All the experiences of life that originate from without enrich the ego; the *id*, however, is its second external world, which it strives to bring into subjection to itself. It withdraws libido from the id and transforms the object-cathexes of the id into ego-structures. With the aid of the *super-ego*, in a manner that is still obscure to us, it draws upon the experiences of past ages stored in the id. [1923b, p. 55]

Against the background of the *D-P-M* systems, we have followed Freud in developing our ideas about the ego on the basis of perception and consciousness. Consciousness, too, is a perceptual process, albeit— according to the foregoing—a specific one, consisting in a projectively mirror-reversed perception of a part of the current activities of the ego "within" the boundary. In formal terms, these ego activities consist in the combinatorial switching (synthesis, coordination, control, etc.) of all processes within the entire psychical apparatus. The ego here does not have direct access to *all* individual process cycles within the various organizational units (that is, within the id and superego subsystems), but only, in effect, uses their output for further processing; the depth of its insights into current id and superego processes, the subtlety and differentiation with which, in its action as a seismograph, it registers and processes the oscillations and movements originating there, remain open and subject to individual variation. Since Freud considers the ego to perform a mediating function of this kind between the id, the superego, and perception, the ego activities "within" the boundary are held to be partly preconscious and partly dynamically unconscious. Indeed, all important ego functions can be seen as taking place outside the conscious mind. Even reality testing, which we recognized as a referencing of pattern formations of wishful perceptions against (external) sensory perceptions, is a process whose outcome may have been settled prior to its becoming conscious. The conscious mind then perceives only the result of this comparison, although, if this process receives an increased cathexis or takes a relatively long time, it may also perceive the process of referencing as such in the form of a pattern formation that then arises. Consciousness, the psychic domain most familiar to us, is thus most certainly not the most interesting part of the ego. Seen in this way, it is little more than a lens that reproduces just a small segment of all results of the ego processes, but it is nevertheless an "active" lens, in that the system *Cs.*—like any structure—"turns upside down" (from the optical point of view) the *drive* processes *"within" the boundary* that impinge on it; or, in our terms, it subjects these processes to a further level of combinatorial switching. This enables us to conceptualize the (limited) possibilities of "conscious control" within the psychical apparatus. Since the system *Cs.* is deemed to perceive less than the preconscious and unconscious ego, the processes taking place within it may also be slowed down: brief cathexes in the ego below the *Cs.* time threshold are thereby lost to conscious perception—in other words, a certain quantity (frequency) of repeated cathexes in the ego are required in order to give rise to the perception of a pattern formation in the conscious mind. This is another reason why the system *Cs.* is assigned only limited functions of integration and control within the ego. Most of the decisive ego processes determining our internal equilibrium take place outside consciousness and before they become conscious; that is to say, we do not (directly) consciously perceive, but we *become conscious* (or not, as the case may be) of what we perceive (of what we have first perceived and processed in our preconscious and unconscious ego). After all, the third major blow to humanity inflicted by Freud's discovery "that *the ego is not master in its own house*" (1917a [1916], p. 143)—because most psychic processes take place unconsciously—also has to do partly with the internal relations between the ego and its system *Cs.*:

> What is in your mind does not coincide with what you are conscious of; *whether something is going on in your mind and whether you hear of it are two different things.* In the ordinary way, I will admit, the intelligence which reaches your consciousness is enough for your needs; and you may cherish the illusion that you learn all of the more important things. But in some cases, as in that of a drive conflict such as I have described, your intelligence service breaks down and your will then extends no further than your knowledge.

In every case, however, the news that reaches your consciousness is incomplete
and often not to be relied on. Often enough, too, it happens that you get news
of events only when they are over and when you can no longer do anything to
change them. [ibid., my emphasis]

The Relations between Id, Superego, and Ego

Now that we have reached this point, our final task is to compare the
dynamic interaction of the three macrostructures[29] as imagined by Freud with
the conception developed here and to combine them with the models used in
our investigation. Let us begin with the superego:

The considerations that led us to assume the existence of a grade in the ego,
which may be called the "ego ideal" or "super-ego," ... still hold good. [1923b,
p. 28]

Thus in the id, which is capable of being inherited, are harboured
residues of the existences of countless egos; and, *when the ego forms its*
super-ego out of the id, it may perhaps only be reviving shapes of former
egos and be bringing them to resurrection. [ibid., p. 38, my emphasis]

Thus *the super-ego is always close to the id and can act as its representative*
vis-à-vis the ego. [ibid., p. 48f., my emphasis]

As you see here, the super-ego merges into the id; indeed, as *heir*
to the Oedipus complex it has intimate relations with the id; it is more
remote than the ego from the perceptual system. [1933a [1932], p. 79,
my emphasis]

[I]t may be said of the *id* that it is totally *non-moral*, of the *ego* that
it strives to be *moral*, and of the *super-ego* that it can be *super-moral* and
then become as cruel as only the id can be. [1923b, p. 54]

---

29 Space limitations preclude a separate account of the situation with the id; for this,
reference may be made to the section on the unconscious in Part II.

The first three quotations concern the position of the superego relative to the id and the ego. In the first, Freud describes the superego as "a *grade in the ego*"; in the second, "the ego forms its super-ego out of the id"; and in the third, "the super-ego is always close to the id and can act as its representative *vis-à-vis* the ego." On the basis of the second and third quotations, the superego could just as readily be conceived as a *grade in the id*, not only formed by the ego out of the id (integrated as a self-contained system complex within its organization), but also performing an intermediary role (representing the id) *between* the id and the ego. Conversely, however, the ego in turn stands (or strives to stand) in the moral middle between the non-moral id and the supermoral superego, which can then be equated with the id in its cruelty (crudely based as it is in the drives). In this conception, then, the ego is the switch between the drive activity of the id and the drive activity (repression) of the superego. It is therefore impossible to determine unequivocally from these passages whether the superego should be reckoned more a part of the ego or of the id, and which agency is considered to perform an intermediary function between which others. On the assumption of a flexible organization within the psychical apparatus, and of in principle equal-ranking positions for all three agencies, each of them is formally in a position to dominate the other two in the higher-order super-position in the hierarchy—that is, to undertake combinatorial switching of their output (drive resultants). The situation as a whole can be visualized as a rotation or tilting of the apparatus, whereby a different macrostructure moves into the "top" position each time, thus possibly giving rise to a partial modification of the organization of excitations within the two macrostructures that have slipped "downward." We can then follow Freud in assuming that, in the normal (waking) state, the ego may be expected to be in the hierarchical superposition (for example, the ego strives to be moral— that is, not too non-moral, but also not super-moral); but the system may also undergo a changeover bringing the superego into the hierarchical super-position, where it becomes as super-moral and cruel "as only the id can be." Seen in these terms, these quotations reflect not indecision but the converse, the thrilling concept of a dynamically flexible mutual organization of the three macrostructures. Another reason for Freud's alleged "indecision" immediately emerges from a glance at his synthesizing account of the ego:

> So far we have allowed ourselves to be impressed by the merits and capabilities of the ego; it is now time to consider the other side as well. *The ego is after all only a portion of the id*, a portion that has been expediently modified by the proximity of the external world with its threat of danger. From a dynamic point of view it is weak, *it has borrowed its energy from the id*, and we are not entirely without insight into the methods—we might call them dodges—by which it extracts further amounts of energy from the id. One such method, for instance, is by *identifying itself with actual or abandoned objects. The object-cathexes spring from the drive demands of the id*. The ego has in the first instance to take note of them. But by identifying itself with the object it recommends itself to the id in place of the object and seeks to *divert the id's libido on to itself*. We have already seen that in the course of its life the ego takes into itself a large number of precipitates like this of former object-cathexes. *The ego must on the whole carry out the id's intentions*, it fulfils its task by finding out the circumstances in which those intentions can best be achieved. [1933a [1932], p. 76f., my emphasis]

The ego, then, is "only a portion of the id." Albeit modified by perception, it nevertheless remains a "portion of the id" (ibid., p. 75); it must "carry out the id's intentions," and has "borrowed its energies from the id." Freud, it seems, is here again categorically warning us not to overestimate this ego, and doing his best to disillusion us as to its possibilities. However, it is interesting to see how he describes the "methods" and "dodges" whereby the ego "extracts further amounts of energy from the id"—namely, by *identification with the id's object cathexes*, which enables the ego to "divert" the id's libido (and lethe) "on to itself" or, if you will, bind it to itself. "In the course of life," it even "takes into itself a large number of precipitates like this of former object-cathexes"—that is to say, in our terms, it converts a high proportion of the system tension emanating from the id and registered in the ego into switch tension. That is the meaning of the famous sentence "Where id was, there ego shall be" (ibid., p. 80).

We learn, then, (1) that object cathexes spring from the *id*; we know (2) that these object cathexes and identifications mold the *superego*, and that the superego was indeed "the first identification and one which took place while the ego was still feeble" (1923b, p. 48); and, in addition, we read (3) that the *ego* identifies with such object cathexes—that it "is formed to a great extent out of identifications which take the place of abandoned cathexes by the id; that the first of these identifications always behave as a special agency in the ego and stand apart from the ego in the form of a super-ego" (ibid.). It now becomes clear that everything revolves around the "*identifications* and *object-cathexes*," and that it is to these that id, superego, and ego alike relate: *all three agencies have a share*—one that is, as it were, *fiercely fought over*—in these (*mainly early*) *identifications and object cathexes, of which the self and object representations are the precipitates.*

We can now link this insight with the two main models of our formalized conception of metapsychology, the *D-P-M* configuration and that of the two tracks of drive organization, in two ways. Let us begin with the *D-P-M* model. If all three macrostructures generate their processes with the involvement of self and object representations (i.e., of the early identifications and object cathexes), *the domain where all three agencies intersect is the P2 system.* Here, in this extended region of memory traces, which is also linked (depending on the degree of organization or consciousness of a process) to the *P3* system and the three *M* systems, is the meeting place of the id, superego, and ego; here the core conflicts are fought out, subsequently undergoing only fine modulation in the "upper" (*P3–M3*) portions of the superego and ego. *P2*— or *P2–M2* (since we are assuming complete *D-P-M* process cycles)—is the location where it is decided what proportions of a subject-objectaffect representation are actualized at id, superego, and ego levels— that is, what functional state of the overall system constituted by the psychical apparatus becomes dominant. Whether a process is then preunconscious, unconscious, preconscious, or conscious depends on whether it is a drive-repression process involving all three *D-P-M* systems (which does not apply to *Pucs.* processes), and on how far "up" it reaches within the systems—that is to say, whether it involves word representations (which does not apply to the *Ucs.*), or whether it includes at least affect representations (in which case it can be both *Ucs.* and *Pcs.*, as well as, of course, *Cs.*).

So far we have left out of account the sense organs in *P*1: Freud's consideration that, for the ego, perception plays the part "which in the id falls to the drive" (ibid., p. 25) might suggest that the *P*1 system represents the (component) drive foundation of the ego, in which case we should be decoupling the ego from the *D* system. Even if Freud's descriptions indicate that a high proportion of all ego processes can substantially be conceived as a circulation of excitations within the three tiers of the *P-M* systems, our present reflections suggest that this circulation of excitations within *P-M* presupposes at least a basic excitation from the *D* system, extending initially as far as the *P*1–*M*1 systems, and then on to the *P*2–*M*2 systems. Hence the area of intersection for the three agencies of the psychical apparatus includes this bottom level of the *P-M* systems.

We stated earlier that *identifications* are deposited on the *subject track* of the psychical apparatus in the various (sub)groups—or aspects—of the *self-representations*, whereas *object cathexes* are recorded on the *object track* in the different structural complexes, called *object representations*. Since, according to Freud, the id (or parts of it, such as the repressed), as well as the superego and the ego, can be traced back to early identifications and object-cathexes, it now also follows that *all three macrostructures partake of the structures of the subject–object track.* The id comprises the most undifferentiated part of these self and object representations (the "base" of our diagram of the two tracks of drive organization, in which we placed the primal self and the selfobject). The superego contains already substantially more differentiated developmental stages of such self and object representations, which protect the foot of the subject and object tracks from structural regressions in the structural complexes of the two stages of the ego ideal and of conscience, and are combined (integrated or balanced) in the higher-order structure of

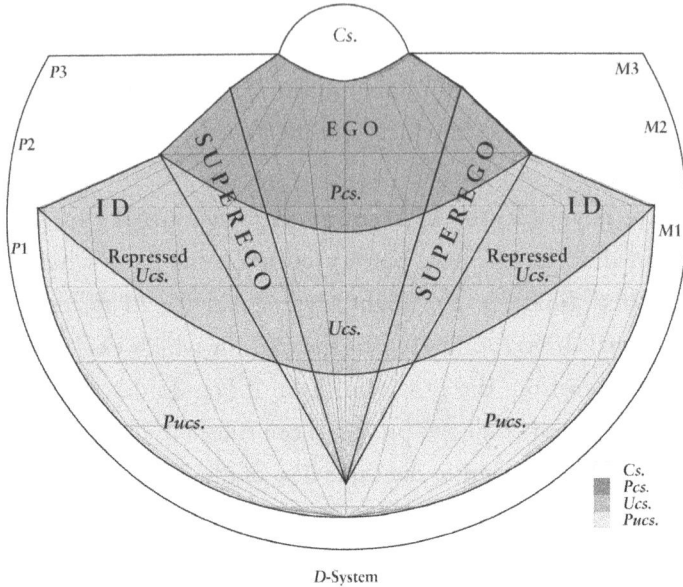

D-System

FIGURE III–7. The psychical apparatus is illustrated here *from the outside* (left) and in *cross section* (right). The diagrams combine the four different frames of reference of our formalized version of metapsychology—namely (1) the *subject–object track*; (2) the *D-P-M systems*; (3) the *systems Pucs., Ucs., Pcs., and Cs.*; and (4) the *agencies* of the *id, superego,* and *ego*. In the *external* view, the subject–object track is depicted as perpendicularly intersecting the *D-P-M* systems. This shows that each self-representation and each object representation on both tracks of drive organization represents an association (pattern formation) that draws its components from all three *D-P-M* systems. Conversely, all processes within the *D-P-M* systems can be said to be related to the subject-object tracks, or, if you will, take place on one of their self and/or object representations. This applies to every process on every functional level—that is to say, equally to the *Cs., Pcs.,* and *Ucs.* (the exceptions concerning the *Pucs.* were discussed in the section on the unconscious), as well as to the ego, superego, and id. In the *cross-sectional diagram*, the systems *Pucs., Ucs., Pcs.,* and *Cs.* (from the first topography) are also shown as perpendicularly intersecting the agencies of the id, superego, and ego (from the second topography, the structural theory) and interpenetrating. Whereas the first topographical configuration took the form of a horizontal stratification,

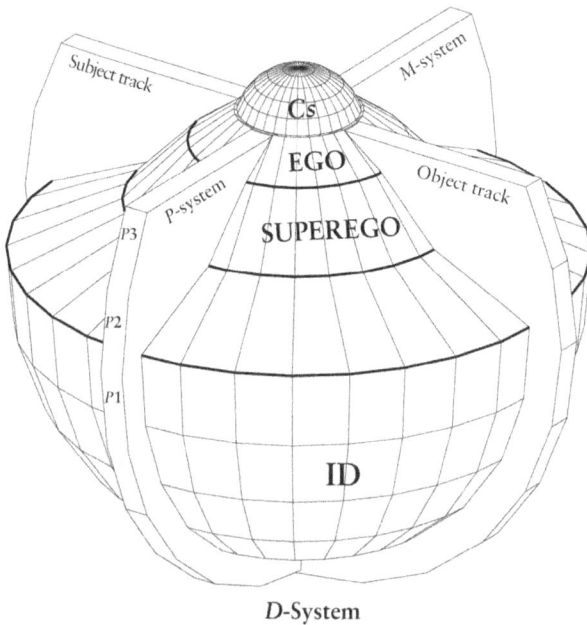

D-System

the agency-based model as it were intersects these strata vertically· as Freud tells us, the ego and superego plunge deep into the id, so that they have not only Cs. and *Pcs.* but also *Ucs.*—and possibly *Pucs.*—portions. It is important to note, too, that all three agencies participate in the bottom-most P1–M1 layer and the P2–M2 layer above it; this applies equally to the id and the *Ucs.* and to the superego, ego, and *Pcs.* It is in this area that all the psychic systems meet or intersect, and that exchanges between the macrostructures take place; conversely, access to the thing and word representations of P3–M3 remains confined to the areas of the superego and, in particular, of the ego that are closer to consciousness. (The most densely structured systems of the psychical apparatus are depicted with the darkest shading [see scale]; the white area of the Cs. indicates the "exchange of figure and ground"—the changeover from the "darkest" area "within" the boundary to the "brightest" area "beyond" it.) The diagram also makes it clear that the conscious mind and the ego occupy only a relatively limited domain within the whole—in accordance with Freud's comment on his drawing of the psychical apparatus (Figure III–5): "The space occupied by the unconscious id ought to have been incomparably greater than that of the ego or the preconscious. I must ask you to correct it in your thoughts" (1933a [1932], p. 79).

the superego. Finally, the ego, which proceeds from portions of the id and superego and develops into the most mature part of the psychical apparatus has, to the extent that it extends into the id, dynamically unconscious access to the relatively undifferentiated self and object representations of the id, and, to the extent that it is influenced by the superego, also partly unconscious and partly preconscious access to the self and object representations of the superego. Hence both of Freud's statements are true: that the superego can represent the id *vis-à-vis* the ego, and that the ego occupies the moral middle ground between the id and the superego.

We are now in a position to draw up a graphic representation of the psychical apparatus in its four dimensions (Figure III–7). Every layer, every individual structure, and every psychic unity in this diagram should be visualized as constituting a highly complex network of *combinatorial drive-repression switching operations* with differing modalities. To help us find our way around in all this complexity, the drawing is based on Freud's "onion" model and on his own diagram (Figure III–5); no attempt has been made to illustrate all the connections within the entire apparatus in complete cybernetic form.

Concluding Remarks

Turning now to our formalized model of metapsychology, one might perhaps object that matters have by no means become simpler! My response can only be: Ought we really to have expected anything simpler? Again, considering that the entire system was developed out of just a small number of assumptions applicable to all of its parts, and that each of these assumptions was in turn validated by each new concept introduced by Freud or added here, I hope that it will after all come to be felt that this formalized version of metapsychology has made it easier, even if not simpler, to find our way about within the theoretical foundations of psychoanalysis.

Freud called an approach that describes "a psychical process in its *dynamic, topographical* and *economic* aspects" a metapsychological presentation (1915e, p. 181, my emphasis). These three aspects are present and interlinked in all our considerations: the dynamic aspect in the drive-repression processes; the topographical aspect in the structural element; and the economic aspect in the switching laws of the structure. Moreover, this applies equally to the microlevel, the sublevel, and the macrolevel of the entire system. Account has also been taken of genetic and adaptive considerations, where deducible from Freud's writings.

The systems-theory approach to metapsychology adopted in this book does *not* claim to reflect "the *real* situation," or "the *true* content of metapsychology"; nor does it assert that "this is how the theory *ought* to be understood and used." It does, however, seek to demonstrate the reasons and consequences—or indeed advantages—of interpreting and conceiving metapsychology in the terms I have developed here. Nevertheless, since this formalized version can lead us to no more than a basic understanding of psychic processes, the only way to progress further is to resume our study of Freud's metapsychological writings, from whose tremendous wealth of ideas and insights we may again and again glean something new.

In the foregoing, then, the various metapsychological concepts developed in the three great theoretical advances of 1895–1905, 1910– 1915, and

1920–1925 have been transposed into a formalized, consistent model of psychoanalytic drive and structure theory. Many questions have, in my view, been answered on our path through the maze of Freud's assumptions and definitions, but many new ones can at the same time be raised. Doubtless, too, many more questions inherent in Freud's writings have remained unmentioned, or have even been overlooked. But that is surely inevitable with texts containing such a rich abundance of ideas as may be found, refound, and yet discovered not only in Freud's metapsychological works, but throughout his oeuvre.

Epilogue: Further Developments

I completed the long metapsychological journey of this book in time for its first publication in German at the centenary of the 1895 *Project for a Scientific Psychology*—that I still regard as the foundation of Freud's psychoanalytic thinking about mental functioning. And yet, it took me another ten years (Schmidt-Hellerau, 2006), before I understood how Freud's first drive theory could be meaningfully integrated into his second, how his original self-preservative drive could be part of and on the same trajectory with his death drive. At no point did I—in a kind of reverence for the founder of psychoanalysis—strive toward justifying Freud's ideas. Rather, considering that Freud's stupendous acuity of thought might have captured an important previously unseen aspect of mental life, namely a force towards death, kept me intrigued. And so too was Freud, when he mused on the death drive ten years after its introduction:

> The assumption of the existence of a drive of death or destruction has met with resistance even in analytic circles (...) To begin with it was only tentatively that I put forward the views I have developed here, but in the course of time they have gained such a hold upon me that I can no longer think in any other way. To my mind, they are far more serviceable from a theoretical standpoint than any other possible ones; they provide that simplification, without either ignoring or doing violence to the facts, for which we strive in scientific work. [1930a (1929), p. 119]

Of course, from the basic point of view of the drives' antagonism, which I deem necessary to maintain the dynamic stability of the "psychic apparatus", it seems obvious that a life drive with its potentially boundless manic exuberance had to be paired with a taming, depressive death drive. But was there a clinical necessity for this new concept? Until today, most analysts reject the notion of a death drive. I maintain that it is an intrinsic element in Freud's metapsychology and offers invaluable insights in our clinical work.

A developmental approach might be helpful (Figure E-I). Keeping Freud's postulate of a (+)life- and a (–)death drive as given primal forces, we can say that at the beginning of an infant's life everything is a matter of life or death. For instance, hunger comes up as a critical surge ("I'm starving") that would lead to death if it were not attended to and allayed. The infant screams, mother comes and nurses the baby, the hunger subsides. The "drive towards death" or death drive (hunger in this case) is stopped as it were by the object who satisfies the need, thereby preserving the infant. The repeated cycle of hunger and satiation by the nursing object is stored as a memory trace (a *D-P-M* unit). Other self-preservative needs are cared for in the same way, e.g., the need to be cleaned, warmed, held, soothed, feel comfortable and safe. All these needs are satisfied by the caring object. The memory traces of these interactions eventually come to represent what self-preservation entails. We can see: self-preservation is not inborn or primary; rather it is a learned capacity based on the experience of what is required in order to be safe and to survive. That's how the interaction with the object structures the death drive and introduces the self-preservative drive with its general goal of survival. We can say: the self-preservative drive is the structured part of the death drive; lethic energies activate the memory traces that indicate what is needed to be well and to prevent death.

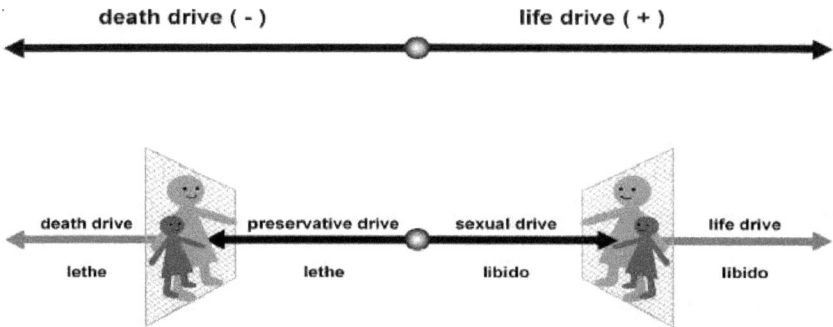

FIGURE E-I (Schmidt-Hellerau, 2018, p. 13) shows the structuring of the death and life drives by the object. The antagonism of the drives departing from a hypothetical mid-point is represented in the (+) and (-) signs; the self-preservative drive cuts as it were the death drive into half and brings the lethic strivings to a halt at the memory traces of the interaction with the caretaking object. Similarly, the object's libidinal interactions with the child structure the life drive and introduce with the erotic pleasure the sexual drive as part of the life drive.

Of course, in these early interactions, the caretaker does not only feed and soothe her baby, she also plays and sings, strokes and rocks her child and showers him with love. Her narcissistic and erotic investment in her child arouses the infant's libidinal energies and begins the structuring of his life drive. Freud captured this concurring stimulation and satisfaction of the emerging sexual drives as their initial "attachment" to the self-preservative drives. "To begin with, sexual activity attaches itself to functions serving the purpose of self-preservation and does not become independent of them until later." (Freud 1905d, p. 182) Thus, the memory traces of these interactions with the early object(s) structure both, the life and the death drives, and introduce the sexual and self-preservative drives as primal forces of the infant's mental activity.

As development continues and the self-object-unit gets differentiated into two distinct representations, the libidinal strivings aim separately at the self (narcissism) and/or at the object (object-love); and equally the lethic strivings not only activate the self (as Freud's notion of a "self-preservative drive" suggests), but also show object-preservative urges (the baby wants to feed the mother/caretaker). Since the drive, by definition, can be directed towards any object, lethic energies can invest not only in the representations of self and mother, but also of father, siblings, the dog, a stuffed animal, as well as in structures that represent certain routines, rights, or ideas (the wish to preserve is the "conservative" streak of mental activity). This variability of potential lethic objects led me to suggest dropping the prefix "self" and rather use the term *preservative drive.*

We can now see that the set-up of solid structures of good self- and object-preservation is decisive for a healthy development and the survival of the self, the object, the community, and the environment. And in line with our focus on the dynamic interaction of both drives, we understand that simultaneously the build-up of libidinally invested structures on the side of the life-drive enhances self- and object-love. As above, erotic desire will encompass interest in and love for the community, for life and all aspects of the world. In the end, mature object relations will require the cathexis of self and object with both libidinal and lethic energies, or simply stated: mature human beings will love and care for themselves, their significant others, and the world around them.

In the case of a disease (Figure E-II), a heightened need to take care of oneself and to be taken care of by others will occur. An increase in lethic strivings will reach beyond normal self-preservation and reach the representations of malady (the memory traces of previously successful interactions with the caretaker, leading to recovery, e.g., measures like resting in bed). To say it differently: the activation of the representations of malady and sorrow will hold and contain the lethic energies (thus preventing them from rushing ahead and reaching the representations of death) thereby indicating the measures necessary in order to retrieve the state of a healthy self and to avoid the potential of death.

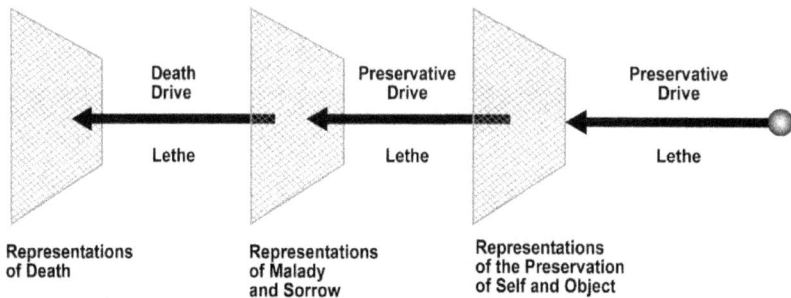

Figure E-II (Schmidt-Hellerau, 2018, p. 401) shows the group of structures that represent different states of the self and the object: a first tier assembles everything that is required to stay healthy and safe; the second tier represents the group of self and object states in (physical) malady and (emotional) sorrow; the third and final tier represents self and object as deadened (traumatized) or dead.

However, if the preservative structures of the first and second tier are not solidly enough established—e.g., if a person cannot take well enough care of herself or her objects—the lethic drives' surge may continuously reach even beyond the realm of disease into the area of threatening death (Figure E-II). A lack of well-structured self-and/or object-preservation is obvious e.g., in addictions or carelessness and risky behaviors as well as in the neglect of dependent others. On the other hand, it may also present itself as an anxious sense of never being safe enough, even as hypochondriacal preoccupation. In short: both, a lack of as well as an excessive need for self-care can indicate fragile or insufficiently well-established preservative structures.

Finally, in the case of trauma (Figure E-III) a breach of structures may disrupt previously normal drive activity, and leave the self or the object represented as dead(ened). Then therapeutic work has to slowly build up new structures, representing the helpless, injured, and hurting self in need of protections as well as a vision of a self that can be safe and well-preserved.

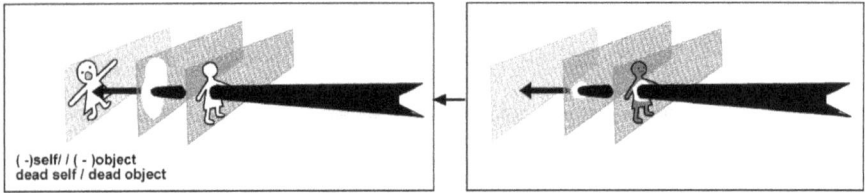

(-)self/ / (-)object
dead self / dead object

Figure E-III (Schmidt-Hellerau, 2018, p. 404) tries to depict how the onslaught of a traumatic impact can punch through the containing structures of self- and object preservation as well as those of malady and sorrow, leaving the self and/ or object represented as dead(end).

Up to now, we have focused on the two primal drives and the structuring effects of self-object-interactions. Within the psychic apparatus the drives' function is to cathect the relevant representations with drive energy. Freud had "discovered that every drive tries to make itself effective by activating ideas that are in keeping with its aims." (1910i, p. 213). Even though he distinguished between the pertinent ideas of the drives, he remained undetermined and even skeptical that they could also be "distinguished by different qualities" (1915c, p. 123). However, a libidinal investment of e.g., the representation "mother" seems to arouse different feelings (erotic, exciting) than a lethic investment (caring, soothing).

Therefore, I propose a clear distinction with regard to the *qualities* of the feeling states aroused by both drives' energies:

Libido promotes alertness, lust, love, liveliness, warmth, joy, lightness, brightness, colourfulness, mobility.... and reaches in the extreme up to mania.

Lethe by contrast tends to oblivion, darkness, slowing down, silencing, emptiness, fatigue, coldness, sorrow, grief and worry.... and in the extreme to depression and catatonic stupor (Figure E-IV).

With this conception we can again conclude that a well-balanced mix of both drives' energies corresponds to the dynamic stability of the system. And any one-sided pre-dominance may give the clinician an idea of the main general trajectory a patient operates on and struggles with.

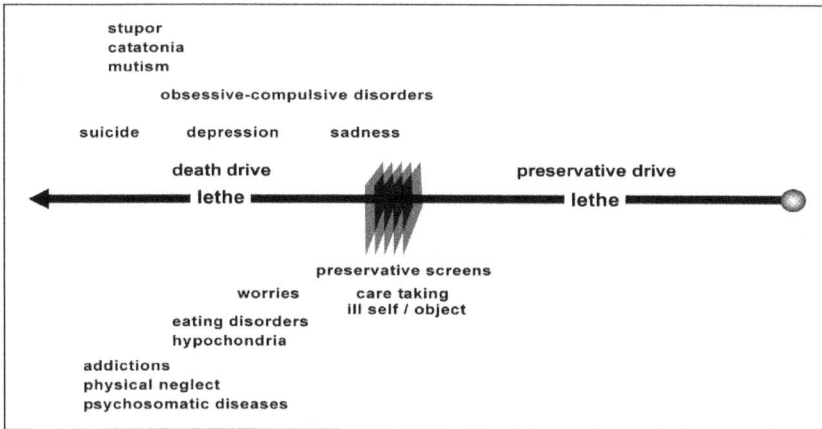

Figure E-IV assorts a number of clinical appearances on the side of the lethic strivings with increasing intensity.

From his early *Project of a Scientific Psychology* on, Freud thought of drive energy as effective in varying *quantities*. As we have seen in the Introduction to this book, this notion became thoroughly disputed as unscientific. Having previously responded to the various critiques on drive theory (Schmidt-Hellerau, 2005), here I want to simply argue for the unavoidability of considering quantities of drive energy. Of course, we cannot determine, measure, or count such quantities. But we constantly think of, feel, and argue by using quantitative terms like more, less, enough, too much, or too little etc. We distinguish between feeling slightly bothered, very angry, or absolutely furious, between being a bit amused, very joyous, or totally enthusiastic; we can feel energized or lacking energy, feel strong or weak etc. All these statements refer to quantitative differences—in metapsychological terms they refer to the intensity of drive arousal and investments.

This finally brings us to reconsider the concept of aggression. Since I didn't accept Freud's 1920 notion of aggression as the representative of the death drive, how would aggression fit in his "psychic apparatus"? In 1909 Freud rejected the idea of "the existence of a special aggressive drive alongside of the familiar drives of self-preservation and of sex" and suggested to leave "each drive

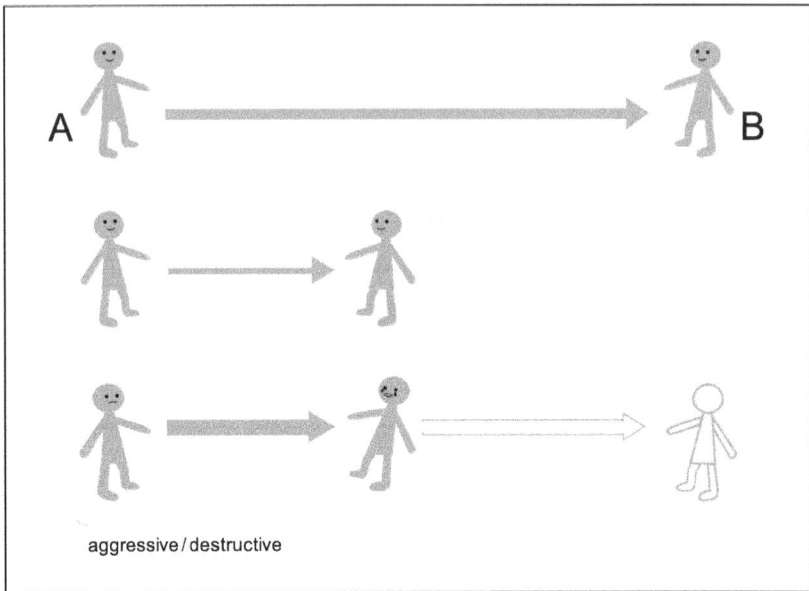

aggressive / destructive

Figure E-V shows in the upper and middle row A applying the appropriate amount of energy to reach B: more is needed when B is further away (distant) than when he is close (attuned). The third row shows a mis-adjustment (or transference): B is perceived far away even though he is close by; A applies as much energy as would be needed to reach a distant object B.

its own power of becoming aggressive" (Freud, 1909, p. 140f.) This idea still makes sense. If by definition a drive strives to reach its goal, then any obstacle or intervention, real or imagined, must lead to an intensification of the drive's effort; that means, *more* energy quantities will be activated in order to reach the object of satisfaction (Figure E-V). As I've elaborated on elsewhere (Schmidt-Hellerau, 2002a, 2023), the reach for every goal will require a specific quantity of drive energy (depending on the object's substance, distance, state etc.). The capacity to anticipate the right amount of drive energy, necessary to get to the object and reach the drive's goal, is developed over time. The structures' function is to modulate and fine-tune the right amount of drive energy, a computational process susceptible to calculus errors and the consequences of (neurotic) misinterpretations. But whether objectively adequate or psychically distorted, drive arousal asserts itself, and its (quantitative) intensification is what we call aggression. Hence aggression is not a primal drive, it is not a drive on its own. Aggression is either a reaction to an experienced interference with the goals of the life/sexual drives or the goals of the death/preservative drives or a combination of both. With the quantitative enhancement of energy, the drives assert themselves in their strivings until they have reached their objects and goals.

In the years since the first publication of this book, I have continued to think about the concept of drives and structures in a way that proved to be useful in my clinical work. In this epilogue I've tried to summarize what I have come to understand on my way. But of course, there will always be more to think about...

Brookline, August 2024

References

Alexander, F. (1921). Metapsychologische Betrachtungen. *Internationale Zeitschrift für Psychoanalyse* 7:270–285.

———— (1929). Strafbedürfnis und Todestrieb. *Internationale Zeitschrift für Psychoanalyse* 15:231–245.

Amacher, P. (1965). Freud's neurological education and its influence on psychoanalytic theory. *Psychological Issues* 4, Monograph 16.

Anzieu, D. (1985). *The Skin Ego. A Psychoanalytic Approach to the Self*, trans. C. Turner. New Haven, CT: Yale University Press, 1989.

Applegarth, A. (1971). Comments on aspects of the theory of psychic energy. *Journal of the American Psychoanalytic Association* 19:379–416.

Arlow, J. A. (1975). The structural hypothesis—theoretical considerations. *Psychoanalytic Quarterly* 44:509–525.

———— (1991). Summary comments: panel on psychic structure. In *The Concept of Psychic Structure in Psychoanalysis*, ed. T. Shapiro, pp. 283–294. Madison, CT: International Universities Press.

Arnold, M. B. (1984). *Memory and Brain*. Hillsdale, NJ: Lawrence Erlbaum.

Ashby, W. R. (1960). *Design for a Brain: The Origin of Adaptive Behavior*. New York: Wiley.

Basch, M. F. (1975). Perception, consciousness, and Freud's "Project." *Annual of Psychoanalysis* 3:3–19.

Beres, D. (1965). Structure and function in psycho-analysis. *International Journal of Psycho-Analysis* 46:53–63.

Beres, D., and Joseph, E. D. (1970). The concept of mental representation in psychoanalysis. *International Journal of Psycho-Analysis* 51:1–9.

Bernfeld, S. (1935). Über die Einteilung der Triebe. *Imago* 21:125–142. Bernfeld, S., and Feitelberg, S. (1930). Der Entropiesatz und der Todestrieb. *Imago* 16:187–206.

Bibring, E. (1941). The development and problems of the theory of the instincts. *International Journal of Psycho-Analysis* 22:102–130.

Bion, W. R. (1957). Differentiation of the psychotic from the non-psychotic personalities. *International Journal of Psycho-Analysis* 38:266–275.

——— (1959). Attacks on linking. *International Journal of Psycho-Analysis* 40:308–315.

——— (1962). *Learning from Experience*. London: Heinemann.

Bowlby, J. (1958). The nature of the child's tie to his mother. *International Journal of Psycho-Analysis* 39:350–373.

——— (1960). Separation anxiety. *International Journal of Psycho-Analysis* 41:89–113.

——— (1969). *Attachment and Loss. Volume 1, Attachment*. London: Hogarth.

Braitenberg, V. (1994). Das Hirn ist in der Seele. Dem Zentralorgan auf der Spur—Abenteuer Gehirnforschung. *NZZ Folio* 3:6–12.

Brenner, C. (1974a). On the nature and development of affects: a unified theory. *Psychoanalytic Quarterly* 43:532–557.

——— (1974b). Depression, anxiety and affect theory. *International Journal of Psycho-Analysis* 55:25–32.

——— (1982). *The Mind in Conflict*. New York: International Universities Press.

Brierley, M. (1937). Affects in theory and practice. *International Journal of Psycho-Analysis* 18:256–268.

——— (1944). Notes on metapsychology as process theory. *International Journal of Psycho-Analysis* 25:97–107.

Brun, R. (1952). Der biologische Charakter der Psychoanalyse Freuds. *Psyche*, 5:561–580.

——— (1953). Über Freuds Hypothese vom Todestrieb. Eine kritische Untersuchung. *Psyche* 7:81–111.

Busch, F. (1999). *Rethinking Clinical Technique*. Northvale, NJ: Jason Aronson.

Cambor, C. G. (1970). Präödipale Faktoren der Überich-Entwicklung. *Psyche* 24:116–128.

Campbell (1905). Reference not available.

Changeux, J.-P. (1983). *L'homme neuronal*. Paris: Fayard.

Chasseguet-Smirgel, J. (1976). Some thoughts on the ego ideal—a contribution to the study of the "illness of ideality." *Psychoanalytic Quarterly* 45:345–373.

———— (1984). *Creativity and Perversion*. New York: Norton.

Compton, A. (1981). On the psychoanalytic theory of instinctual drives. *Psychoanalytic Quarterly* 50:190–392 (I. The beginnings of Freud's drive theory: 190–218. II. The sexual drives and the ego drives: 219–237. III. The complications of libido and narcissism: 345–362. IV. Instinctual drives and the ego-id-superego model: 363–392).

Crutchfield, J. P., Farmer, J. D., Packard, N. H., and Shaw, R. S. (1989). Chaos. In *Chaos und Fraktale*. Heidelberg: Spektrum der Wissenschaft, pp. 8–20.

Damson, W. (1974). Book review: Peterfreund, E., Information, Systems, and Psychoanalysis. An Evolutionary Biological Approach to Psychoanalytic Theory. *Psyche* 28:269–274.

Danneberg, E. (1968). Dynamische und ökonomische Aspekte der Entwicklung des Über-Ichs. *Psyche* 22:365–383.

Detrick, D. W., and Detrick, P. (1989). *Self Psychology. Comparisons and Contrasts*. Hillsdale, NJ: Analytic Press.

Dollard, J., Doob, L. W., Miller, N. E., et al. (1939). *Frustration and Aggression*. New Haven, CT: Yale University Press.

Donnet, J. L., and Green, A. (1973). *L'Enfant de ça. Psychanalyse d'un entretien: la psychose blanche*. Paris: Minuit.

Dornes, M. (1993). *Der kompetente Säugling. Die präverbale Entwicklung des Menschen*. Frankfurt: Fischer.

Drews, S., and Brecht, K. (1982). *Psychoanalytische Ich-Psychologie. Grundlagen und Entwicklung*. Frankfurt: Suhrkamp.

Edelheit, H. (1976). Complementarity as a rule in psychological research. Jackson, Freud and the mind/body problem. *International Journal of PsychoAnalysis* 57:23–29.

Etchegoyen, R. H. (1991). "On Narcissism: An Introduction": text and context. In *Freud's "On Narcissism: An Introduction,"* ed. J. Sandler, E. S. Person, and P. Fonagy, pp. 54–74. New Haven, CT: Yale University Press. Federn, P. (1930). Die Wirklichkeit des Todestriebes. Zu Freuds "Unbehagen in der Kultur." *Hippokrates* 3 (1931), Almanach der Psychoanalyse:68–97.

Feigl, H. (1958). The 'mental' and the 'physical.' In *Minnesota Studies in the Philosophy of Science*, ed. H. Feigl, M. Scriven, and G. Maxwell, pp. 370–497. Minneapolis: University of Minnesota Press.

Fenichel, O. (1935). Zur Kritik des Todestriebes. *Imago* 21:458–466.

Freud, A. (1936). *The Ego and the Mechanisms of Defence.* London: Hogarth, 1976.

——— (1972). Comments on Aggression. *International Journal of PsychoAnalysis* 53:317–333.

Freud, S. (1891b). *On Aphasia: A Critical Study*, ed. and trans. E. Stengel. London: Imago, 1953.

——— (1894a). The neuro-psychoses of defence. *Standard Edition*, 3.

——— (1895d [1893–1895]) (with J. Breuer). Studies on hysteria. *Standard Edition*, 2. ("Theoretical," by J. Breuer.)

——— (1900a). The interpretation of dreams. *Standard Edition*, 4–5.

——— (1901b). The psychopathology of everyday life. *Standard Edition*, 6.

——— (1905c). Jokes and their relation to the unconscious. *Standard Edition*, 8.

——— (1905d). Three essays on the theory of sexuality. *Standard Edition*, 7.

——— (1906c). Psycho-analysis and the establishment of the facts in legal proceedings. *Standard Edition*, 9.

——— (1908a). Hysterical phantasies and their relation to bisexuality. *Standard Edition*, 9.

——— (1909b). Analysis of a phobia in a five-year-old boy ("Little Hans"). *Standard Edition*, 10.

——— (1910c). Leonardo da Vinci and a memory of his childhood. *Standard Edition*, 11.

————— (1910i). The psycho-analytic view of psychogenic disturbance of vision. *Standard Edition*, 11.

————— (1911b). Formulations on the two principles of mental functioning. *Standard Edition*, 12.

————— (1911c [1910]). Psycho-analytic notes on an autobiographical account of a case of paranoia (dementia paranoides). *Standard Edition*, 12.

————— (1912g). A note on the unconscious in psycho-analysis. *Standard Edition*, 12.

————— (1912–1913a). Totem and taboo. *Standard Edition*, 13.

————— (1913j). The claims of psycho-analysis to scientific interest. *Standard Edition*, 13.

————— (1914c). On narcissism: an introduction. *Standard Edition*, 14.

————— (1914d). On the history of the psycho-analytic movement. *Standard Edition*, 14.

————— (1915b). Thoughts for the times on war and death. *Standard Edition*, 14.

————— (1915c). Instincts and their vicissitudes. *Standard Edition*, 14.

————— (1915d). Repression. *Standard Edition*, 14.

————— (1915e). The unconscious. *Standard Edition*, 14.

————— (1916a [1915]). On transience. *Standard Edition*, 14.

————— (1916–1917a [1915–17]). Introductory lectures on psycho-analysis. *Standard Edition*, 15–16.

————— (1916–1917f [1915]). A metapsychological supplement to the theory of dreams. *Standard Edition*, 14.

————— (1916–1917g [1915]). Mourning and melancholia. *Standard Edition*, 14.

————— (1917a [1916]). A difficulty in the path of psycho-analysis. *Standard Edition*, 17.

————— (1920g). Beyond the pleasure principle. *Standard Edition*, 18.

————— (1921c). Group psychology and the analysis of the ego. *Standard Edition*, 18.

————— (1923a [1922]). Two encyclopaedia articles. *Standard Edition*, 18.

————— (1923b). The ego and the id. *Standard Edition*, 19.

————— (1924c). The economic problem of masochism. *Standard Edition*, 19.

————— (1925a [1924]). A note upon the "mystic writing-pad." *Standard Edition*, 19.

————— (1925d [1924]). An autobiographical study. *Standard Edition*, 20.

————— (1925e [1924]). The resistances to psycho-analysis. *Standard Edition*, 19.

————— (1925h). Negation. *Standard Edition*, 19.

————— (1926d [1925]). Inhibitions, symptoms and anxiety. *Standard Edition*, 20.

————— (1930a [1929]). Civilization and its discontents. *Standard Edition*, 21.

————— (1933a [1932]). New introductory lectures on psycho-analysis. *Standard Edition*, 22.

————— (1933b [1932]). Why war? *Standard Edition*, 22.

————— (1937c). Analysis terminable and interminable. *Standard Edition*, 23.

————— (1940a [1938]). An outline of psycho-analysis. *Standard Edition*, 23.

————— (1950c/1950a [1895]). A project for a scientific psychology. *Standard Edition*, 1.

————— (1985a [1915]). *A Phylogenetic Fantasy: Overview of the Transference Neuroses*, ed. and with an essay by Ilse Grubrich-Simitis, trans. A. Hoffer and P. T. Hoffer. Cambridge, MA, and London: Harvard University Press, 1987.

————— (1985c [1887–1904]). *The Complete Letters of Sigmund Freud to Wilhelm Fliess 1887–1904*, trans. and ed. J. M. Masson. Cambridge, MA: Belknap Press of Harvard University Press.

Friedlander, K. (1940). On the "longing to die." *International Journal of PsychoAnalysis* 21:416–426.

Friedman, L. (1972). Difficulties of a computer model of the mind. A critical review of Emanuel Peterfreund's book *Information, Systems, and Psychoanalysis. An Evolutionary Biological Approach to Psychoanalytic Theory. International Journal of Psycho-Analysis* 53:547–554.

Gill, M. (1963). Topography and systems in psychoanalytic theory. *Psychological Issues* 3, Monograph 10.

————— (1976). Metapsychology is not psychology. In *Psychology Versus Metapsychology. Psychoanalytic Essays in Memory of George S. Klein*, ed. M. Gill and P. S. Holzman, pp. 71–105, *Psychological Issues* 9, Monograph 36. New York: International Universities Press.

———— (1977). Psychic energy reconsidered—discussion. *Journal of the American Psychoanalytic Association* 25:581–597.

———— (1988). Metapsychology revisited. *Annual of Psychoanalysis* 16: 35–48.

Gillespie, W. H. (1971). Aggression and instinct theory. *International Journal of Psycho-Analysis* 52:155–160.

Glover, E. (1932). A psycho-analytic approach to the classification of mental disorders. *Journal of Mental Science.* (Volume unavailable.)

———— (1956). *On the Early Development of Mind.* London: Imago.

Goldberg, A. (1991). Changing psychic structure through treatment: from empathy to self-reflection. In *The Concept of Psychic Structure in Psychoanalysis*, ed. T. Shapiro, pp. 211–224. Madison, CT: International Universities Press.

Graber, H. G. (1953). Entwurf zu einem Ausbau der Trieblehre Freuds. *Psyche* 7:365–379.

Green, A. (1973). *Le discours vivant. La conception psychanalytique de l'affect.* Paris: Presses Universitaires de France.

———— (1980). The dead mother, trans. K. Aubertin. In *On Private Madness*, pp. 142–173. Madison, CT: International Universities Press, 1986.

———— (1983). *Narcissisme de vie, narcissisme de mort.* Paris: Minuit.

———— (1986). Pulsion de mort, narcissisme négatif, fonction désobjectalisante. In *La Pulsion de Mort. Premier Symposium de la Fédération Européénne de Psychanalyse*, pp. 49–60. Paris: Presses Universitaires de France.

———— (1993). *Le travail du négatif.* Paris: Minuit.

Greenspan, S. I. (1991). The development of the ego. Insights from clinical work with infants and young children. In *The Concept of Psychic Structure in Psychoanalysis*, ed. T. Shapiro, pp. 3–56. Madison, CT: International Universities Press.

Grossmann, S. (1989). Selbstähnlichkeit: Das Strukturgesetz im und vor dem Chaos. In W. Gerok (1990), *Ordnung und Chaos in der unbelebten und belebten Natur*, pp. 101–122. Stuttgart: Wissenschaftliche Verlagsgesellschaft.

Grubrich-Simitis, I. (1988). Trauma or drive—drive and trauma—a reading of Sigmund Freud's phylogenetic fantasy of 1915. *Psychoanalytic Study of the Child* 43:3–32.

———— (1993). *Back to Freud's Texts. Making Silent Documents Speak*, trans. P. Slotkin. New Haven, CT: Yale University Press, 1996.

Grünbaum, A. (1988). *Die Grundlagen der Psychoanalyse. Eine philosophische Kritik.* Stuttgart: Reclam.

Grunberger, B. (1971). *Narcissism: Psychoanalytic Essays*, trans. J. S. Diamanti. New York: International Universities Press, 1979.

———— (1974). Gedanken zum frühen Über-Ich. *Psyche* 28:508–529.

———— (1988a). *Narziss und Anubis. Die Psychoanalyse jenseits der Triebtheorie.* Band 1. Munich: Verlag Internationale Psychoanalyse.

———— (1988b). *Narziss und Anubis. Die Psychoanalyse jenseits der Triebtheorie.* Band 2. Munich: Verlag Internationale Psychoanalyse.

Guttman, S. A. (1973). Psychoanalysis and science: the concept of structure. *Annual of Psychoanalysis* 1:73–81.

Haken, H., and Haken-Krell, M. (1989). *Die Entstehung von biologischer Information und Ordnung.* Darmstadt: Wissenschaftliche Buchgesellschaft.

Hartmann, H. (1939). *Ego Psychology and the Problem of Adaptation*, trans. D. Rapaport. London: Imago, 1958.

———— (1948). Comments on the psychoanalytic theory of instinctual drives. *Psychoanalytic Quarterly* 17:368–388.

———— (1950). Comments on the psychoanalytic theory of the ego. *Psychoanalytic Study of the Child* 5:74–96.

———— (1952). The mutual influences in the development of ego and id. *Psychoanalytic Study of the Child* 7:9–30.

Hartmann, H., Kris, E., and Loewenstein, R. (1946). Comments on the formation of psychic structure. *Psychoanalytic Study of the Child* 2:11–38.

———— (1949). Notes on the theory of aggression. *Psychoanalytic Study of the Child* 3/4:9–36.

Hebb, D. O. (1955). Drives and the C.N.S. (conceptual nervous system). *Psychological Review* 62:243–254.

Hinshelwood, R. D. (1989). *A Dictionary of Kleinian Thought.* London: Free Association Books.

Holt, R. (1965). A review of some of Freud's biological assumptions and their influence on his theories. In *Psychoanalysis and Current Biological Thought*, ed. N. S. Greenfield and W. C. Lewis, pp. 93–124. Madison, Milwaukee: University of Wisconsin Press.

———— (1976). Drive or wish? A reconsideration of the psychoanalytic theory of motivation. In *Psychology Versus Metapsychology. Psychoanalytic Essays in Memory of George S. Klein*, ed. M. Gill and P. S. Holzman, pp. 158–197. *Psychological Issues* 9, Monograph 36. New York: International Universities Press.

———— (1985). The current status of psychoanalytic theory. *Psychoanalytic Psychology* 2:289–315.

Jacobson, E. (1964). *The Self and the Object World*. New York: International Universities Press.

———— (1971). *Depression. Comparative Studies of Normal, Neurotic, and Psychotic Conditions*. New York: International Universities Press.

Jones, E. (1953–1957). *The Life and Work of Sigmund Freud* (1953: Volume 1; 1955: Volume 2; 1957: Volume 3). New York: Basic Books.

Joseph, B. (1975). The patient who is difficult to reach. In *Tactics and Techniques in Psychoanalytic Therapy, Vol. 2: Countertransference*, ed. P. L. Giovacchini. New York: Jason Aronson.

———— (1982). Addiction to near-death. *International Journal of Psycho-Analysis* 63:449–456.

Kaplan-Solms, K., and Solms, M. (2000). *Clinical Studies in NeuroPsychoanalysis. Introduction to a Depth Neuropsychology*. London: Karnac. Kernberg, O. F. (1969). A contribution to the ego-psychological critique of the Kleinian school. *International Journal of Psycho-Analysis* 50:317–333.

———— (1976). *Object Relations Theory and Clinical Psychoanalysis*. New York: Jason Aronson.

———— (1980, 1983). *Internal World and External Reality. Object Relations Theory Applied*. London: Mark Paterson, 1985.

———— (1984). *Severe Personality Disorders*. New Haven, CT: Yale University Press.

———— (1991a). Sexual excitement and rage: building blocks of the drives. *Sigmund Freud House Bulletin*, 15(1):3–38, Vienna.

———— (1991b). A contemporary reading of "On Narcissism." In *Freud's "On Narcissism: An Introduction,"* ed. J. Sandler, E. S. Person, and P. Fonagy, pp. 131–148. New Haven, CT: Yale University Press.

———— (1993). The current status of psychoanalysis. *Journal of the American Psychoanalytic Association* 41:45–62.

———— (1993a). Sadomasochismus, sexuelle Erregung und Perversion. *Zeitschrift für psychoanalytische Theorie und Praxis* 8:319–341.

———— (1993b). Psychoanalytische Objektbeziehungstheorien. In *Schlüsselbegriffe der Psychoanalyse*, ed. W. Mertens. Stuttgart: Verlag Internationale Psychoanalyse.

———— (1996). Thirty methods to destroy the creativity of psychoanalytic candidates. *International Journal of Psycho-Analysis* 77:1031–1040.

King, P., and Steiner, R. (1991). *The Freud–Klein Controversies 1941–1945*. London: Tavistock/Routledge.

Kirk, G. S. (1974). *The Nature of Greek Myths*. Harmondsworth: Penguin, 1976.

Klein, G. S. (1973). Two theories or one? *Bulletin of the Menninger Clinic* 37:102–132.

———— (1976). *Psychoanalytic Theory. An Exploration of Essentials*. New York: International Universities Press.

Klein, M. (1933). The early development of conscience in the child. In *PsychoAnalysis Today*, ed. S. Lorand, pp. 149–162. New York: Covici-Friede.

———— (1946). Notes on some schizoid mechanisms. *International Journal of Psycho-Analysis* 27:99–110.

———— (1948). A contribution to the theory of anxiety and guilt. *International Journal of Psycho-Analysis* 29:114–123.

Klein, M. H. (1989). Throwing out the baby with the bathwater: a historical analysis of the antimetapsychology movement. *Psychoanalysis and Contemporary Thought* 12:565–598.

Kohut, H. (1971). *The Analysis of the Self. A Systematic Approach to the Psychoanalytic Treatment of Narcissistic Personality Disorders.* New York: International Universities Press.

———— (1975). *Die Zukunft der Psychoanalyse. Aufsätze zu allgemeinen Themen und zur Psychologie des Selbst.* Frankfurt: Suhrkamp.

———— (1977). *The Restoration of the Self.* New York: International Universities Press.

Koukkou-Lehmann, M. (1987). *Hirnmechanismen normalen und schizophrenen Denkens.* Berlin: Springer Verlag.

Kutter, P. (1989). Nachwort und abschliessende Evaluierung. In E. S. Wolf, P. Ornstein, A. Ornstein, et al., *Selbstpsychologie. Weiterentwicklungen nach Heinz Kohut*, pp. 125–133. Munich: Verlag Internationale Psychoanalyse. Lampl-De Groot, J. (1956). The theory of instinctual drives. *International Journal of Psycho-Analysis* 37:354–359.

———— (1962). Ego ideal and superego. *Psychoanalytic Study of the Child* 17:94–106.

Langs, R. (1989). Models, theory, and research strategies: toward the evolution of new paradigms. *Psychoanalytic Inquiry* 9:305–331.

Laplanche, J. (1970). *Vie et mort en psychanalyse.* Paris: Flammarion.

———— (1986). La pulsion de mort dans la théorie de la pulsion sexuelle. In *La pulsion de mort.* Paris: Presses Universitaires de France.

Laplanche, J., and Pontalis, J.-B. (1967). *The Language of Psycho-Analysis*, trans. D. Nicholson-Smith. London: Hogarth, 1983.

Lester, E. P. (1982). New directions in affect theory. *Journal of the American Psychoanalytic Association* 30:197–211.

Lichtenberg, J. D. (1991). A theory of motivational-functional systems as psychic structures. In *The Concept of Psychic Structure in Psychoanalysis*, ed. T. Shapiro, pp. 283–294. Madison, CT: International Universities Press.

Loewald, H. W. (1980). On motivation and instinct theory. In *Papers on Psychoanalysis.* New Haven, CT: Yale University Press.

Loewenstein, R. (1940). The vital or somatic instincts. *International Journal of Psycho-Analysis* 21:377–400.

Löfgren, B. L. (1968). Psychoanalytic theory of affects. *Journal of the American Psychoanalytic Association* 16:638–650.

Lorenz, K. (1981). *The Foundations of Ethology*. New York: Springer. Lorenzer, A. (1970). *Sprachzerstörung und Rekonstruktion. Vorarbeiten zu einer Metatheorie der Psychoanalyse*. Frankfurt: Suhrkamp.

Luria, A. R. (1973). *The Working Brain. An Introduction to Neuropsychology*, trans. B. Haigh. New York: Basic Books.

Mandelbrot, B. (1991). Fractals—a geometry of nature. In *The New Scientist Guide to Chaos*, ed. N. Hall, pp. 122–135. London: Penguin.

Martienssen, W. (1989). Gesetz und Zufall in der Natur. In W. Gerok (1990), *Ordnung und Chaos in der unbelebten und belebten Natur*, pp. 77–99. Stuttgart: Wissenschaftliche Verlagsgesellschaft.

Meissner, W. W. (1981). Metapsychology—who needs it? *Journal of the American Psychoanalytic Association* 29:921–938.

Mertens, W. (1981). Krise der psychoanalytischen Theorie? In *Neue Perspektiven der Psychoanalyse*, ed. W. Mertens, pp. 7–83. Stuttgart: Kohlhammer.

Miller, J. G. (1965). Living systems. *Behavioral Science* 10:337–441.

Modell, A. (1991). Changing psychic structure through treatment. Preconditions for the resolution of the transference. In *The Concept of Psychic Structure in Psychoanalysis*, ed. T. Shapiro, pp. 225–240. Madison, CT: International Universities Press.

Moser, U. (1964). Zur Abwehrlehre. Das Verhältnis von Verdrängung und Projektion. *Jahrbuch der Psychoanalyse* 3:56–85.

——— (1989). Wozu eine Theorie in der Psychoanalyse? Gedanken zum Problem der "Metapsychologie." *Zeitschrift für psychoanalytische Theorie und Praxis* 4:154–174.

Nagera, H., ed. (1977). *Psychoanalytische Grundbegriffe. Eine Einführung in Sigmund Freuds Terminologie und Theoriebildung*. Frankfurt: Fischer.

Noy, P. (1977). Metapsychology as a multimodel system. *International Review of Psycho-Analysis* 4:1–12.

Opatow, B. (1999). Affect and the integration problem of mind and brain. *NeuroPsychoanalysis* 1:97–110.

Ornstein, P. H. (1989). Die Entwicklung der Selbstpsychologie. In E. S. Wolf, P. Ornstein, A. Ornstein, et al., *Selbstpsychologie. Weiterentwicklungen nach Heinz Kohut*, pp. 27–42. Munich: Verlag Internationale Psychoanalyse. Panksepp, J. (1999). Emotions as viewed by psychoanalysis and neuroscience: an exercise in consilience. *Neuro-Psychoanalysis* 1:15–39; commentaries 40–69; response to commentaries by J. Panksepp 69–89.

Parens, H. (1973). Aggression: a reconsideration. *Journal of the American Psychoanalytic Association* 21:34–60.

Pasche, F. (1993). Des pulsions et de leur sujétion. *Cahiers*. Centre de Psychanalyse et de Psychothérapie 26, Les Pulsions II:3–10.

Peitgen, H.-O. (1989). Fraktale: Computerexperimente (ent)zaubern komplexe Strukturen. In *Ordnung und Chaos in der unbelebten und belebten Natur*, ed. W. Gerok, pp. 123–152. Stuttgart: Wissenschaftliche Verlagsgesellschaft, 1990.

Penrose, L. S. (1931). Freud's theory of instinct and other psychobiological theories. *International Journal of Psycho-Analysis* 12:87–97.

Peterfreund, E. (1971). Information, systems, and psychoanalysis. An evolutionary biological approach to psychoanalytic theory. *Psychological Issues* 7, Monograph 25/26. New York: International Universities Press.

———— (1975). The need for a new general theoretical frame of reference for psychoanalysis. Symposium on the ego and the id after fifty years. *Psychoanalytic Quarterly* 44:534–549.

Peters, R. (1960). *The Concept of Motivation*. 2d ed. London: Humanities Press. Pribram, K. H. (1962). The neuropsychology of Sigmund Freud. In *Experimental Foundations of Clinical Psychology*, ed. A. J. Bachrach. New York: Basic Books.

———— (1965). Freud's "Project": an open, biologically based model for psychoanalysis. In *Psychoanalysis and Current Biological Thought*, ed. N. S. Greenfield and W. C. Lewis, pp. 81–92. Madison, Milwaukee: University of Wisconsin Press.

———— (1969). The foundation of psychoanalytic theory: Freud's neuro-psychological model. In *Brain and Behaviour* 4:395–432.

——— (1989). Psychoanalysis and the natural sciences: brain-behaviour connection from Freud to present. In J. Sandler, *Dimensions of Psychoanalysis*. London: Karnac.

Pribram, K. H., and Gill, M. M. (1976). *Freud's "Project" Re-assessed. Preface to Contemporary Cognitive Theory and Neurology*. New York: Basic Books.

Pulver, S. E. (1991). Psychic structure, function, process, and content: toward a definition. In *The Concept of Psychic Structure in Psychoanalysis*, ed. T. Shapiro, pp. 165–190. Madison, CT: International Universities Press.

Rank, B. (1949). Aggression. *Psychoanalytic Study of the Child* 3/4:43–48.

Rapaport, D. (1953). On the psychoanalytic theory of affects. In *The Collected Papers of David Rapaport*, ed. M. Gill, pp. 795–811. New York: Basic Books, 1967.

——— (1960). *The Structure of Psychoanalytical Theory: A Systematizing Attempt*. New York: International Universities Press.

——— (1967). On the psychoanalytic theory of motivation. In *The Collected Papers of David Rapaport*, ed. M. Gill, pp. 853–915. New York: Basic Books.

Rapaport, D., and Gill, M. (1959). The points of view and assumptions of metapsychology. *International Journal of Psycho-Analysis* 40:153–162.

Rawn, M. L. (1979). Schafer's "Action Language": a questionable alternative to metapsychology. *International Journal of Psycho-Analysis* 60:455–565. Rizzuto, A.-M., Sahshin, J. I., Buie, D. H., and Meissner, W. W. (1993). A revised theory of aggression. *Psychoanalytic Review* 80:29–54.

Rosenberg, B. (1991). *Masochisme mortifère et masochisme gardien de la vie*. Paris: Presses Universitaires de France.

Rosenblatt, A. D., and Thickstun, J. T. (1970). A study of the concept of psychic energy. *International Journal of Psycho-Analysis* 51:265–277.

——— (1977). Modern psychoanalytic concepts in a general psychology. Part One: General concepts and principles. Part Two: Motivation. *Psychological Issues* 11, Monograph 42/43. New York: International Universities Press.

Rosenfeld, H. (1952). Notes on the psychoanalysis of the superego conflict of an acute schizophrenic patient. *International Journal of Psycho-Analysis* 33:111–131.

———— (1971). Contribution to the psychopathology of psychotic states: the importance of projective identification in the ego structure and the object relations of the psychotic patient. In *Problems of Psychosis*, ed. P. Doucet and C. Laurin, pp. 115–128. The Hague: Excerpta Medica.

Rubinstein, B. (1965). Psychoanalytic theory and the mind–body problem. In *Psychoanalysis and Current Biological Thought*, ed. N. S. Greenfield and W. C. Lewis, pp. 35–56. Madison, Milwaukee: University of Wisconsin Press.

———— (1967). Explanation and mere description: a metascientific examination of certain aspects of the psychoanalytic theory of motivation. In *Motives and Thought: Psychoanalytic Essays in Honor of David Rapaport*, ed. R. Holt, pp. 18–78. *Psychological Issues* 5, Monograph 18/19. New York: International Universities Press.

Sandler, J. (1960a). The background of safety. In *From Safety to Superego*, pp. 1–8. New York: Guilford, 1987.

———— (1960b). On the concept of superego. *Psychoanalytic Study of the Child* 15:128–162.

———— (1962). The classification of superego material in the Hampstead Index. *Psychoanalytic Study of the Child* 17:107–127.

Sandler, J., Dare, C., and Holder, A. (1973). *The Patient and the Analyst. The Basis of the Psychoanalytic Process*. London: Allen & Unwin.

Saul, L. J. (1958). Freud's death instinct and the second law of thermodynamics. *International Journal of Psycho-Analysis* 39:323–325.

Schafer, R. (1970). An overview of Heinz Hartmann's contributions to psychoanalysis. *International Journal of Psycho-Analysis* 51:425–446.

———— (1976). *A New Language for Psychoanalysis*. New Haven, CT: Yale University Press.

———— (1978). Action language—an alternative to metapsychology. In *Language and Insight*, pp. 175–200. New Haven, CT: Yale University Press.

———— (1991). Discussion of panel presentations on psychic structure. In *The Concept of Psychic Structure in Psychoanalysis*, ed. T. Shapiro, pp. 295–312. Madison, CT: International Universities Press.

Schmidt, R. F., ed. (1983). *Grundriss der Neurophysiologie*. Berlin: Springer.

Schmidt, R. F., and Thews, G, eds. (1987). *Physiologie des Menschen*. Berlin: Springer, 23d, fully rev. ed.

Schmidt-Hellerau, C. (1988). Über das Rätsel der Weiblichkeit. Neue Thesen zur weiblichen Entwicklung, herausgearbeitet aus dem Werk Sigmund Freuds. *Psyche* 42:289–306.

———— (1990). Über Berufsethos und persönliche Integrität. Zur Geschichte der deutschen Psychoanalyse im Dritten Reich. *Zeitschrift für psychoanalytische Theorie und Praxis* 5:262–272.

———— (1991). Das Es und das Ich. Metapsychologische Überlegungen zum Thema Schlafstörungen. *Zeitschrift für psychoanalytische Theorie und Praxis* 6:198–231.

———— (1993). Überbau oder Fundament? Zur Metapsychologie und Metapsychologiedebatte. *Psyche* 47:1–30.

———— (1997). Libido and lethe. Fundamentals of a formalised conception of metapsychology. *International Journal of Psycho-Analysis* 78:683– 697.

———— (2000). Zur Metapsychologie der Aggression. Paper presented to the Swiss Psychoanalytical Society on 26 February and to the Vienna Psychoanalytical Society on June 27 (to be published).

———— (2002a). Why aggression? Metapsychological, clinical and technical considerations. *International Journal of Psycho-Analysis* 83(6):1269-1289.

———— (2002b). Where models intersect. A metapsychological approach. *Psychoanalytic Quarterly*, 71(3):503-544.

———— (2005a). We are driven. *Psychoanalytic Quarterly, 74(4):989-1028.*

———— (2005b). The other side of Oedipus. *Psychoanalytic Quarterly, 74(1): 187-217.*

———— (2006). Surviving in absence. *Psychoanalytic Quarterly, 75(4):1057-1095.*

———— (2008). The lethic phallus. Rethinking the misery of Oedipus. *Psychoanalytic Quarterly, 77(3): 719-753.*

———— (2010). The Kore Complex. On a woman's inheritance of her mother's failed Oedipus complex. *Psychoanalytic Quarterly, 799(4):911-933.*

———— (2018). *Driven to survive. Selected papers on psychoanalysis.* New York: International Psychoanalytic Books.

———— (2023). Asserting oneself. On aggression and suicide. A metapsychological (economical / quantitative) approach. The Scandinavian Psychoanalytic Review, 45:14-23.

Schönle, O. (1981). Die Konzeption Roy Schafers und ihr Resultat, die "action language." In *Neue Perspektiven der Psychoanalyse,* ed. W. Mertens, pp. 124–161. Stuttgart: Kohlhammer.

Schur, M. (1966). *The Id and the Regulatory Principles of Mental Functioning.* New York: International Universities Press.

Segal, H. (1957). Notes on symbol formation. *International Journal of PsychoAnalysis* 38:391–397.

Shapiro, T., ed. (1991). *The Concept of Structure in Psychoanalysis.* Madison, CT: International Universities Press.

Shapiro, T., and Emde, R. N., eds. (1992). *Affect: Psychoanalytic Perspectives.* Madison, CT: International Universities Press.

Shevrin, H., Bond, J., Brakel, L. A. W., et al. (1996). *Conscious and Unconscious Processes. Psychodynamic, Cognitive, and Neurophysiological Convergences.* New York: Guilford.

Simmel, E. (1924). Die psycho-physische Bedeutsamkeit des Intestinalorgans für die Urverdrängung. *Internationale Zeitschrift für Psychoanalyse* 10:218–221.

———— (1933). Prägenitalprimat und intestinale Stufe der Libidoorganisation. *Internationale Zeitschrift für Psychoanalyse* 19:245–246.

Smith, H. F. (1999). Subjectivity and objectivity in analytic listening. *Journal of the American Psychoanalytic Association* 47:465–484.

Solms, M. (1997). What is consciousness? *Journal of the American Psychoanalytic Association* 45:681–703; commentaries 704–765; response to commentaries 765–778.

Spitz, R. A. (1951). The psychogenic diseases in infancy: an attempt at their etiologic classification. *Psychoanalytic Study of the Child* 6:255–275.

———— (1958). On the genesis of superego components. *Psychoanalytic Study of the Child* 13:375–404.

Stern, M. (1974). Das Problem der Aggression. Bemerkungen über Trieb, Trauma und Tod. *Psyche* 28:495–507.

Stolorow, R. D. (1978). The concept of psychic structure: its meta-psychological and clinical psychoanalytic meanings. *International Review of PsychoAnalysis* 5:313–320.

Sulloway, F. J. (1979). *Freud, Biologist of the Mind. Beyond the Psychoanalytic Legend.* New York: Basic Books.

Tinbergen, N. (1951). *The Study of Instinct.* Oxford: Clarendon.

Treurniet, N. (1991). Introduction to "On Narcissism." In *Freud's "On Narcissism: An Introduction,"* ed. J. Sandler, E. S. Person, and P. Fonagy, pp. 75–94. New Haven, CT: Yale University Press.

Tyson, P. (1988). Psychic structure formation: the complementary roles of affects, drives, object relations, and conflict. *Journal of the American Psychoanalytic Association* 36, Supplement:73–100.

Waelder, R. (1962). Psychoanalysis, scientific method, and philosophy. *Journal of the American Psychoanalytic Association* 10:617–637.

Wallerstein, R. S. (1983). Defenses, defense mechanisms, and the structure of mind. *Journal of the American Psychoanalytic Association* 31, Supplement:201–225.

——— (1991). Assessment of structural change in psychoanalytic therapy and research. In *The Concept of Psychic Structure in Psychoanalysis*, ed. T. Shapiro, pp. 283–294. Madison, CT: International Universities Press.

——— , ed. (1992). *The Common Ground of Psycho-Analysis.* Northvale, NJ: Jason Aronson.

Weinshel, E. M. (1991). Structural change in psychoanalysis. In *The Concept of Psychic Structure in Psychoanalysis*, ed. T. Shapiro, pp. 263–280. Madison, CT: International Universities Press.

Weiss, E. (1935). Todestrieb und Masochismus. *Imago* 21:393–411. Weizsäcker, C. F. von (1971). *Die Einheit der Natur.* Munich: Deutscher Taschenbuch Verlag, 1974.

Westerman Holstijn, A. W. (1930). Tendenzen des Toten, Todestriebe und Triebe zum Töten. *Imago* 16:207–231.

Wiener, N. (1948). *Cybernetics or Control and Communication in the Animal and the Machine.* New York: Wiley.

Winnicott, D. W. (1963). The development of the capacity for concern. *Bulletin of the Menninger Clinic* 27:167–176.

———— (1984). *Deprivation and Delinquency.* London: Tavistock.

Wolf, E. S., Ornstein, P., Ornstein, A., et al. (1989). *Selbstpsychologie. Weiterentwicklungen nach Heinz Kohut.* Munich: Verlag Internationale Psychoanalyse.

Wollheim, R. (1971). *Sigmund Freud.* New York: Viking.

Zelmanowits, J. (1971). David Rapaports Gesammelte Schriften. *Psyche* 25:400–409.

www.ingramcontent.com/pod-product-compliance
Lightning Source LLC
Chambersburg PA
CBHW062118020426
42335CB00013B/1013